A COMPANY
OF **HEROES**

A COMPANY
of HEROES

PERSONAL MEMORIES ABOUT THE
REAL BAND OF BROTHERS
AND THE LEGACY THEY LEFT US

MARCUS BROTHERTON

BERKLEY CALIBER, NEW YORK

THE BERKLEY PUBLISHING GROUP
Published by the Penguin Group
Penguin Group (USA) Inc.
375 Hudson Street, New York, New York 10014, USA
Penguin Group (Canada), 90 Eglinton Avenue East, Suite 700, Toronto, Ontario M4P 2Y3, Canada
(a division of Pearson Penguin Canada Inc.)
Penguin Books Ltd., 80 Strand, London WC2R 0RL, England
Penguin Group Ireland, 25 St. Stephen's Green, Dublin 2, Ireland (a division of Penguin Books Ltd.)
Penguin Group (Australia), 250 Camberwell Road, Camberwell, Victoria 3124, Australia
(a division of Pearson Australia Group Pty. Ltd.)
Penguin Books India Pvt. Ltd., 11 Community Centre, Panchsheel Park, New Delhi—110 017, India
Penguin Group (NZ), 67 Apollo Drive, Rosedale, North Shore 0632, New Zealand
(a division of Pearson New Zealand Ltd.)
Penguin Books (South Africa) (Pty.) Ltd., 24 Sturdee Avenue, Rosebank, Johannesburg 2196,
South Africa

Penguin Books Ltd., Registered Offices: 80 Strand, London WC2R 0RL, England

The publisher does not have any control over and does not assume any responsibility for author or third-party websites or their content.

PRINTING HISTORY
Berkley Caliber hardcover edition / May 2010
Berkley Caliber trade paperback edition / May 2011

Berkley Caliber trade paperback ISBN: 978-0-425-24095-3

The Library of Congress has catalogued the Berkley Caliber hardcover edition as follows:

Brotherton, Marcus.
A company of heroes : personal memories about the real band of brothers and the legacy they left us /
Marcus Brotherton.
  p. cm.
ISBN 978-0-425-23420-4
1. United States. Army. Parachute Infantry Regiment, 506th. Company E.   2. World War,
1939–1945—Personal narratives, American.   3. World War, 1939–1945—Regimental histories—
United States.   4. World War, 1939–1945—Campaigns—Western Front.   5. United States.
Army—Parachute troops.   6. Soldiers—United States—Biography.   I. Title.
D769.348506th .B75 2010
940.54'12730922—dc22

                              2009050664

PRINTED IN THE UNITED STATES OF AMERICA

10   9   8   7   6   5   4   3   2   1

INTERVIEWS WITH THE FAMILIES OF:

Albert Blithe

Gordon Carson

Burton "Pat" Christenson

Bill Evans

Tony Garcia

Walter "Smokey" Gordon

Herman "Hack" Hanson

Terrence "Salty" Harris

Frederick "Moose" Heyliger

Paul "Frenchy" Lamoureux

George Lavenson

Joe Liebgott

C. Carwood Lipton

Robert Marsh

Warren "Skip" Muck

Patrick O'Keefe

Alex Penkala

George Potter

Robert Rader

Mike Ranney

LaVon Reese

Eugene "Doc" Roe

Ron Speirs

Floyd Talbert

Joe Toye

Robert Van Klinken

To the Men of Easy Company

Mike Ranney's famous quote from a letter to me on January 25, 1982, will live forever.

"In thinking back on the days of Easy Company, I am treasuring my remark to a grandson who asked, 'Grandpa, were you a hero in the war?'

"'No,' I answered, 'but I served with a company of heroes.'"

—MAJOR RICHARD WINTERS
Easy Company Commander

CONTENTS

PREFACE

Are you familiar with the Band of Brothers? Let me introduce you to a few.

Meet Tab Talbert, the best soldier in Easy Company, and Robert J. Rader, a man so community-minded he has a bridge named in his honor in California.

Meet Moose Heyliger, who set muskrat traps as a child and could name every bird in the sky by the time he led Easy Company, and Pat Christenson, unofficial artist of Easy Company. Pat sketched pictures of the combat he saw—soldiers, tanks, rifles, explosions—always mindful, as he wrote in his journal, that "the true picture of war is impossible to convey, even by those who did the bleeding and the fighting."

Meet Robert Marsh, a married seventeen-year-old father who lied about his age to get into the Army, and Eugene Roe, a no-show at his own wedding. (As his bride waited at the altar, Doc Roe was parachuting into Normandy—how's that for an excuse?)

Meet Patrick O'Keefe, who once, although hungry, put all the money he had—thirty-five cents—into a collection box for the poor, and Robert Van Klinken, a backwoods mechanic who showed a remarkable skill for writing. As you read portions of Van Klinken's letters in the pages ahead, watch for his creative use of language, his frequent use of "swell" (definitely the superlative of the day), and expressions such as "pill squirter" for a rifle, and "honey" for a guitar. Van Klinken's personality comes through strongly, and because you feel you know him after reading what he wrote, his death comes hard.

Within a company filled with heroes, each man has a story worth telling. In my previous book, I interviewed twenty members of Easy Company who are still alive. In this new book I interviewed the families of twenty-six of the Band of Brothers who have departed. These are their life stories.

Although this is a book that shows a lot of death, it also shows a lot of life. I must warn you that not everything in this book reflects the stuff of heroics, particularly what transpires after the war. This is a tribute book, yes, and is meant to represent the men warmly, but it's also about real people. It shows their lives, warts and all. This book is about the authentic Band of Brothers, who they truly were, how they lived, served, fought, worked, loved, and ultimately died.

Within a Company of Heroes

Who were the Band of Brothers? If you're completely new to the subject, they were the men of the now-legendary Easy Company, 506th Parachute Infantry Regiment, 101st Airborne Division, an elite group of World War II war fighters. They formed and trained at Camp Toccoa, Georgia, under the tough and controversial Captain Herbert Sobel. After training stateside, the men rode the troop ship *Samaria* to Aldbourne, England, for further battle preparation. They parachuted into Normandy on D-day and, later into Holland for Operation Market-Garden. They fought their way through Belgium, France, and Germany, survived overwhelming odds, liberated concentration camps, and drank a victory toast in April 1945 at Hitler's hideout in the Alps. Along the way they encountered horrors and victories, welded themselves into a family of soldiers, and helped swing the tide of World War II and, ultimately, the course of history.

Although twenty-six men's life stories are featured in this book, many more men's stories could be told. At the start of the war, some 140 men formed the original Easy Company at Camp Toccoa. By the end of the war, due to transfers and (mostly) to men getting shot, 366 men are listed as having been a part of Easy Company.

The company was first chronicled in 1992 by historian Stephen Ambrose in the book *Band of Brothers*. In 2001, Tom Hanks and Stephen Spielberg turned Ambrose's book into a ten-part HBO miniseries by the same name. The series won six Emmys and numerous other awards, and still runs frequently on various networks around the world.

The essays that follow differ from other books in that they do not trace the war's chronology. Rather, they act as snapshots from the company as a whole. For readers seeking to learn more about Easy Company or to build a complete library, a number of other books about the Band of Brothers have been published over the years. The books are:

* *Parachute Infantry* by PFC David Kenyon Webster. Webster was an English literature major at Harvard who fought with Easy Company. He died in a shark fishing accident in 1961. His memoir was published posthumously in 1994.

* *Beyond Band of Brothers* by Maj. Richard Winters and Colonel Cole Kingseed. Winters commanded Easy Company for part of the war and later went on to serve as battalion staff. This is the first of his memoirs.

* *Biggest Brother* by Larry Alexander is the second of Dick Winters' biographies and covers more about Winters's life after the war.

* *The Way We Were* by Cpl. Forrest Guth and Michael de Trez. This is a coffee-table collection of Guth's wartime pictures, published by a European company.

* *Brothers in Battle, Best of Friends* by S/Sgt. Bill Guarnere and PFC Babe Heffron with Robyn Post is an oral-history account of the war by two friends from Easy Company.

* *Call of Duty* by Lt. Buck Compton with Marcus Brotherton. Compton, a child actor and college sports star, went on to have careers after the war as a detective, attorney, and judge. He prosecuted Sirhan Sirhan for the murder of Robert F. Kennedy.

* *Easy Company Soldier* by Sgt. Don Malarkey with Bob Welch is a poignant memoir that describes Malarkey's fight through the war years.

* *Easy Company—In Photographs*, published by Genesis Publications, is a limited edition, large-format collector's book from the UK.

* *We Who Are Alive and Remain* by Marcus Brotherton is an oral-history book released in 2009 featuring twenty of the last few surviving members of Easy Company.

Feel free to either read this book straight through or skip around from chapter to chapter. The book works in two ways. First, if you're new to the Band of Brothers, you'll be inspired and challenged by the biographies of each man profiled. These were ordinary men who trained to become the best, and ultimately did extraordinary things.

Second, if you're already a fan, this book adds insight to understanding the overall profile of the company. Read this book, then watch the HBO series again. Your increased knowledge of each man prompts a deeper sense of identification. For instance, watch the scene in Episode 7 (*"The Breaking Point"*) where Joe Toye loses a leg during heavy shelling at Bastogne. This is the same Joe Toye you've now come to know as the toughest man in Easy Company. This is the same Joe Toye who, if he had been offered better opportunities before joining the army, undoubtedly could have become a professional athlete. This is the same Joe Toye who, after the war, spent his last years caring for the daily needs of a severely handicapped son. After reading this book, you'll never watch the series the same way again.

I've spoken with the family members who knew the men closely, as well as relied on firsthand accounts from writings, journals, and letters. My hope is that you will benefit from the intrigue and poignancy that comes from reading the stories of each man featured.

Please enjoy.

Marcus Brotherton
Bellingham, Washington,
September 2009

EASY COMPANY TIMELINE

July–November 1942: 506th PIR activated at Camp Toccoa, GA. Basic Training. Hike from Toccoa to Atlanta in late November.

December 1942: Parachute training at Fort Benning, GA. Additional training at Benning through February '43.

February–May 1943: Additional training exercises at Camp Mackall, NC. More training jumps.

June–August 1943: Additional training in Kentucky and Tennessee, then to Fort Bragg, NC.

September 1943: Regiment moves to Camp Shanks, NY, boards SS *Samaria* for England. Arrives in Swindon and moved to Aldbourne.

September 1943–May 1944: Additional training in Aldbourne. In May regiment moves to marshalling area near Exeter, England, then to Upottery Airfield.

June 6, 1944: Jump into France.

June 7–8, 1944: Various battles in Normandy.

June 8–16, 1944: Battle for Carentan.

June 29, 1944: Company is relieved and returns to Aldbourne.

September 17, 1944: Company jumps at Zon, Holland, and advances into Eindhoven, heading for Arnhem. Series of intense battles along "Hell's Highway" throughout September.

October 3, 1944: Company is relieved from duty around Eindhoven and transported by truck to the Island, the area between the Waal and the Neder Rhine. Patrols and battles until November when the Company is relieved and sent to Mourmelon, France.

December 17, 1944: Company sent to Bastogne, Belgium, to fight in Bois Jacques woods.

January 13–16, 1944: Fighting around Foy, Noville, and Rachamps.

January 19–February 25, 1944: Company is relieved and moved to Haguenau. Fights along the Moder River.

March 1945: Now back at Mourmelon, the entire 101st Airborne Division receives the Presidential Unit Citation. This is the first time an entire division has been honored in this way.

April 1945: Company heads into Germany. Finds concentration camps. Occupies Berchtesgaden.

May 8, 1945: Victory in Europe day.

April 6–10, 1945: Company moves to Kaprun, Austria. Begins occupation duties.

May–November 1945: High-points men are rotated home.

A COMPANY
OF HEROES

PART I

ENLISTED MEN

THE KEY TO VICTORY

ALBERT BLITHE

Interview with Gordon Blithe, son

Band of Brothers came down on me like an atom bomb. I had never heard of the book, never even heard of it on TV, until a friend of mine, a WWII buff, came over to my house one day. I had all this WWII memorabilia from my dad around the house, which my friend knew about. He asked, "Was your dad in Easy Company in WWII?"

"I don't know what company he was in," I said. "All I know is that he was with the 506th PIR, 101st Airborne."

"So far, so good," he said. "Was your dad's name Albert?"

"Yeah."

"Was he born in Philadelphia?"

"Yeah."

"Buddy, you better come over to my house and watch this thing on HBO," he said. "I think it's about your dad."

So I went over, and things started to click. There was this character named Albert Blithe, played by the actor Marc Warren. I didn't recognize the specific stories because my dad had never talked about the war, so that didn't mean anything to me. Then, in one episode that featured him, I saw his RA [Regular Army] number. That's when I realized this was about my dad.

There were two mistakes with the series when it came to Albert Blithe—one little, one big. The first issue was not as important to me. It showed that my father had been wounded in the neck. Well, it wasn't actually the neck. It was his upper right shoulder. Growing up, I had seen the scar hundreds of times. He received a partial wartime disability because of the injury. When he came home from WWII he was on disability payment for one year, then he waived it and went back into the army. A man from Texas got in touch with me who had known my dad, and said that my dad had a permanent profile where he didn't have to salute anymore because his shoulder was so messed up.

But the second mistake, the bigger one, I knew I had to have it corrected. The series said that Albert Blithe never recovered from his wounds and died in 1948. That simply wasn't true.

I became obsessed about finding out more and setting the record straight. For five days straight I left messages on Internet sites. I got a lot of e-mails in reply, then a woman in Maryland, Linda Switzer, came to my aid in a big way. She helped me get word out even more, and soon I actually received e-mails from Tom Hanks and Steven Spielberg apologizing for the oversight.

It seems that Bill Guarnere and Babe Heffron had sworn up and down that they attended my dad's funeral in 1948. I have the utmost respect for those guys and I can see how that made sense to them. The last thing they knew about Albert Blithe was that he had been seriously wounded, somewhere near the face, head, or neck area, near Carentan. They never saw him alive again. But it must have been another Albert Blithe's funeral they went to (there are a few of them out there—for instance, I have a cousin named Albert Blithe), or else they were simply relying on their memories when the book was being researched and had been to so many funerals over the years that they were thinking about somebody else. I have documents (they're now posted at the 506th Infantry Web site)[1]

1. http://www.506infantry.org/his2ndbnwwiiphoto24.html, accessed August 2009.

that show my dad at Fort Bliss, Texas, in 1948, so he couldn't have died then.

At first the task of convincing people that Albert Blithe had lived beyond 1948 was a bit of a hard sell. I got some pretty nasty e-mails from people who couldn't believe that Stephen Ambrose and HBO had actually made a mistake. They felt simply that because my last name was Blithe I was jumping on the Band of Brothers bandwagon and wanted attention for myself. One person, who had done a lot of research into Easy Company and has a pretty well-known name in these circles, basically called me a liar. "Send me your dad's DD-214s [military records]," he said. I did that. But even then he wasn't convinced. He had a picture of Albert Blithe's grave in Philadelphia.

That didn't matter to me. I knew it wasn't my father's grave. I was there when my dad died. My mother was there. We buried him. My dad died December 17, 1967, and is buried at Arlington National Cemetery.[2] I have a picture of the gravestone, which I sent to this man.[3]

My dad and Gordy Carson were close friends during the war. His son, Gary Carson, lives in Seattle. Gary showed me a wartime diary his dad had written that said, "I don't know what I'd do without Al Blithe." I had a sack of documents and Gary and I went through them. One of the documents is a signed and stamped military affidavit showing that my dad jumped with E Company during WWII, then went on to jump with the 82nd Airborne in the 1950s—so he couldn't have died in 1948, according to this affidavit. I'll tell you, Gary Carson is a prince of a gentleman. When we met, we hit it right off. He gave me Bill Guarnere's phone number, but I didn't have the courage to phone Mr. Guarnere up and tell him he went to the wrong Al Blithe's funeral. So I just let it lie. Evidently Mr. Guarnere was convinced in the end because he and Babe Heffron mentioned in their book that although they never saw my dad again, they later heard he ended up back in combat in Korea.[4]

2. http://www.arlingtoncemetery.net/albert-blithe.html, accessed August 2009.
3. http://www.506infantry.org/his2ndbnwwiiphoto24.html, accessed August 2009.
4. William Guarnere and Edward Heffron with Robyn Post, *Brothers in Battle, Best of Friends* (New York: Berkley Caliber, 2007), 79-80.

For some time I did whatever I could to prove that my dad wasn't dead [in 1948]. For instance, I interviewed with the 506th Infantry's webmaster for about three hours and showed him all the documents I had. In the end, all the people who needed to be convinced were convinced. The error in the book and the miniseries were never corrected, but I guess it's hard to correct something when it's been that widely distributed. But the new Blu-ray version of *Band of Brothers* has an interactive guide called "In the Field with the Men of Easy Company," stating correctly that Albert Blithe died in 1967. So that's good. In Dick Winters's memoirs, he sets the record straight as well.[5] That was good for me to see. I felt I had done my job.

The Real Albert Blithe

Albert Blithe was born June 25, 1923, in Philadelphia. His mother worked in the garment district. His father worked for the United Parcel Service as a deliveryman.

Now, it's hard to say this, and I don't know how you're quite going to put this in a book, but my dad was a thug. There's no other way to say it. He was raised on the rough side of the tracks and was always in trouble, even though he came from a very religious extended family. Most of them on his mother's side were missionaries. I can't say any of that faith ever rubbed off on my dad. He always said that their religion was forced on him as a kid. Later, he became an agnostic. He didn't know one way or another if there was a God. My mother told me that when he was a kid my grandmother used to give him money to put in the offering plate. My dad would skip out on church and gamble the money away in the alleyways of the city.

Dad graduated from high school and worked at the Westinghouse plant after he graduated. As a young man he got in so much trouble that he finally concluded he had to get out of Philadelphia, away from his old

---

5. Richard Winters with Cole Kingseed, *Beyond Band of Brothers* (New York: Berkley Caliber, 2006), 105, 107.

friends and influences, and the only way to do that was to join the Army. The war was going on by then, so he enlisted, and the rest is history. I'll tell you all I know about his wartime experiences in a minute.

My dad was married twice. His first wife's name was Flora Mae, from West Virginia. When Dad was wounded and sent back to the states, he was in a veteran's hospital in Ashland, West Virginia. I assume he and Flora Mae met there. When he went back into the Army he was sent to Fort Bliss, Texas. That's where my half-sister Barbara was born, in 1948, at Fort Bliss. I know the family went to Germany about that time, then came back. My dad and his first wife divorced around 1951.

My parents—his second marriage—were married in 1957. My mother's name is Sadie, but she went by Kay. She had two daughters from a previous marriage, Sandra and Pinky. My mom and dad met on a blind date at the USO in Fayetteville, NC, where my dad was stationed with the 82nd Airborne out at Fort Bragg. The date was set up by my oldest half sister, Pinky. I was born in 1959.

Fayetteville is mostly where I grew up. In many ways it was a lot of fun to grow up with my dad. He was a chronic alcoholic, probably due to the war, but he was a Good Time Charlie, too. He was always fun to be with. We went to the beach and to carnivals. In many ways we were a happy, small, army family. Mom and Dad loved to go out dancing. In her later years, my mom says the happiest she had ever been was when she was with my dad. Those years encompass my best memories of him, too. It's good that I have some good memories, because the rest of my father's life became pretty ugly.

In the Mind of Albert Blithe

My dad died when I was just eight years old. He never talked about the war to me, but my mom told me several times, "You just don't know how badly the war messed up your dad's mind."

When I was maybe seven, I asked my dad two questions straight-out. The first was: "Did you kill anybody?"

He nodded his head slowly, but didn't say anything more.

"Were you scared?" I asked. That was the second question.

"Yeah, of course I was scared," he said.

I'm pretty sure he told my mom a lot more about what happened during the war, but those were the only two questions I ever asked him about it.

We know now from other sources that Dad was one of the original Toccoa men who trained under Captain Sobel.

We know that my dad liked to gamble. Apparently, they had a little business going on that Dad was in the midst of, running a dice game back in the barracks in England.

The big story of Dad in the war is when he became temporarily blind [hysterical blindness], after the battle of Carentan. I asked Mom about it in later years and she never doubted that it happened to Dad. The men all went through so much and saw so much. Carentan was a fierce battle. Dick Winters wrote about it as fact in his memoirs. He also states that Dad immediately returned to duty as soon as he regained his vision, which speaks about the guts and determination it took to keep going.[6] Dad evidently was brave, despite the incident with the blindness, because later he fought in Korea and earned both a Silver Star and a Bronze Star. He was a private in World War II, but he achieved the rank of master sergeant in Korea. He was proud of his military career. It meant the world to him. I don't think I ever saw my dad out of uniform. The uniform was always a part of who he was.

In a letter to my mother dated December 18, 1967, from the Department of the Army, it describes how my dad died. He was on active duty with the 8th Supply and Transport Battalion, 8th Infantry Division, in West Germany. A week before his death he had attended a commemorative weekend in Bastogne, Belgium, and returned from the event feeling unwell. He was taken to the emergency room and diagnosed with a perforated ulcer. Emergency surgery was performed the next day. Complications set in, his kidneys failed, and he died December 17.

I don't doubt that's all true. But I will say that what's in that letter is

---

6. Ibid., 105.

mostly polite talk. My dad drank himself to death. That's how it really happened.

My dad drank every day. After work he went to the NCO club until it closed at two in the morning. He came back home bringing a couple bottles of Seagram's 7 with him, which was his favorite. My mom and he were drinking buddies, and most times they drank until five in the morning. My dad would sleep an hour, shave, shower, get on his uniform, go to work, and perform duties like it was nothing. That's how it went pretty much every weekday for my dad. He'd sleep more on the weekends, but even then, as soon as he got up and ate something, it was back to the drinking again. I've never seen a man drink as much as my father. He could drink enormous quantities of alcohol. At least he was a happy drunk: that was about the only good thing about his addiction.

There were other problems in the marriage. Mom and Dad split up a couple years before he died. Dad liked to gamble as well as drink. My mom put up with that for eleven years. Mom handled the money and gave him a lot of leeway in how much money he used for gambling. He used to gamble away the rent money until Mom put a stop to that.

We were stationed at Fort Lee for a time where he got a job as a parachute-rigger instructor. Then he had a ministroke, so they put him on temporary retirement. But dad loved the Army and worked to get his strength back. Finally he was strong enough, so they let him go back in. He had eighteen months to go before he retired. They stationed him in Germany in June, 1967. He was dead by December of that year. He was forty-four years old when he died.

My mom and dad always loved each other, I don't doubt that. When my dad died, it just destroyed my mom. She started drinking more and eventually became a severe alcoholic herself. Toward the end she would sometimes drink twenty-three out of twenty-four hours in a day. She drank herself into dementia. She grew very sick at the end; she was in the hospital on full life support. I don't think she ever got over the death of my dad. She died in 1996.

I went through a lot of the same problems as my dad. I got in trouble a lot as a kid. As a teenager I liked to drink. I figured the Army was the only way I could get straightened out, so I joined the service. I was mostly stationed at Fort Lewis. I put in my four years but didn't want to enlist again. I liked the Seattle/Tacoma area in Washington State a lot and settled down there after the service. I got married and had a son, then got divorced. For a while I had custody of my son. He lives across the country now, but we're still close. Washington State treated me good and is my home now. Good people. Good fishing. I'm happy here. Washington's where I love to be.

I know my dad certainly had his share of problems, but nobody is perfect. I want people to remember my father this way: He was a true American paratrooper who put his life on the line for this country and thousands of other people in this world. He fought for people he didn't even know. I'm proud of him, so proud. That's how I want people to remember Albert Blithe.

2

TONY GARCIA

Interview with Greg Garcia, son
With additional information from Kelly Garcia, daughter,
Carmen and William Deshler, sister and brother-in-law,
and Suzanne Eckloff, niece

When I was a kid and asked Dad about his combat experiences, I always asked in general terms—"Did you kill any Germans?"—that type of thing, and my dad's answers were equally vague—"Oh, I don't know. Maybe." After *Band of Brothers* came out, we learned to ask more specific questions, and in turn, Dad gave us more specific answers. But even then there was a lot that remained unsaid. I wish that thirty years ago we had known how to ask questions better. Maybe we all wish that with our parents.

You first see a glimpse of my dad, Tony Garcia (as portrayed by actor Douglas Spain), toward the end of episode 3 of the *Band of Brothers*, the one titled "*Carentan*." Then in episode 4, titled "*Replacements*," when the original men of Easy are back from Normandy, three very young-looking privates—Les Hashey, James Miller, and my dad—are sitting at a table in the Blue Boar Inn in England. The now battle-hardened Bill Guarnere sits down with them, tells them an off-color joke about getting inside a plane named Doris, then warns them to listen closely to whatever their squad leader, Bull Randleman, tells them. Later, while on the ground outside the plane just before the jump for Operation Market-Garden, my dad's character is seen nervously trying to get his rifle and gear in order, and Bull gives him some last minute advice about jumping, which sets Dad's mind at ease.

We learned a lot about our dad's combat experiences only after the miniseries came out. Dad talked as we watched TV together. It was the most we had ever heard from him about it. As a rule, Dad kept the war to himself. I believe he didn't want to burden anyone else with it. He had seen such awful things—the shellings, the concentration camp, his buddies getting killed and wounded. But even though he didn't say much, you could tell that the war had affected him. Every so often Mom would say, "Your dad had a nightmare again." His dreams would usually be about fighting in combat or jumping out of a plane. On several occasions the dreams must have been intense. When I came over to visit, he might have a new scratch or cut, or maybe a bruise on his forehead. He'd fallen out of bed and hit his head on the nightstand during a nightmare, thinking he was fighting or jumping from a plane.

I saw evidence of these dreams firsthand a few times. In 2000, Dad, my sister Kelly, and I went to an Easy Company reunion in New Orleans where we all shared a hotel room. (Mom didn't travel by plane anymore because she was disabled with multiple sclerosis.) We could hear Dad in the night mumbling and thrashing around. I called out to him: "Relax. It's okay. Everything's going to be fine." He went back to sleep, and we didn't mention it the next morning. We also saw this while on the trip to France for the premier of *Band of Brothers*. The vivid memories surfaced in his dreams, making for troubled sleep. I can imagine that any kind of event relating to Easy Company or the war brought back the memories and dreams.

There were things that he readily shared, though, from his wartime experiences. Once after watching a war movie as a kid, I remember asking him how a bazooka destroyed a tank. He drew me a detailed diagram and explained how the bazooka shell worked. He was happy to share that kind of information.

What was my dad really like? Some details are lost forever, and we'll never know, but this is what we do know:

A Considerate Kid

Anthony Garcia was born in 1924, in Inez, Texas. The timing of his birth came as a surprise. His family lived in Cheyenne, Wyoming, but my grandmother was visiting relatives in Texas when she gave birth to him prematurely. When the baby was strong enough to travel, they rejoined the rest of the family in Wyoming.

Dad's parents were full-blooded Mexicans who had moved to the United States in search of a better life. My grandmother, Isabel, was the daughter of a sharecropper, and came to the states first. My grandfather, José, came later. They met and married and moved about the country following work—everything from coal mining in Appalachia to handling freight for the Union Pacific Railroad, where José eventually gained permanent employment. My dad was the fourth child in the family. All of José and Isabel's seven children were born in the United States. They spoke Spanish in the house and picked up English as time went on. Dad spoke it fluently by the time I knew him. He didn't have any accent at all.

My dad's family wasn't wealthy by any means. My grandfather decided to build the family a house. By hand, he and the boys dug the basement. For a while they actually lived in the hole in the ground. The family joke is that dad was born in a foxhole. Then, gradually, they built the rest of the house, much of it with salvage wood that my grandfather brought home from work. That house still stands today.

My dad learned early how to be self-reliant. He and his brothers and sisters picked cotton, tended turkeys, and helped out with the calves, which he and his siblings sometimes saddled for fun and rode around the farm. His sister remembers him as a laid-back kid, an average student, someone who got along with all of his siblings and was especially considerate to the younger children. Dad had a large paper route. Come rain, shine, or Cheyenne snow, the papers always got delivered on time.

Only in the Movies

When the war began, Dad's older brother Ben had already enlisted and survived the Pearl Harbor attack on December 7, 1941. That clinched Dad's decision to join up, so he dropped out of high school in 1943 to enlist.

My dad and a buddy first tried to enlist in the Marines. At the recruiter's office, they were told, "Sorry, we're all full up. Why don't you try the Army?" So they did. His first assignment was with a searchlight battalion.

He saw posters advertising the Airborne and had his mind set on joining it, but he failed the physical twice because his heart rate was irregular. Someone gave him a couple of pills to help steady his heart rate. Not knowing any better, he took more pills than necessary, which made his heart race during the exam. The doctor commented, "I guess they worked you guys really hard in physical training today," to which my dad, not missing a beat, said, "They sure did!" And with that, he passed the exam and got into the Airborne.

Even though the military was segregated at the time, I don't recall Dad ever talking about incidents of prejudice because he was Mexican-American. I think he always fit in well with the rest of the guys.

Dad wasn't one of the original Toccoa men. He trained stateside then was shipped to England and arrived just before the D-day invasion. They kept the newer replacements out of that jump, holding them back to replenish the ranks when the invasion forces returned. He remembered being on the bus coming into the camp area and seeing the other guys gearing up for the invasion. It was quite a way to join Easy Company, he said.

Market-Garden was his first combat jump. He jumped, battled all through Holland with the other men of Easy, and continued on with the company through the end of the war.

In the "Crossroads" episode, the miniseries shows a scene where Easy was about to attack a German machine-gun nest at night. My dad was shown firing a rifle but was actually on the mortar squad with Skip Muck and Alex Penkala. Muck and Penkala were setting up the mortar tube, and the mortar squad was so close to the enemy that it looked like the mortar tube was practically straight up and down. My dad remembered thinking, "If there's any wind, that shell's gonna come right back down on our heads." Fortunately, there wasn't, it didn't, and the shell took out the German machine-gun nest.

The next morning they were off the top of the dike and had taken cover at the base of it. Dick Winters decided that they should attack the Germans and had the men fix bayonets. A close-up is shown of my dad as he's putting the bayonet on the end of his rifle. When my dad saw the scene, he said he remembered the exact moment back in 1944, and recalled that at that moment in his past he had thought, "This kind of stuff only happens in the movies." How ironic.

In a later episode, during the mission to cross a river and capture German prisoners, the miniseries shows him and some other men falling into the river near Haguenau. Dad told me he was actually in the first boat going across, and they got across okay. But after they got to the other side, one of the following boats capsized: the one with the group's lieutenant. Times like these, my dad's sense of humor tended to show up, although it wasn't the best timing. You can picture it: a cold, dimly lit night, and my dad's on the far bank of the river with the other guys from his boat. The lieutenant comes up the bank, soaking wet, and my dad, being a smart-ass, whispers, "Hey lieutenant, you fall in the water?" The comment probably didn't get a very good reception. Another detail he remembered about that mission was that he helped clear out some buildings. He had three grenades with him but dropped one, losing it in the mud, gave one to another guy, and tossed the last one into a cellar. It was also on this mission to get prisoners that he managed to collect a couple of souvenirs. After the patrol brought the German prisoners back to their quarters, my dad took out his bayonet and approached one of the prisoners in order to cut off some German patches. My dad remembered how the German's eyes "went wide when he saw me walking towards him with me holding that knife."

My dad apparently could make situations a little lighter without intending to. Once, after the major fighting of the Battle of the Bulge had taken place and Easy was moving away from Bastogne, the men were in the woods getting shelled. His buddy Les Hashey got hit by a tree splinter while in his foxhole. Hashey yelled out, "Hey Tony, I'm hit. I need help." Dad asked, "How do you know?" Hashey yelled back, "My shoulder's bleeding." My dad felt pretty silly for asking the question. He and Hashey were the closest of friends, but my dad didn't take too much to Hashey's constant volunteering for patrols. I remember him telling us about one time Hashey was trying to get my dad to go along with him on a patrol, and my dad jokingly telling him, "You're crazy. Get away from me."

In the wintery cold of Bastogne, Dad was jumping across a stream while carrying an ammo bag containing six rounds of mortar ammunition. He misjudged the distance, broke the ice, fell into the stream, and got soaked. By the time the men reached the next town, his clothing had frozen, causing a crackling sound as he walked. There were no clean or dry clothes to change into, and the incident kept him out of duty that night because the men didn't want to risk the noise. That was the only good thing about walking around in ice-covered clothes all day, he said.

I think that's one of the ways my dad survived—by choosing to see things in the most positive light he could. He certainly saw the difficult experiences, too. In Bastogne he remembered seeing a horse in the snow with one of its legs shattered by a shell fragment, which he later wrote Stephen Ambrose about. The incident is mentioned in the book.[1] Fortunately, one of the noncoms put the horse out of its misery. The incident affected my dad deeply. Consistently, he talked about how he couldn't believe how brutal the war was. It didn't matter who or what got in the way of shelling—men, buildings, horses—it was *all* destroyed in the end.

Family Man

After the war, Dad reentered high school in a different program and got his diploma. He graduated from high school in 1948, at the same time as his youngest sister. Although he attended a different school than she did,

---

1. Ambrose, *Band of Brothers*, 215.

she remembers him as a popular guest at her senior prom. She was deluged with requests from her girlfriends for him to dance with them. He was a good looking "older man" to them, and a war hero. He was also an excellent dancer. He had excellent rhythm, and he and our Aunt Carmen used to enter and win dance contests. He enjoyed dancing throughout his life, and at the 2002 Easy Company Reunion in Phoenix, it was a real treat to see him and Aunt Carmen "cutting a rug" to some swing music, smooth as ever.

Dad spent about a year and a half at university. He drove a cab in San Francisco back then. In 1951, Dad left school to reenlist for the Korean War, along with his brother, Emilio, who we knew as Uncle Jay. Dad and Uncle Jay served in the same unit while in the Army. He was in the Airborne again, but not with the 101st, since it had been deactivated at the end of WWII. He had been a private during WWII, but was a sergeant in Korea because of his experience in WWII. Dad never talked about why he reenlisted other than he enjoyed the discipline of the Army. It was probably also out of a sense of duty, or even fun and adventure.

He didn't talk a lot about that period of time, either. About the only story he ever told was on the humorous side. He was in the barracks with his brother, Uncle Jay, when a runner from headquarters came in, stood at the door, and yelled, "Hey *Garcia*, the lieutenant wants to see you."

Dad yelled back down the length of the room: "Which *Garcia*? Ya gotta be more specific."

The orderly said, "Doggone it, I don't know," left, went back to HQ, then returned to the barracks and said, "*Sergeant* Garcia."

Dad yelled back down again, "*Which* Sergeant Garcia?" (He and his brother were both sergeants.)

The orderly shrugged again, went back to HQ to check again, then finally came back to the barracks and yelled, "Sergeant *Tony* Garcia."

My dad yelled a simple "Okay—be right there," and went to see the lieutenant. It wasn't like there was a whole bunch of other Sergeant Garcias in the outfit (just the two of them); they were just messing with the guy for fun.

After Korea, Dad returned to San Francisco in the late 1950s and lived in a boardinghouse where he met our mother, Nancy, who lived in the same boardinghouse. During their dating, my dad, being somewhat presumptuous, said to my mom, "So, after we're married . . ." and continued on with the conversation they were having. That was how he "proposed." They were married in December 1958 at St. Dominic's Catholic Church. Dad was working for Macy's then as a warehouseman. He moved furniture around, stocking and restocking, and enjoyed the physical nature of the work. He stayed with Macy's for about twenty-five years until he retired in the early 1980s.

Mom had been born in 1938, so there was fourteen years' difference between them, but the age difference never seemed to affect my parents. Mom wasn't of Mexican heritage, either. She was of English, Scottish, Irish, and Cherokee ancestry, and had been born and raised in Little Rock, Arkansas. She moved out to San Francisco with her good friend in 1957 where they both worked for Pacific Bell. Growing up, we mostly weren't aware of our mixed heritage. San Francisco was a strong collection of ethnicities even then, so we weren't much different than most other families in our community.

Mom was the classic American housewife. She took care of us kids while Dad worked. She had been very active in high school, played basketball, and was a high school homecoming queen. As we grew older, she worked outside of the home for Pan Am, at the San Francisco International Airport, first in the statistics office, then she switched to being a PBX operator. Dad was a bit slower to adjust to her working outside the home. Once, Mom was working swing shift, and Dad was in charge of making dinner, which he almost never did. He set the table, boiled the spaghetti, and grated the parmesan cheese. He looked so proud. But then when he called us for dinner, he realized he forgot to make the sauce. We got to go to Pan Am that night and have an automat-style dinner with Mom.

They had four children together, two boys and two girls. We were a typical American family in many ways, just growing up eating macaroni and cheese, watching TV, always having fun among ourselves. One of my sister's favorite memories is when we were little and went to the city swimming pool. All of us kids took turns climbing on Dad's shoulders to jump off. He was tireless and could play like that for hours. Dad could be strict on the exterior, but he was mostly a softy inside. If us four kids got loud at the dinner table, his method of discipline was to say, "One more word out of any of you, and you'll go eat dinner sitting at the top of the stairs." The view from the top of the stairs wasn't too bad, according to my sister Kelly. He could be hard on us, but it was all in the hope of keeping us out of danger. My sister remembers getting in trouble as a kid a few times, but no matter what she did wrong, whenever the punishment or fight was over, Dad would tell her that she was still his little princess. She always loved that he said that.

Dad enjoyed working with his hands. He enjoyed woodworking and kept a full workbench of tools and assorted paraphernalia he accumulated over the years. He'd rather fix something than buy it again.

He was an involved father and helped out with us kids. My brother and I joined the Boy Scouts. Dad also joined and went with us to Scout meetings and on hiking/camping trips. He helped us make Pinewood Derby cars, which we still have and are treasured possessions. One of my all-time favorite memories I have about my dad is when he built plastic models with my brother and me. I still have one of the first models I ever built.

You could say our religious life was fairly average. We were regular churchgoers at St. Elizabeth's. We kids all took our first Holy Communions there, and my sisters went to the Catholic grade school for a couple of years. Mom grew up Baptist, but converted to Catholicism because my dad was Catholic. Both of my sisters were also married at St. Dominic's, and my parents renewed their vows after my sister Kelly's wedding ceremony.

In 1972, along with many other families in the neighborhood, we moved out of San Francisco to the suburbs in San Bruno, about twelve miles south of San Francisco. Dad kept the same job, transferring to a newer location in Colma, CA.

Dad always seemed well adjusted to us. He never succumbed to addictions or disturbing behavior. Except for the nightmares, the war never really showed outwardly. Essentially, he put the war aside and moved on with his life. He went to reunions and was heavily involved with the Northern California Chapter of the 101st Air Division. He was president of the chapter for a year. He went to the occasional Easy Company reunion, more so early on. It was harder to go when he was raising a family, and later while taking care of my mom. Dad had a strong network of friends and especially kept in contact with buddy Les Hashey, who lived in Maine. Periodically he phoned or wrote his commanding officer, Dick Winters.

I'm thankful we never had to worry about an insecure family life. What helped promote that? I think it's because he came from a large, supportive family in the first place. He had a healthy, down-to-earth childhood, and learned to appreciate things because he went through the Depression as a kid. He had a good marriage to our mom, that's for sure. And he was sure of himself. There was a real confidence about him. It's as though he always knew what to do, and never had problems deciding on one course or another.

Dancing to the End

When the book *Band of Brothers* came out, Dad was very proud of the book and gave copies to friends and family. When the miniseries came out he was even more excited. We all were. We met Doug Spain, who came up from LA to meet us and to get to know my dad, the character he'd be portraying in the miniseries. That was one of the first times I ever heard dad talk openly in detail about the war. My parents didn't have HBO, but they subscribed to it just to watch the miniseries. Doug Spain drove up from LA when the fourth episode aired to watch it with us. We had a big gathering with friends and neighbors to watch the episode.

HBO held premieres in various cities, with one in Sacramento. At first my dad didn't want to go because of the difficulty of transporting, housing, and caring for my mom, but arrangements were made with the help of HBO and he decided to go. At the theater, after watching part of the first two episodes of the series, the four vets in attendance were invited up on stage and each given a plaque of appreciation by a local state representative.

Every five years, to commemorate the liberation of southern Holland, the Dutch hold a celebration in Eindhoven and invite the allies who had served there to join them. My dad started going to those events in the 1980s. The vets are treated like royalty. They are featured in parades, taken on bus tours of where they had fought, and invited to participate in ceremonies at war memorials. Dutch children come up to them to get autographs and hear stories. The Dutch hold a commemorative jump for those vets who want to jump again onto the drop zone that they jumped on for Operation Market-Garden. Several times my dad did his pre-qualifying jumps here in California, then jumped again with the vets in Holland. His last jump was in 1999, when he was 75. We were all a bit concerned for that one. As soon as he landed safely, my sister Stephanie ran up to him and gave him huge hugs of relief. I called my mother to let her know (and my Aunt Carmen and Uncle Bill, who had come out from Virginia to be with her) that he had jumped and was fine. He was one of about half a dozen vets to jump.

My mom retired in the early 1980s after she was no longer able to work due to multiple sclerosis. My dad retired in the late 1980s, basically to care for her full-time. He took on her care as his new life's work. Her disease grew progressively worse. Eventually she lost the ability to use her arms and legs. He dressed her, fed her, bathed her, kept the house clean, and cooked meals. Even though my mom was confined to a wheelchair, my dad would still "dance" with her, moving around the dance floor. Dad always called mom "his girlfriend." His devotion and loyalty were total.

Dad passed away first. In 1993 he had a mild stroke. Fortunately it didn't affect him much physically, but he found it harder to put words together, and you could tell it was very frustrating for him. Plus, his hearing was starting to go. Then, he had a major stroke in August 2005, and he died twelve days later of complications. Dad was almost eighty-one when he died. I was on my way to work when my sister Kelly called me with the news. Dad was in the hospital when he passed. One of the last communications I had with him was shortly after he went into the hospital. I told him I loved him and was proud to be his son. His eyes were closed and he wasn't able to speak, but he squeezed my hand in response, which meant the world to me.

We held a memorial service for him. It was touching to hear so many people talk well about him. Former coworkers from Macy's talked about him having a good sense of humor. Several others talked about how they didn't even know he had been in the military. The president of the Northern California 101st chapter spoke, "Taps" was played, then he gave my mom an American flag. It was a fitting tribute to his life.

My mother died as a result of the MS. Her body had gradually grown weaker as happens with MS. She died in October 2006. Both he and my mom wanted to contribute even after they had passed away and had made arrangements to have their bodies donated for scientific research. Their ashes sit next to each other in the home where they spent so many years in San Bruno.

As for the war, sure, there were bad memories there for Dad, but he was able to put them aside and not let them jeopardize or seriously affect the rest of his life. He was devoted to raising a family and taking care of his wife and kids. I think that focus helped him a lot. He didn't make a lot of money. He never became an executive. He worked with his hands his whole life, but I would still call him successful. Dad had a tough exterior, but was truly a softy inside. He was a selfless father and loved his family deeply. He was a good man, a man who truly loved his family and worked so hard to keep us safe and happy. He was always a gentleman and could laugh so easily.

One of my favorite memories comes from when we were little kids; we would take turns playing "airplane." Dad would lie on his back on the floor, we would stand over him and he would put his foot on the middle of our chests and raise us up in the air, holding our hands, so we could pretend we were flying. That's the picture of success I hold today. Tony Garcia was a man who loved his country, loved the men he fought with, loved his wife, and loved us kids. He loved us all to the end.

3

PAUL "FRENCHY" LAMOUREUX

Interview with Jerry Lamoureux, son

We had never heard anything at all about the Band of Brothers.

I was doing some genealogy research at the beginning of 2001 and asked my father for his discharge papers. Out of curiosity I typed in "Easy Company 506th" on the Internet and found out about the book, that they had just made a movie, and that they were looking for veterans of Easy Company. I told my father, and his only comment was "Oh yeah?" I bought him the book, and, after he read it, he couldn't sleep for a week. Literally. All those memories flooded back to him.

Dad had never talked about the war to us when we were growing up, or at least very seldom. About all we knew was that he had been a paratrooper in the 101st Airborne. He never went to any of the reunions. He was one of those "lost" men of Easy Company you hear about. There was one other veteran from Easy Company, George Luz Sr., who also lived in Rhode Island near where we lived, and he and Dad met together once after the war. About all Dad ever talked about from his combat days was an incident about a soldier he had been with in Bastogne who had accidently shot himself in the leg and bled to death. Dad never mentioned him by name, but we found out later it was Don Hoobler. The experience is shown in the miniseries.

HBO wanted to bring the veterans over to France for the premiere of the miniseries. At first, my father was reluctant to go. But he couldn't give any really good reasons for not going, so eventually we convinced him. My mother went also, along with my wife and me. It was the first time in fifty-seven years that Dad had met up with those guys.

First thing in Normandy, Dad caught sight of Dick Winters. He had always thought highly about Winters. He was really happy to see him. Back during the war, Winters and the rest of the men had given Dad the nickname "Frenchy" because he could speak French. Winters used him for an interpreter back in the war, then also relied on his language skills again at the premiere. We thought that was a good connection to make again.

All in all, I think Dad was glad he went to the premiere. When he came back he started getting phone calls and letters from fans of the Band of Brothers. Dad always said, "I don't understand why people want my signature." He was proud of his service, but never bragged about it. He always told people that he was not a hero but merely did his duty for his country.

First Platoon Man

My father was born in Rhode Island on May 19, 1925. He was the youngest of thirteen children. Some of my aunts and uncles were born in Canada, but Dad was born in the States.

My grandparents were French Canadians and had immigrated in the 1920s to America from Quebec. They came to New England primarily to work in the mills because there was no work for them in Canada. My grandparents only spoke French at home, and Dad picked up English from friends in the neighborhood and at elementary school.

Dad grew up during the Great Depression. There wasn't much money for the family in spite of the millwork. My grandfather also worked as a farmer. I think everybody grew food back then. The family depended on income brought in from the older children to buy the food for the rest of the family.

Times were hard all around, and Dad quit school to work. He never reached high school. He joined the service in 1943 when he was just 17. My grandfather needed to sign for him to get him in.

Dad wasn't one of the original Toccoa men. He trained in Georgia at Fort Benning, then was sent to Aldbourne, England, where he was assigned to E Company as a rifleman in February 1944. He was eighteen when he got to England. He turned nineteen on May 19, 1944, then jumped into Normandy two weeks later on June 6. He was one of the youngest men in the company.

Dad was assigned to the first platoon. We have a roster dated May 1, 1944, that shows Dad, along with privates Van Klinken, Miller, and Webb (who went to company headquarters), all in the fourth squad. Dick Winters was the platoon leader then, and Harry Welsh was assistant platoon leader. Dad was in Winters's plane when they jumped in Normandy.

Dad told me that when he first got into the company he was kind of frowned upon by the older guys, even though none of them had been through any combat yet. If you weren't one of the originals, you weren't part of the company—that's how some guys felt, anyway.

Once in a while he told us some funny thing about what happened in the service. For instance, because of his language skills, the older guys in the company had him line up the French girls and prostitutes for them when they were in France. I guess that's how he became friends with them. After they found out he could get girls for them, they became his buddies.

When we went to France in 2001, we met Carwood Lipton, whom Dad always respected a great deal. My father started talking to Carwood. He said, "You remember that time I brought some French girls to the barracks, and you came in and yelled at me, 'Frenchy, get those whores out of here!'" Carwood and Dad had a good laugh over that.

When Dad jumped into Normandy, he landed in an apple tree near the outskirts of Ste. Mère-Église. He had a map but no idea where he was, so he sat in the field awhile and watched other soldiers dropping in. He could see tracers hitting people, and men getting killed. When it became light the next morning he spotted a farmhouse nearby. He took the map to the farmhouse and asked the farmer in French where he was and where he should be heading.

Dad met up with a few other guys and they headed out to where they were supposed to meet up with Easy Company. He was separated from E Company for about thirty-six hours after landing. He was finally able to rejoin the company and fought in the battle of Carentan. He survived all of that fierce fighting. He never got hurt, not that he told me.

Dad made it through Normandy, then jumped again in Holland for Operation Market-Garden, then went on to Bastogne. That was the roughest part of the war for him, he said.

Bastogne was his last full-fledged battle. Sometime in January 1945, his feet grew really bad from trench foot. Then he got bronchitis so bad he could hardly breathe. So they took him out of Bastogne and sent him to a hospital in England where he recuperated.

Then they sent him back to Easy Company when they were in Austria, just before the end of the war.

He was one of the very few members of Easy Company who never got wounded. I used to kid him, "You must have been hiding pretty good." He laughed at that. He was discharged from the Army in December of 1945 and returned to Rhode Island.

One of the Guys

When my father first got home from the war he started doing odd jobs, then he found work in the mills. He married my mother, Rita, in April 1947. I was born in October 1948. Eleven months later, my sister, Susan, was born. We're the only kids in the family.

Growing up, we lived in a small town in Massachusetts, right near the border of Rhode Island. As a hobby, he liked to play cards with his friends. His favorite card games were poker and blackjack.

Dad worked in mills for most of the rest of his career, but at one time he had his own business, a small machine shop, and ran that for a while. Sometimes, as kids, we worked for him part-time if he needed us to help out. Mostly, he made parts for machines in the lace industry, which is big in Rhode Island. He retired in the late 1980s.

He was a good father. Sometimes he was even more like a friend than a father. When I was a teen, my friends liked to come over to the house. Dad often sat down and played cards with us. In some ways, I think my father had lost his youth because he went into the service so young. So, as I was growing up in my teens, he was often like one of us. He took us fishing, bowling, different things like that. He was never mean or anything. He was just another one of the guys. At times he had that paratrooper cockiness about him and he liked to tease a lot. Undoubtedly when he was in Easy Company he caught the brunt of a lot of teasing himself for not being one of the originals and being one of the youngest in the company.

Though Dad talked about the funny things in the service, he never talked about the killings or anything, though I'm sure he saw a lot of action. For some reason, the war didn't seem to burden him as much as it did some of the others. I think that when he got out, he was just happy he made it out alive. Once he got out, he was out of it, and he went on living his life—that's how he saw things.

Or maybe he adjusted well because he had all those brothers and sisters praying for him. My grandparents were very religious, and Dad was religious, too. He went to church every Sunday. We were Catholics. St. Joseph's Church in Woonsocket, Rhode Island, was the last parish he was involved with.

In mid-January 2005 Dad and Mom left to go on vacation in Florida. On their way back home they were bringing the car back to the rental place at the airport. He pulled the car off the road, passed out, and died. My mother was with him. That was it. He didn't really suffer or anything. He had been a little bit overweight and had some problems from that, and he had some problems with chronic bronchitis. I think that came from smoking over the years.

My mother is still living here in Rhode Island. She is doing pretty well for her age. She doesn't drive anymore, but we look after her and try to take her out once a week. Mom and Dad were married for fifty-seven years. They have two children, four grandchildren, and five great grandchildren. All of us miss him a lot.

★ 4 ★

PATRICK O'KEEFE

Interview with Kris O'Keefe, daughter

In his memoir, *Parachute Infantry*, Easy Company veteran David Kenyon Webster described my father as "one of our younger and more gentle-manly replacements."[1] Both parts of that description seem to fit my father well: young, and gentlemanly.

My father's name, Patrick O'Keefe, is perhaps best associated with a scene in the miniseries where he and Frank Perconte are talking while on guard duty in Germany. It's toward the end of the war, and my father has just come in as a replacement and is eager to see action. Frank has already seen two years of fighting by then and doesn't want to be bothered by a greenhorn's enthusiasm. Frank is trying to read a paperback while my father snaps together his machine gun and hums, "She'll be coming round the mountain." Frank tells my dad to relax and calls him by the wrong last name—O'Brien—for the second time. When my dad corrects him—*I told you, it's O'Keefe*—Frank tells him to shut up, then launches into a tirade about how no one cares what his last name is anyway, because there are

---

1. David Kenyon Webster, *Parachute Infantry* (New York: Dell Publishing, 1994), 244.

too many replacements showing up all gung ho for the war who will soon be shot and wounded, screaming for a medic, begging for their mamas.

In several other places in the miniseries, my father is epitomized as one of the younger, greener replacements. He's seen looking very shocked, in contrast to the other more experienced men who smoke and relax, as they travel in the back of a truck while French soldiers shoot German prisoners in the head by the side of the road. Then he's seen looking nervous while patrolling with his squad right before they find the concentration camps. Bull Randleman asks him why he's so jumpy, and says that he can hear his heart pounding in Arkansas. Someone has even assembled a video about my dad that's posted on YouTube about how many times he needs to correct the men about his last name.

My father was indeed young when he fought with Easy Company. He was only seventeen when he went into the service. He was a paratrooper who made all his qualifying jumps and had his wings but never made a jump into combat. Years later when I met many of the men at the Emmy awards, they were still teasing Dad about being a kid. And Dad was good naturedly taking it. "Yeah, I'm just this green kid," he said, though he was well into his seventies.

That shows his personality. He was always known for his good nature, his kindness, and for a life well lived after the war.

Living on Purpose

Patrick O'Keefe was born April 3, 1926, in Northampton, Massachusetts. He was one of the youngest of the Band of Brothers.

His parents had both been born in Ireland and had married after moving to the states. His father, Cornelius O'Keefe, worked as a policeman in Northampton and was referred to by the nickname "*Connie Keefe, the Cop*." His mother cleaned houses for professors at nearby Smith College. Family members described Northampton as a beautiful, safe, small town, an ideal place to grow up.

Dad had two older sisters, Ellen and Breeda, a younger brother, Mike, and two younger sisters, Mary and Johannah. They all liked to ride their bikes up to Look Park in Northampton. The O'Keefe kids hung out at the library and at Smith College. They played kick the can, hide-and-seek, and different kinds of ball. Dad was a Boy Scout.

Everyone in the family was a devout Catholic. Life revolved around the church. Pat was an altar boy and always attended Sunday Mass and First Friday seven a.m. Mass, even when it was cold outside in winter. A younger sister remembers Pat walking her to seven a.m. Mass one time and pointing out Venus in the early morning sky. The family went to novena, special prayer meetings held on nine consecutive days. As a child, Pat heard that missionary priests were needed in China and thought that might be his calling.

Dad went to St. Michael's Catholic High School. He was on the basketball team but was a substitute, not one of the regular players or big stars. During the big championship game versus the next town over, he got his big break. He was put in the game for the last thirty-seven seconds and scored five points, which prompted a championship win for his team.

Dad worked for the city of Northampton's recreation department while he was in high school, coaching young students in track and field. His sister, Mary, was one of the kids he coached.

His younger brother, Mike, was a strong athlete. He played baseball and was scouted by the pros. At age eighteen, he went into the Marines near the end of the war but was never sent overseas. Tragically, Mike died at age nineteen of a heart attack.

His brother's death affected Pat a lot. He often wondered why he was the one to live when his younger brother died. He continually vowed to make something of his life because his brother didn't have the chance. He vowed this again after the war. Why had others died when he had lived? Again, he vowed to live purposefully in their honor.

The Irish Replacement

Toward the end of high school, Dad figured he'd go into the priesthood. But he felt he also had a duty to serve his country, so he enlisted while still in school. He graduated at seventeen, started college and took civil engineering college courses, then went through jump school, and shipped out from New York on the *Queen Elizabeth* in late January 1945.

In a radio interview right around when the book *Band of Brothers* came out, Dad described his first jump. "I was scared at first, but once the chute opened, I remember saying what a grand and glorious feeling, a spectacular way of getting to the ground."

Years after the war he wrote friends of his, describing his first jump. It says as much about his character as it does about the jump.

> *On the day of my first parachute jump at Ft Benning, Ga as I approached Lawson Field aboard a C-47 for my first airplane ride, I suddenly felt scared and a prayer popped into my head: "O Holy Ghost, spirit of truth and holiness, enlighten my mind and strengthen my will to shun evil and to do good."*
>
> *Lo and behold I calmed down and went through my first jump without a hitch. In the long haul any good accomplishment can be laid at God's feet.*

After his first jump, Dad said he always prayed the *Magnificat* anytime before he jumped or headed out on duty. Some of the text of the prayer is taken from Luke 1:46–55.

Being Irish was extremely important to Dad, and he talked about his heritage all the time. He never actually visited Ireland. On the boat ride over the Atlantic, he passed by Ireland but fell asleep for that part of the voyage. That was as close as he ever got to Ireland. He always kicked himself for that.

Dad described joining Easy Company in France. From a replacement depot, he came to camp about eight o'clock at night. It was cold and blustery. The replacements came off their truck, were told simply to find a cot, and were sent to a tent. When Dad went inside the tent he saw a group of the men playing cards. Although most were around twenty-one or twenty-two, to Dad they looked "tough, old, and grizzled," and he said to himself, "I think you've bitten off more than you can chew, O'Keefe." He was assigned to 1st platoon, under Lieutenant Jack Foley and Sergeant Pat Christenson.

The book talks about how on his third night in Mourmelon, Dad went out on a night problem at midnight. As the men walked in the dark in single file, Dad lost sight of the man in front of him. He tensed, looking around. A quiet voice from behind him said, "You're okay son. Just kneel down and look up and you can catch sight of them against the sky." Dad did and caught sight of the troops.[2] Only later he learned that the voice had been from Major Dick Winters, then battalion staff, who had come back and was leading an all-night exercise for an outfit now full of replacements, which speaks highly of Winters.

Once in France the men were all hungry and went looking for something to eat. Dad reached into his pocket and pulled out all he had—thirty-five cents. It wouldn't have bought much. Then he saw a church and decided to put his last money in the collection box for the poor. He believed that God would provide for him and the men. There was no immediate miraculous provision of food, but the men kept going and eventually found some food somewhere. Dad said he wasn't seeking a miracle; what mattered was that he was trusting God and giving all he had.

Dad rode into Germany with the outfit where they saw little fighting. Mostly they were involved in occupation duties. In his interview with HBO, Dad mentioned that at the end of the war he saw a dead German soldier on the ground still holding a Catholic missal (prayer book). It struck him how alike they all were, young men just doing their jobs.

On May 8, the last day of the war in Europe, he and Harry Lager went to a storage space to look for eggs. When they kicked in the door, two Italian deserters were inside. They jumped up, and Dad and Lager pointed their rifles. There was a bottle of champagne on the table and one of the Italians said, "Pax," and they drank a toast to peace.

On the way back to camp, Dad and Lager met a German officer with a bum leg who had been in the North Africa campaign. He invited them in for wine and they toasted the end of the war. "It was the best thing they could do," Dad said, "to all say yes, that darn war was finally over."

---

2. Steven Ambrose, *Band of Brothers* (New York: Touchstone, 1992), 239.

One Hundred Ways to Say Hello

Dad returned home and went to college at the University of Ottawa in Canada for two years, then switched to Maryknoll Seminary in New York, still thinking about entering the priesthood. That's when his younger brother, Mike, died. There are various family theories as to why Pat decided against the priesthood. Most likely it was because after Mike's death Dad was the only remaining son in the family. Dad earned his bachelor's degree in philosophy from the State University of New York.

After university, he returned to his hometown of Northampton and did odd jobs, but felt stifled there, so he moved to California in the late 1950s where he worked as a civilian for Edwards Air Force Base, a type of work that became his life's career. He was a position classification specialist, a type of personnel manager. In 1968, our family moved from California to Washington, DC, where Dad continued similar work spending most of his career at the Pentagon. Dad lived in Rockville, Maryland, from 1968 until his death.

He had many more interests besides his career and job. Mostly he just loved his family. Although working for the government, whenever people asked him who he worked for, he said, "I work for my wife and kids."

Dad married our mom, Gloria Lopez, in 1961. He was thirty-five when he got married. She was twenty-seven. My mom is Mexican-American, and came from a family with eleven children. She grew up in La Junta, Colorado. Her oldest brother, Edward Lopez, had been killed in WWII when she was in elementary school.

When Dad met Mom, she was a junior high school English teacher at Edwards Air Force Base. They met at church. They were married quickly, less than a year after first meeting. They had two children, a boy, Kevin, and a daughter, me, Kris. Kevin grew up to be an Army military intelligence officer in Panama in the 1980s during the Noriega years. He was commissioned by Colin Powell. Later, Kevin worked as an ATF field agent in Miami, and later at the ATF headquarters in Washington, DC. I have a master's degree in special education and work in mental health.

Dad was a wonderful father. As a very little girl I remember not wanting to go to sleep. He held me and walked around singing this old Irish lullaby, "*Too Ra Loo Ra Loo Ra*." He could be a lot of fun, too. Sometimes my brother and I watched scary movies, and Dad hid behind the couch to scare us.

He always told these stupid jokes. His favorite was:

Did you hear about the three holes in the ground . . . ?

Well, well, well.

My dad cracked up whenever he said it, like we had never heard it before.

He was always doodling, a bit of a dreamer. He worked complex math problems just for fun. He played a banjo, mostly in our backyard. He collected oddly shaped rocks.

Dad attended all of our school events, athletic games, piano recitals, and swim meets. He coached basketball and soccer, his son's best sport. Dad was a voracious reader and a regular at the Aspen Hill Library. He read several books each week, everything from historical fiction, to detective novels, to books about ancient languages, cave drawings, and early civilizations. He kept a bookcase at home in the bathroom downstairs—that's how much he loved reading.

Dad's faith involved more than going to church. He saw his spirituality as a guiding force throughout his life. It affected how he saw things and treated people. Several times I remember asking him for advice, and Dad instructed me to discern what God wanted me to do. I remember feeling a sense of purpose, that God had an overarching control of all things, of hope, that I would see God in Heaven after death, and of security, that God accepted and loved me. All of Dad's children and his three grandchildren, Brian, Alexandra, and Ella, are very involved with church today.

Dad loved to meet people everywhere he went and learn little bits of different languages. He wasn't a super-social type of person, but he could talk very easily to strangers. He credited that to his war experiences, how the travel overseas had expanded his world view. He was always trying to learn about other countries, people, groups, and customs. Before the subway was built in DC, he took buses to work, and met all kinds of people on his commute. He always tried to meet and befriend as many people as he could. He learned to say, *"Hello, how are you,"* in more than one hundred different languages.

He retired in 1986, just after he turned sixty, the same year I graduated from college. They were getting computerized at work, and he decided he didn't want to go through the hassles of learning the new system. Dad made a great retiree. He was still young and active. Many days he met with other retired friends and veterans at a McDonald's in town to swap war stories, politics, and current events. Dad always wore his Airborne cap and smoked a pipe.

After Ambrose's book came out, and then the miniseries, he exploded as a local celebrity. There were news stories about him. He spoke to schools and community groups about his war experiences. Young fathers brought their kids to McDonald's to get his autograph. I think it almost made some of the other guys jealous that he got all this attention.

Dad seldom talked about his war years with us, but whenever he watched the evening news and a story came on about another war, Dad shook his head sadly and said, "You know, WWII was supposed to be the war to end all wars."

Dad absolutely loved going to the Easy Company reunions. He was closest with Clancy Lyall, Chris Christensen, Tony Garcia, Shifty Powers, Bill Guarnere, Babe Heffron, and Don Malarkey. I remember him talking about those men quite a bit. Dick Winters and Dad corresponded. Winters still sends bits of news to my mom.

One Last Jump

In Dad's later years, he got arthritis in his feet and that slowed him down a lot. But he still loved to walk down by Rock Creek, and found it very peaceful there. He always mentioned different animals he saw down by the creek.

In the spring of 2002, Dad got very sick and they had a hard time diagnosing him. He had a lot of tests done, including one at Walter Reed Army Medical Center, to figure out if he had picked up some sort of strange infection during the war. But he hadn't. Finally they diagnosed him with two types of cancer, bladder cancer and a type of lymphoma. Dad had been a cigarette smoker his whole life. He had switched from cigarettes to pipes a few years before the diagnosis.

In spite of the diagnosis, doctors didn't know how to treat him. In August 2002, I was visiting, and Dad was really down. His weight had dropped considerably and he was barely moving off the couch. All he ate was vanilla ice cream, because he said nothing else tasted good. Doctors were suggesting various plans for treatment, but Dad wasn't being cooperative at all. "It's my time to go," he kept saying. "I survived the war, but this is my time to die."

During that visit, he received an invitation in the mail to go to the Emmys in California with all his Easy Company friends. He perked up when he saw that. "You know," he said, "I really want to go to that."

It sounded great, but I wanted to make sure. "You think you're well enough to fly cross-country?" I asked.

"I'm going to tell the doctors that they need to get started on me, and that I need to be well enough to go," he said.

Dad met with his oncologist immediately. "Do whatever you need to do," he said. "Start the chemo."

About six weeks later, in September, we went to the Emmys. My mom had her fiftieth high school reunion in Colorado the same weekend, so she asked me if I could go with Dad. He was so excited. He didn't seem as sick as he really was. He was trying to eat regular food again, and he could often eat a little bit.

HBO treated us royally. We flew first class and were put up in a great hotel. After the Emmys, everyone went to the restauant Spago for a celebration. Dad was in a wheelchair then, and Tom Hanks was at the restaurant, too. Dad couldn't get in the line where everybody was talking to Tom, but Tom came over to Dad and bent down to his level. They had a good talk.

When we came home, Dad finished his course of chemo and radiation, but grew sicker. He was in and out of the hospital during the next few months. We spent a very enjoyable Christmas together where all the family was together one last time. By the first week of February 2003 his body grew very weak.

We got the call on a Wednesday that Dad had grown very sick. We travelled to be with him, and my brother flew in from Florida. My mother and brother and I spent the day with him in the hospital. It was snowing heavily, and we went home that night. I've heard this from several wives of paratroopers before, that sometimes their husbands will jump out of bed in the middle of the night, like they're dreaming of parachuting again. Dad was extremely weak, but the next morning when we went back to the hospital, a nurse told us that Dad had jumped out of bed during the night. I like to think he was dreaming of one last jump.

On his last day alive, he was in and out, not talking, just resting. As I sat by his bed, I held his hand and prayed. I had this strange spiritual experience; I can't quite explain it. I saw somebody come into the room—I could just barely see movement in the air—and it was like some sort of spirit moved Dad's body up to a standing position. I think it was an angel coming to get Dad. I couldn't actually see anybody, but I could see motion in the room—I don't know how else to describe it other than that.

When Dad died, we were all in the room with him holding his hands. Again I felt this strange presence, it's hard to describe, but it was like I touched Heaven when I was holding his hands. I was feeling Heaven through him.

Dad didn't fear dying. He felt like he had lived a long life and done what he wanted to do. He felt that death was simply going home to be with God.

He passed away on Saturday, February 8, 2003. At his funeral we had two photo displays of him, one with his family, the other with his war buddies. We played the *Band of Brothers* CD in the lobby for the wake. People told us how beautiful it all was.

The next day at his Mass, we played a song called "On Eagle's Wings," based on Psalm 91, that talks about how God will lift you up on eagles' wings and make you shine like the sun. Then a friend played "Amazing Grace" on the flute. I wouldn't call the funeral sad. I would call it joyful, like Dad would have wanted it to be.

Dad's body was transported to Gate of Heaven Cemetery, where he was buried, and an Army representative came out and played "Taps". It was a very cold day, it had just snowed, and the sound of a single bugle filled the air. The day was extremely clear, and as the sound rang out across the snow, it seemed to resonate forever.

5

GEORGE L. POTTER JR.

Interview with Daniel Potter, son

I was never quite positive that the stories my father told me about the war actually happened. At least from my perspective as a young boy, they didn't seem real. We'd watch war movies with Dad, and he'd talk about all these far-flung places and horrific action scenes with familiarity, saying things like, "Yeah, that looks about right," or "I was nearby there when that happened." His stories seemed so extraordinary. I just couldn't fathom how my dad—how anybody—had actually gone through all those experiences and lived.

Dad didn't help us understand much, either. If I ever asked Dad a question about his combat experiences, he wouldn't say anything in return. He'd grunt or look away or make it clear somehow that he wasn't going to answer any questions about the subject. Whenever he talked about the war, it was on his terms, and he talked mostly about the funny parts. I believed those more. He'd have a drink in his hand and tell stories about life in the barracks, his friends, and the good times they had, poaching deer in England, avoiding the officer of the day while stowed-away British girls fell through the attic of the barracks, things like that.

My father, George L. Potter Jr., was one hell of a man. He lived creatively and intensely and was an innovator in his industry. He also died broken and bitter. Those were his life's contradictions. He did much more than most men ever dream of doing, and he made it through the war physically. But psychologically, I don't think he ever really survived the war. I think that's the best way to put it.

And what about me believing his war stories?

Everything changed the night before the D-day museum opened in New Orleans. I was over there at the time and met someone by chance who put everything in perspective for me.

At the museum opening, a woman named Lies Staal was introduced as a guest. She had been a fifteen-year-old girl living in Eindhoven at the time of the Market-Garden jump. The night before the opening we had a banquet. After the meal was over, I wandered over to her table to ask her a few questions. I was curious about what it was like to live under Nazi occupation. She told me all about it, how her father was in exile in the UK, and how she and her brother needed to walk to the town of Sonne to pick potatoes out of a field. They had heard there was some food there, and that's what they ate to survive.

This girl had witnessed the Allied parachute landing for Operation Market-Garden, and she and her brother had made their way back from the potato field to Eindhoven. The next day, when the troops came through, her mother had allowed her to stand in front of their house as the troops walked by. She had asked several of the troops to sign her autograph book. Years later, she had brought this book with her to the banquet, and she let me look at it.

On the very first page was unmistakable handwriting. It was my dad's signature: George L. Potter. It completely stunned me—when you think of the coincidences—it still chokes me up today. Dad had obviously made the jump into Holland. He needed to have walked down the correct side of the street where she was standing. That book needed to survive the bombing of Eindhoven a few days later. The woman needed to care for that book all of those years, and then hear about this D-day museum opening, and then bring the book to the banquet. Then I needed to go over and talk to her, and she needed to show me the book. What are the chances?

Seeing Dad's signature brought everything together for me. The piece of paper was tangible and the handwriting was his own, the scrawl that was so familiar to me. His stories and experiences were validated in my mind. I had no doubt that he had told me the truth all those years. His stories were horrific and far-fetched and fantastic—and it's true. Real men actually lived through those extraordinary experiences.

On a Motorbike in Swindon

From moment one, my father was a military man. He was born in 1923 at Fort Benning. His dad was an officer from WWI and had fought in Europe with the 5th Infantry regiment. Later, my grandfather went into the ministry, which was quite a change from his previous career. After my dad was born, the family moved around from Fort Benning to Long Beach then to Arizona—Tombstone, Mesa, and Winslow—working at different churches in those cities, then to Spokane, Washington, then to Hood River, Oregon. That's where my dad lived in 1942 when he turned eighteen and enlisted.

When Dad enlisted, he came home and told everybody. His mother was really upset. But his dad said, "Well it's not too bad. At least he's enlisted, so he'll be with a good group." Then he asked what unit my dad had enlisted with. "The paratroopers," Dad said. My grandfather shook his head and immediately hauled him back to the recruiter, trying to get him transferred out. But he was unsuccessful, and Dad stayed with the paratroops.

When Dad enlisted he was still attending Hood River High School where he was a good athlete and track star. He held the state record for the quarter mile. He went into the military his senior year and received his diploma as part of his enlistment.

Dad wasn't one of the original Toccoa men. He was one of the very first replacements in Easy Company. He went through boot camp at Camp Roberts in California (Vandenberg Air Force Base today), and later joined the company February 22, 1943, while they were still training either in North Carolina or across the river at Benning. I've got Dad's records. Captain Herbert Sobel initialed all the lines.

Dad was never happy about joining Easy Company late. He was one of the original guys in many ways, but he always felt a bit slighted by the original Toccoa men for being a replacement.

Although Dad seldom talked about combat, we've confirmed that he made the Normandy jump with Easy Company. He was in Stick 69. He lost his rifle on the jump because the aircraft was traveling too fast and it flew out of his hands. He landed on the roof of a farmhouse near Ste. Mère-Église. He heard lots of shooting going on, so he slid off the roof into a walled yard where he found another trooper from another company. They both made it to safety and found weapons soon.

We have a photo that shows a group of Easy Company men standing across a road outside Carentan. All the troopers have been identified except one, who we think is Dad. He looks just like Dad and is standing much like Dad stood at times. Next to this man is Don Hoobler with his arms crossed, and tipping his helmet is Bill Dukeman, who were both known to be friends of Dad's.

We have another group photo of Easy Company men where we have confirmed that Dad is in the group. Dad is standing with his arm on Dukeman and on the other side of him is Vernon Menze, both killed in action in Holland.

As a kid, Dad would show us the official 506th scrapbook and point out pictures of himself in that book. There's a photo of troopers marching in Ste. Marie-Du-Mont. He's in that photo. When I visited Europe so many years later, I went to the mayor's office in Ste. Marie-Du-Mont, and there's a big blowup of that picture.

I can remember Dad talking about his records. The military said he never officially made the jump into Holland, although that's where he was wounded and why he received his Bronze Star, although the medal was given to him in 1949. It seems that Dad had stolen a motorcycle to go to a pub in Swindon with some of the guys—borrowed maybe, but the word he always used was "*stolen.*" On the way back to Aldbourne he crashed the bike and was put in a cast, so the rosters show him in the hospital. Dad heard that the jump into Holland was coming. He didn't want to miss it, so he broke the cast off his leg, went AWOL from the hospital, and made it back to the airfield in time for the jump. He was wounded within a few days of the fighting in Holland, sent back to another hospital, and his records never caught up with him. So there's no record of him ever being on the Holland jump.

After the war, Dad wrote to the medic who had treated him. Fortunately, the medic had kept very accurate records and was able to verify that he had treated my dad, and on what day it happened. So Dad got his Bronze Star a few years late.

I remember Dad's feet were always kind of messed up from frostbite in Bastogne. Once while over there, Dad saw a dead soldier with better boots than his, so he swapped boots with him. I remember him telling us this story as kids and me thinking, "Why would you ever want to take some dead guy's boots?" But now I understand it was to survive.

In Austria the enlisted men found a truck and rode around in it just for fun. A lieutenant wanted the truck. The enlisted men weren't too happy about this, so Dad shot out the engine first, then handed it over.

At Zell am See, the enlisted men found a speedboat and zipped around the lake, having a great time. Some officer wanted it for his own, but the enlisted men held their ground this time. They were hauled in before Colonel Robert Sink, who announced that the boat was now the property of the 506th and that the enlisted men could continue to use it as long as they gave all the other men rides in it. So that became one of Dad's jobs in the army—giving speedboat rides, which he always chuckled about. Pat O'Keefe confirmed this story.

Dad never attended reunions. I think he still carried some bitterness from never feeling fully accepted as a replacement. Plus, I think he really just wanted to be done with the war and not think about it again. Apparently he was in contact with somebody in the company, because he always seemed to know what was happening. For instance, in 1961 Easy Company veteran David Kenyon Webster got lost at sea while out shark fishing. My father was working as a TV news photographer at the time. He convinced the TV station to rent an airplane, and he flew around searching for Webster, who was never found.

An Innovative Journalist

When Dad came home from the war, his folks were living again in Winslow, so he moved there. He married a girl from that city, Emely Davis (not my mom), and had a daughter with her, my half-sister.

I think Dad struggled for direction at first. He went to college some, worked some, but really was kind of a wash for the first few years after the war. I talked to his first wife and she said he felt the government owed him something. Physically, he didn't suffer any permanent disabilities except for his feet and the frostbite issues. But the war was always in his mind and he never could seem to shake it. Dad, like many of his generation, chose to self-medicate with alcohol. In my memory (I was born in 1954), I don't ever remember a time when alcohol wasn't an issue for him. Later on, it became much worse.

Dad divorced his first wife around 1949 or 1950, then married my mom, Lois Larson, in 1953. At the time, his folks had moved to Lompoc, California, so Dad moved with them. He worked at the prison in Lompoc. His second wife went to nursing school in Santa Barbara. There were six or seven years between them, not a big age difference. They had four children together.

After Lompoc, Dad and Mom moved to Fresno where my dad wrote stories for the *Fresno Bee*. He tried to break into journalism as a freelancer but never could quite make enough to support a family. They moved to San Diego, where he worked security as a day job and freelanced for the TV stations. Finally, he was hired full-time by one of the TV stations, channel 10 at the time. I think it was an NBC affiliate.

Dad was a cameraman, but it was more like reporting in the early days of TV news. They gave cameramen these Bell & Howell 16 mm cameras and put them in cars with radios. Dad's job was to drive around and shoot film footage of whatever news was happening. They didn't have on-camera reporters in those days, just anchormen back at the studios, so the cameramen took the film back and spliced up the stories. Then the anchormen would read the stories while the film Dad took provided footage of the action.

He was really good at his job and dreamed up a variety of innovative ways to shoot film of people. For instance, Harry S. Truman toured San Diego just after his presidency was finished, and my father was sent to cover the story. He knew Truman would be doing a lot of walking around, and he wanted to get a stable shot, but these were the days before steadycams. So Dad rigged up a child's red wagon with his camera and sat in it while someone pulled him. United Press International did a story on Dad's innovation with the headline "Another First for KOGO-TV and San Diego."

What was life like growing up with my father? Mostly a huge adventure. Nothing was ever exciting enough for him. Adrenaline fueled whatever he undertook. I've got videos of him as a newsman in San Diego. They were building high-rises, and he decided to do a story on the ironworkers. So there he is walking on steel girders thirty stories up. Or when parasailing first started in early 1960s, he tried parasailing as part of a news story. He was the first newsman on the West Coast to fly Mach 2 in a fighter jet. That's the kind of stuff he regularly did.

Dad loved outdoors and camping, and did a lot of that with us. It didn't matter the season, he'd take us camping year round. He was an active father in many ways. He took us tobogganing in winter. He was active when we were Boy Scouts. He could always add more adventure to a situation. That's how he liked it. Dad could be a lot of fun. He had a tremendous personality and could make friends with anybody.

Haunted and Consumed

Dad never really struck the balance between being a family man and alcohol—it overtook him, particularly in the end. As a child and teenager, there was a lot of insecurity in the family. I always felt dread going home because I was never sure what I'd find. That was tough. When I was a kid I didn't understand what was going on. I remember finding bottles around the house that he had hidden. Today, that's not surprising to me because I understand alcoholism much better.

When I was probably nine, Dad took us camping one winter at a cabin in Julian, just north of San Diego. It was my dad, my sister, me, and my brothers. Dad became intoxicated and started hallucinating. He piled the beds against the windows because the Germans were "just outside," he kept yelling. That kind of thing was terrifying for a kid, and it gives a good indication of the extent to which he continued to be haunted by the war, how the horrors he had seen spilled over to postwar life.

There were times where he became extremely introverted, such as around Christmas, which is when the men were in Bastogne. One Christmas he started talking about how Don Hoobler got killed (he had mistakenly shot himself in the leg with a Luger), and how Dad had been right there when it happened and had tried unsuccessfully to stop the bleeding. Some of the people in the company don't remember my dad being there, but I can remember Dad talking about it. In the movie it's portrayed as happening during the daytime, but Dad said it was more at night, and the men couldn't locate where Hoobler had been shot. They weren't able to get a good light on him because they could hear German tanks idling not far away.

It was about 1990, and we were trying to determine what unit Dad was in. We called his brother Bob. This was before the book or series came out. Bob Potter confirmed Dad was in Easy Company, 506th. We asked who his friends were, and Bob said, "Well, Hoobler was his best friend," so that helped explain Dad's introverted tendencies around Christmas.

I'd characterize the relationship he had with my mother as difficult. They divorced in 1967 or '68. He was remarried twice more, although he didn't have any more children. He was still married to his fourth wife when he died, so three divorces total.

In his last years Dad lived in Mt. Shasta, an outdoorsy type of town where he was able to be outside whenever he felt well enough. He's buried there in the Mt. Shasta cemetery. He died from the flu. His health was not good by then, and the flu just kind of overwhelmed him.

I wasn't interacting with him much toward the end. The last time I saw him was about ten years before his death. He wasn't doing well then, from alcoholism, Valium addiction, and whatever else he could find. I went to his apartment to check on him, and he was really a mess. It's tough to go into detail. He had lost much of his sense of reality. I guess as his son I needed to protect myself. I chose to put distance between us.

We kept in touch, on and off. He tried to regain some sense of control over his life, I think. He went to some kind of ministry school, one of these fringe religions, and became some kind of minister, perhaps working with other alcoholics, I'm not quite sure. The religion wasn't enough to save him. The substances had pulled him down so far that he was never really able to climb back out. There were a lot of people at his funeral, though, maybe a hundred and fifty friends of his, so he was able to connect with people on a good level to some extent during his last few years. He died January 7, 1985.

It's not easy being the child of an alcoholic. In my own life I've tried hard to break the cycle of addictions. I never drank much, but when my oldest daughter reached high school, I quit drinking altogether. It wasn't like I ever drank much anyway: a six-pack of beer could sit in my fridge untouched for months. But I wanted her to see that alcohol didn't automatically need to be part of every social gathering. If I went to a party, I didn't need to drink to have a good time. That's what I wanted to show her—to lead my family from the front. Seven or eight years went by where I didn't drink at all. Occasionally I'll have a beer now at dinner, but that's it.

Remembering George L. Potter Jr.

In the early 1990s I was a representative for Honeywell as a test engineer. I was commuting to Florida quite frequently at the time, almost on a weekly basis, and reading a lot. I had seen *Band of Brothers* on the bookshelf, but I didn't know what unit Dad was in at the time. I had thumbed through the book but hadn't seen any pictures of Dad, and his name wasn't listed in the index, so I didn't buy it.

A few years later, in the summer of 1997, my brother Tim was in an army surplus store in Connecticut where he lives. He talked to the store owner about our dad being a paratrooper, and the guy asked him what unit he was in. When Tim said, "Easy Company, 506th," the guy recommended reading *Band of Brothers*. Tim went and bought the book, read it, and told me I needed to get it, so that's when I bought it and read it cover to cover.

It was well worth the read. I recognized many of the stories Dad told us through the years. I was able to call Stephen Ambrose and we talked for some time. He put me in touch with Dick Winters, E Company's commander, who gave me some other stories about my dad. I called and wrote other survivors of E Company, and have developed a good relationship with many of them. We've been invited to their reunions and have attended several. It's been very good to go and connect with these men.

It's true, Dad led a complicated life. When he wasn't drinking, he could be a great father. I know he was always proud of his service. He volunteered, stepped up and did what needed to be done. That's how I'd want people to remember George L. Potter Jr.

PART II

NON-COMMISSIONED OFFICERS

The Backbone of the Army

6

GORDON CARSON

Interview with Gary Carson, son

My father's story is inextricably linked with my mother's. Stephen Ambrose described her at the end of *Band of Brothers* with one simple line: "Carson fed an educated, beautiful, sophisticated Polish blond."[1]

That one line has raised questions over the years. Who was this Polish blond? Why was my father feeding her? And what was the mystery behind how they met and married?

Here's how the story unfolds.

The Polish Blond

My mother was a blue-eyed dynamo who became a wife, widow, smuggler, slave, parent, and killer all before she turned twenty-three. Her name was Antonia Puchalska. Friends called her Toni.

When Toni was seventeen, she lived with her parents in Warsaw, the capital of Poland, right when the city was bombed by the Germans. Imag-

---

1. *Band of Brothers*, 278.

ine it: Here was this pretty teenage girl, intelligent, sensitive, and full of dreams. One morning as she was getting ready to walk to school, bombs started falling out of the sky. Her childhood and young adulthood stopped at this point. It was September 1939, just before the official start of WWII, and Germany and Russia acted in tandem to simultaneously invade, ransack, and occupy Poland. Germany attacked from the west, Russia attacked from the east. The Polish army didn't stand a chance, although it fought valiantly. It was vastly outnumbered and fell quickly. Thousands of Poles were arrested, executed, or deported to Siberia. Poland was divided between the Soviets and Germany and occupied by armed fighters.

Toni had been a child of wealth and privilege up to this point. Her mother was a doctor and her father was an engineer for the Polish government. They lived a cultured lifestyle in a large house on the outskirts of the city but were forced out of their house by the German army, who used it for a command center and officers' barracks. Toni's family was abruptly homeless with the war just beginning. A botanist family friend took them in elsewhere in Warsaw.

My mother was being courted by a young Polish army officer by the last name of Lewandowski. He was a longtime family friend, and they wished to marry soon, but delayed wedding plans because of the war.

Toni's father and older brother were part of the Polish army and survived the initial invasion, but were soon murdered by the Russians while on a mission at a dam site.

In just weeks, Toni had lost her father, brother, and home. She longed for her homeland to return to a place of security and freedom and vowed to do whatever she could do to fight for her dreams—and her survival.

Her First Marriage

Despite her losses, Toni decided to press forward with her life. She went ahead and married her longtime love, the Polish officer Lewandowski, when she was just eighteen. Almost immediately they had a little blond-haired baby named Richard. It was a horrible time to bring a baby into the world. Toni's new husband was a quick casualty of war. He died

March 5, 1940, during the Katyn Forest massacre when some 22,000 Polish officers, policemen, intellectuals, and civilians were murdered by the Soviets.

In her grief both for her husband and her country, Toni, along with many other Polish young people her age, joined the Polish resistance. It was tough going for all. Her specific job was to smuggle bread to the Polish fighters at night, the fighters' only source of food. Being associated with the Polish underground carried risks, but the botanist friend who sheltered Toni, her mother, and young son, Richard, had a secret double basement in his house. For the next year and a half my mother hid in the basement during the day while Nazis searched for her and other resisters. Sometimes she could hear the Nazis walk right over her head. She feared for her life every time she heard the familiar click of their heels.

Her mother looked after baby Richard during daylight hours. Even that task carried peril. Once, while grandmother and baby were outside, a bomb went off and the baby was hit in the stomach by shrapnel. Fortunately, he survived, although with permanent scars. At night, Toni continued to sneak out and take food to the Polish resistance. Each move by any family member was filled with danger.

Then one day the unthinkable happened. Toni came home and found that her mother and Richard had vanished. Toni had no idea what had happened until she started talking to neighbors and found out they had been picked up by the Nazis, thrown in the back of a truck. Nothing could be done. The grandmother and baby had been taken away to a concentration camp, but Toni didn't know where. Toni was beside herself. There was absolutely nothing she could do but continue on alone.

Auschwitz

Toni's perilous work with the resistance movement continued. It was dangerous, secretive, and sometimes horrible work. One night while on a routine bread run some distance outside of Warsaw, Toni and her cousin Marie encountered an unforeseen Russian roadblock at a crossroads. A Russian colonel heard them from a distance and came out to investigate.

Being caught would have meant certain death. The women hid in a ditch. Toni and Marie were armed. They ambushed and killed the Russian officer. Toni felt avenged, to a degree, for the killing of her husband, brother, and father by the Soviets, but knew she now had blood on her own hands. She was convinced the Russians were looking for her—and she was right. She needed to hide, even more than before.

Despite her extra precautions, she was more than ever motivated to help the resistance and help free her country. A strict ten o'clock curfew was imposed all over Warsaw. It was 1942, just before the start of the Warsaw ghetto uprising, and one night Toni was still outside five minutes after ten o'clock. She was caught by the Nazis for violating curfew. Toni was arrested, thrown on a truck with other prisoners, then herded onto a cattle train and sent to Auschwitz. The rumors of what was really happening at Auschwitz were just coming out in 1942. Being sent there was basically the same as a death sentence.

In Auschwitz, a prisoner was sent either to this line or that line: those marked for immediate extermination and those to be registered as prisoners. Some three million people eventually died in the camp. People often talk about how Hitler targeted the Jews—and that's correct—yet he also targeted many other groups. Hitler didn't just kill Jews. Anyone who got in the way of the Nazis was imprisoned. They usually ended up in the ovens. The Nazis considered Polish people *Untermenschen*, meaning subhuman, or less than human. Included in this group were Jews, Gypsies, Slavic people, and anyone else who was not an Aryan according to Nazi race terminology.

It was fortunate that Toni had blond hair and blue eyes, and that she spoke German fluently. (She had been raised by a German nanny who taught her the language.) Her captors found her both useful and attractive, so they didn't kill her. Still, conditions in Auschwitz were horrible. Everywhere around her was death and dying. She knew she had to get out. Toni could think of only one plan—it was a long shot and risky, but she decided to take it. From prewar times, Toni's family was acquainted with an influential German countess. Toni was able to smuggle a letter out to her, telling the countess her family's story and begging for help. The countess received the letter, was able to pull some strings from the out-side, and had Toni transferred to another Nazi labor camp, this one still severe, but less murderous than Auschwitz. The countess was more pow-erful than Toni realized. On the first night inside her new prison cell, Toni heard a familiar voice in the next room. She couldn't believe it. It was Toni's mother, along with baby Richard. The little family was reunited in the new prison camp.

The next three and a half years passed slowly and harshly. Toni re-mained in the prison camp with her aging mother and young son, some-times hearing the Allied bombing of nearby railroads. Toni was not used as a translator this time; she worked at hard labor with a pick and shovel. Her specific job was to carry buckets of railroad ties and help repair the bombed railways. It was slave labor, but every night she was able to see all the family she had left in the world.

The grandmother, named Irene Puchalski, continued to act in her profession as a doctor, and constantly took care of people in the prison camp, giving away her provisions. Toward the end of the war, Irene grew sick with dysentery. She had helped other people, but in the end she could not help herself. The grandmother died in the camp. Toni had now lost her father, brother, husband, and mother. It was just her and her young son. Toni herself was sick, thin. One picture survived of her during that time. She has sunken, drawn cheekbones. Her eyes convey hopelessness. There wasn't much time—or hope—left for her.

Gordy Carson's Story

Hold that thought, and let me tell you about my father.

Gordon Carson (known as Gordy to his friends) was born July 30, 1924, in Geneva, New York. Unlike Toni, he wasn't a child of wealth or privilege and he didn't have an easy upbringing. Gordy's dad was a former WWI Marine: hardnosed, alcoholic, and a real roaring drunk. Life at home was chaotic, loud, unpredictable, and frightening. His mother was an alcoholic, too. This little short thing, maybe four-foot-ten, could put away an eighteen pack a day and still walk.

Despite the hard times, Gordy grew up learning to be charming, even a bit of a smooth talker. Friends referred to him as the "lovable scoundrel." He found solace from a difficult home life in sports and threw himself into athletics. At Geneva High School he was the only athlete to letter in five sports in one year: lacrosse, track, basketball, football, and baseball. He dreamed of playing professional baseball someday and had the potential to make it. Everybody said so, except his father. Gordy had a quieter side to him, too, one he rarely showed to anybody. For fun he read Plato and Socrates. He dreamed of going to college one day and studying philosophy. He wanted to make something of his life.

WWII hit, and Gordy and his classmates put plans on hold and enlisted. Gordy found out there was an extra fifty bucks a month for being a paratrooper, so he signed up and was soon on a train bound for Camp Toccoa.

Gordy threw himself headlong into the training. He was one of five men in the company who received highest scores in the physical competition at Toccoa. Yet there was still time for his other "hobbies." Gordy developed a reputation among the men as a real ladies' man. The guys in the company even gave him the nickname "Loverboy."

Gordy kept an extensive journal while at Toccoa, which described the training jumps from airplanes, the running, the marching, the endless physical exertion, and the other members of the outfit. He didn't like training at Toccoa much, yet on November 29, 1942, wrote of the joy of camaraderie he was experiencing:

> Our 13 weeks of training, as I look back on it, has been one mass of countless days. We came here raw, very raw, recruits and go from here soldiers. We have learned to live with each other, and with all our grumbling, swearing, and noise, we have learned to know that you have to have buddies to get along in the service.

While at Camp Benning, he wrote about the thrill of jumping, which also shows you a bit of his personality:

I think I am getting jump crazy because when I am on the ground I want to jump some more. The feel of that rush of the prop blast cannot be told in writing. It gets you after a while. You jump out excited and then you feel that rush of the wind. I don't know whether I close my eyes or not, but all of a sudden I feel that opening jerk and I shout with all my might.

From America, Gordy and Easy Company boarded the troop ship *Samaria* and sailed to England, where more training occurred in Aldbourne. Gordy's journal also covered this time extensively. He wrote about first seeing England on September 17, 1943:

Kissed the Samaria good-bye and put our feet on good old ground for the first time in 11 days. We organized as a battalion and marched 1½ miles to the railroad station. The people are the same the world over, and we looked at them as much as they did at us. We saw some spots that were bombed bad. It is really awful and some of the buildings are just stripped. The people here really know that there is a war going on, for their homes have been bombed in front of them.

He wrote simply and poignantly on December 31, 1943:

Last day of 1943. Tomorrow shall be a new year, and I wonder what it shall bring, wonder how many of us will see 1945.

Wartime England was its own world, filled with dread of the combat that was to come. Some of the men used the opportunity to experience life to the fullest while they still could. Gordy was one of them. Once, Gordy and Sgt. Bill Guarnere smuggled two English girls back to their barracks. They hid the girls in the attic while the tight-lipped Lt. Peacock made rounds. One of the hidden girls slipped, and her legs fell through the ceiling. Peacock busted the soldiers, and Guarnere took the rap for my dad.

The high jinks stopped very soon. Gordy parachuted into Normandy on D-day and survived the intense fighting that followed over the next month as Easy Company helped liberate various French towns.

Gordy jumped again into Holland for Operation Market-Garden. The fighting was fierce, but again, he survived.

Then, in the harsh cold of winter, from December 1944 to February 1945, Easy Company fought the Germans in Bastogne. Conditions were horrible. The men of Easy Company had little food and no proper winter clothing. Days passed, filled with bloodshed. The men endured the constant pounding of German shells. Gordy was in his foxhole one day during a shelling. A German 88 flew in and hit the tree above him and exploded, driving a large jagged arrow of wood into his leg. He was sent to the frontline aid station in the surrounded hospital in Bastogne. Supplies were low in the hospital, and a medic gave Gordy a bottle of booze for pain. It was crème de menthe, and Gordy drank half the bottle. The Germans bombed the town that night and Gordy got on his hands and knees in the hospital to brace himself against the concussions. He threw up—green—in his helmet.

Gordy recovered from his wound and rejoined Easy Company just as they headed through Germany. The war was nearly over, yet there was much work still to be done. For three days and nights as Easy Company drove south, wave after wave of German soldiers marched north in the center of the autobahn, still in ranks but defeated, heading home.

In Germany, Gordy became a clerk for Captain Ron Speirs, who was then Easy Company's commander. One of Gordy's jobs was to pick out a company command post (CP) each night in the different occupied villages they came to. Gordy, who had a smattering of high school German, would pick out the best house in each town, knock on the door, and tell the people inside to leave. One evening he knocked on an apartment complex and the residents came out, including one elderly lady who reminded him of his grandmother. Out of compassion, Gordy told her not to worry, and stay where she was.

By the time they got to the Eagle's Nest, Hitler's hideout in the Alps, Speirs and Gordy were good buddies. Together they drank bottles of wine, then got out their .45s and shot wine bottles off the Nest's railing in celebration.

Gordy found Hermann Goering's car, and he and Speirs immediately hopped in and went for an extended joyride. Upper Brass wanted the car, but before they turned it over, they wondered if the windows were bulletproof. They paced off ten yards, aimed their M1s and fired. The windows were not.

From Germany, the company was sent to Kaprun, Austria, for occupation duties.

How They Met

Mercifully, the war ended in 1945, and Toni's captors deserted the prison camp. But she was not free yet. Along with many in the prison camp, she was transferred to a displaced persons' (DP) camp, which just happened to be in Kaprun, Austria. It was part of the huge humanitarian effort that began to take place. Following World War II, some eleven to twenty million people were considered displaced persons. Allied military and civilian authorities faced considerable logistic, linguistic, and transportation challenges in helping displaced persons find their way home to resettle. It was no simple task. Many DPs were sick, extremely malnourished, and in need of food and medical care. Many, including Toni, had no homes to return to or no way of getting there.

It's hard for people today to fully understand the depth of what happens during a war the size of World War II. What is it like to displace several million people? That's the size of several large-scale American cities. Imagine just New York City. Its population is about eight million people today. More than eleven million people died in the Nazi ovens during WWII. A million and a half of those were children. And millions more were displaced from their homes and were taken for slave labor, like my mother, Toni. I don't think we can fathom the scope of that—how traumatized people were, how scattered they were all over the globe. My whole extended family on my mother's side disappeared—she and my brother Richard were the only two out of nineteen on that side of the family left alive.

One of Easy Company's tasks was to help with the DPs. As Easy Company drove into Kaprun, all the DPs were together outside the DP camp on the grass. Gordy, ever the ladies' man, immediately noticed Toni's blond hair and went out of his way to meet her. Gordy didn't speak any Polish, and Toni didn't speak any English, but they both spoke German and made a connection. Toni and Gordy began to see a lot of each other. He introduced her to his commander. Because Toni spoke five languages, Speirs put her to work for Easy Company as a translator, helping with the DPs. On the side, Speirs also gave Toni a Luger to defend herself, because of all the drunk GIs around. Mom always said you couldn't imagine how happy people were that the war was over. An atmosphere of jubilance permeated the region.

Toni became a familiar face to Easy Company men. Once, Easy Company was having a party complete with ever-present beer kegs. Toni's son, Richard, who was about three or four years old by then, turned on the spigot of a keg and emptied out all the beer. Joe Lesniewski, Pat Christenson, and George Luz caught him at it, but laughed it off good-naturedly. Richard became known around Easy Company as "that little blond kid." We have a picture of Toni with Sgt. Ralph Spina and young Richard. The child is wearing clothes made of parachute material given to Toni from the paratroopers. There weren't any stores around there where a person could get cloth or baby clothes.

Toni and Gordy were very close, constantly. They spent the summer of 1945 together in Kaprun, taking in the beauty of the countryside, going for long walks, and falling deeper and deeper in love. But by August, many of the men from Easy Company were officially done with their duties, and plans were made to ship them back to Cherbourg, then back to the states. Gordy, as a high-points man, was one of these men. Gordy and Toni parted. Gordy was still in the Army. It wasn't like he could cart a wife along with him, particularly one with a young Polish son. Or could he? Perhaps it was just a fun summer, they concluded, one bright spot in years of horror. They wondered if they would ever see each other again. They concluded probably not.

Speirs remained in Austria for a short time. With Gordy gone, Speirs discovered that Toni was pregnant with Gordy's child. Speirs sent word to Gordy, who was then in Cherbourg, inches away from heading home.

Gordy had a decision to make. Like other GIs, he could have claimed that the baby was not his and skipped the country and kept going. Being with Toni would also mean taking on the responsibility of Toni's other son, Richard. Gordy still had college ahead of him. And dreams of playing professional sports. He had always been known as a ladies' man—this was just one of those things that happens, right?

Nothing But Hopes Ahead

Well, it must have been true love, because my father returned to Austria and proposed. On the day of the wedding in October 1945, George Luz had found some kind of rickshaw, like those in Asia. Luz pulled Toni around Kaprun while Gordy finished his day's duty. All DPs needed to wear white arm bands, but Toni didn't have hers on. A major drove by in a jeep, stopped, and ordered Toni to put on her arm band. She did, but as soon as he was out of sight, the affable Luz told her not to wear such a thing on her wedding day.

They married, but because there was no married housing, Toni and Richard continued to live in the DP camp while Gordy stayed in the Army camp. The family waited for clearance to come back to the States. It wasn't easy. Thousands of American men were coming home, some with new families, and America had so far closed its doors to receiving displaced persons.

The night their baby was born, Gordy secured a house in town for Toni so she could be inside and comfortable. A doctor came from Vienna to deliver the baby. Immediately after the birth, mother and baby went back to the DP camp. Their new son, Gary Carson, was born on March 3, 1946. That little baby was me. I was the first son of Easy Company born in Europe. It staggers me when I think about the odds against me being born. Fortunately, my mother had regained her health from her days in the prison camps, and I weighed in at a whopping nine pounds.

Finally the red tape parted and clearances were allowed. My mother and father, along with my half-brother, Richard, and me, came to the States on a troop ship through Ellis Island. My mother and Richard were listed as being Polish, but I was listed as an American citizen, born to an American GI. My brother and I both caught whooping cough while on the ship. I was the sickest, and they thought they were going to lose me. But we both survived. We returned home, a free family, to our new life in the United States. My dad had survived the war. My mother had found her place of freedom and security at last. We were all together, a young family with nothing but hopes ahead.

The Trauma of War

I wish I could say we all lived happily ever after.

The trauma that both my parents had been through during the war affected the family forever after. I remember some of Mom and Dad's early arguments. He would say things like, "Well, you don't know what I went through." And she would say, "Bullshit, you don't know what I went through." I always got a kick out of that, because Dad could never bluff her as to how horrible war is. She went through it all.

After the war, Dad went to Springfield College in Massachusetts where he majored in physical education and minored in philosophy. He graduated and they moved to the West Coast where he got a job. Dad did okay for a while, but, like a lot of the other guys, he drank a lot. I think that was that generation's drug of choice. Fortunately, he was a gentle drunk, always an easygoing guy, and always a gentleman. You couldn't help but love him. He told me once that after World War II and all he had seen, his philosophy of life was that he was simply going to have as much fun as he could. That was basically what he lived by even years later when he found out he had liver cancer. We were sitting near the ocean on a log down in Olympia and he said, "Well, I've had my fun." That's how he viewed life and death—enjoy each day while you're still alive—and boy, he sure did. But his fun often trumped any sense of responsibility.

I was twelve when my parents divorced. I stayed with my mom for a while then went to live with my dad in Seattle. He remarried soon and encountered the same problems in his relationship with my stepmother; she just put up with him longer. Mom never did remarry. I think she always loved Dad—and he always loved her—they just couldn't live together and make it work. There was always the language difference. She didn't have any extended family nearby. Then there was Dad's drinking.

When Dad first got out of college he worked for the YMCA in Bellingham as athletic director. He got involved with the Jaycees, and that led to a job as a life insurance salesman, which is what he worked at the rest of his life. When he moved to Seattle he worked for Olympic National Life. Later he moved to Olympia, and he and my stepmom bought a beautiful home on the beach. He worked for Midland National Life then and that's where he finished his career. He sold life insurance to the GIs up at Fort Lewis. Being an old Airborne Ranger, he had an instant bond with them and was quite successful in his business.

Mom was an accountant after the war. She was a hell of a mathematician. There were five children in the family and three in Dad's second. A few years after the divorce, Pat Christenson helped get my mother a good job down in California. They had stayed good friends since the war and had always written letters back and forth. Every year he sent Christmas cards of drawings he had done. She packed up the three younger kids and moved down to Sacramento. After a few years, she moved back up to the Pacific Northwest.

How My Parents Died

I wanted my kids to know their grandparents well, so we used to go often down to Olympia where my dad lived. My stepmother, Susan, was always kind to me and my family, and I have always loved my three sisters from my father's second marriage. One day Susan took me aside and said, "Your father's got liver cancer. It's terminal."

I was in shock. They had just found out that week. After that, my wife, Marci, and I made an effort to see as much of my father as we could.

It was just a few months after the diagnosis that he passed away. He never really talked about his feelings or what he had been through, but one day we walked out into the garage together. I asked him if there was anything he wanted me to know about. I was thinking more business thoughts, if he had his will all in order, but he really snapped at me. "Nobody ever did anything for me," he said. That was the only time I ever saw he had had a hard life himself, how his father had never really been there for him, and about the things he had seen in the war.

Dad didn't want anybody to know he was dying. He flew to the Easy Company reunion that October in South Carolina to see his old buddies one last time again. He didn't tell anyone it was going to be his last reunion.

I saw Dad the night before he died. Susan was taking care of him at home. He was in one of those hospital beds and was so weak he couldn't even talk, but I remember looking into his eyes and knowing that he could understand what I was saying. I told him I loved him. I knew it would be soon. He died at home November 13, 1998.

Dad was cremated and is interred at Tahoma National Cemetery. His plaque reads, "For the good times," the title to an old country song by Kris Kristofferson.

Several years later, when Mom was eighty-three, she was diagnosed with liver and lung cancer. Doctors caught it early enough so they could have treated it, but she refused. She was always a strong woman, very tough and stubborn. She believed in the afterlife and said she wanted to join her father and mother. Dying is a process, and as she was passing away, we'd catch her talking to her father in Polish like he was right next to her. I hadn't heard my mother talking Polish in years. She lived with my two sisters toward the end, and I saw her consistently before she passed. On her last night I told her that I loved her, that I realized what she'd been through had been so difficult. She died just a few hours after our conversation, at home, on March 11, 2006.

Because of These Events

The same year Dad got sick, we found out that Tom Hanks and Steven Spielberg had bought the rights to the book. We didn't know there was going to be a miniseries or anything yet. I said, "Well, Dad, if they make a movie and you're in it, who would you want to play you?"

"Tom Cruise," he said.

He had been very proud when the book had come out a few years earlier. He gave me a copy right away and wrote on the inside, "Because of these events, this is the way life was."

I always had fun with my dad. In my earlier years I drank with him a lot. Dad loved singing. Whenever Dad got drunk he sang. He loved Frank Sinatra and Harry Belafonte. He'd get me singing with him, too.

Was he an alcoholic? Oh, yeah. Absolutely. At the reunion in Seattle in 1993, Dad got so drunk he couldn't tie his shoes. Basically it was a four-day booze fest for him. We heard Dad got so drunk at a reunion in Vegas that he passed out in a parking lot. If the men hadn't reached him in time he would have died of sunstroke. I hate to write that down, but it's something that children of alcoholics need to wrestle with. Twenty-five years ago I had some problems of my own when it came to drinking. Fortunately that's behind me now.

Dad's big problem was that he was never responsible. He never paid attention to anything—bills, rent, child support—he was definitely lucky that Susan took care of him the rest of his life. But there wasn't a mean bone in his body. No one ever hated him; they excused much because he was so kind and funny. I think he simply didn't have a clue about how to be a father or husband. I doubt he ever realized how much his irresponsibility affected other lives or hurt people.

It was never easy to get either of my parents to talk about their experiences during the war, but Mom opened up to me quite a bit toward the end of her life. I may be slightly off about a few details, but what I've just described is how I remember my mother telling me things. It was her horror story and she always told it through tears.

What's one thing I'd want people to remember about my parents? Well, I'd want people to know that we're not far removed from the generation who lived through World War II. People who went through all that horror really existed. If you see documentaries on the History Channel about how horrible it was in Europe or the Pacific during the war, you know what I mean. I'd want people to know my parents went through some incredibly hard things. It was "because of these events" that they were the way they were. They had their flaws, but they also had a lot of good in them, too. What they went through is part of my heritage. World War II still affects this country—and the world—today. People need to realize that the war was very real. It was very horrible. And it wasn't all that long ago.

7

BURTON "PAT" CHRISTENSON

**Interviews with Chris Christenson, son,
and Gary Van Linge, nephew**

"The true picture of war is impossible to convey—even by those who did the bleeding and the fighting."

So wrote Burton "Pat" Christenson at the start of a pictorial journal he made for his three sons after the war. The journal is the size of a large picture album and runs more than fifty pages. Inside are pictures drawn by Pat, exquisitely detailed pencil sketches of the war he lived through. Underneath each drawing is an excerpt from a journal he kept about his season of fighting in Europe. Sometimes the journal excerpts show straight descriptions of battle scenes; sometimes they are poems or analyses. The art flows from him in various forms as he's ever seeking to communicate his experiences.

Pat's art is graphic, vivid, not something you'd show to a six-year-old. One page shows a soldier clutching his hand over one eye. The soldier's just been hit by shrapnel. Blood gushes from his hand and spills over his face. The soldier's other eye is still open, shocked, looking straight ahead. "Only those who were wounded severely know the conflicting emotions and anxieties that race through a person's brain," wrote Pat underneath, "if one is still conscious after being hit."

Pat also left an additional journal, the thickness of a small phone book. He wrote in pencil, sometimes printing the words, sometimes writing in large, clear cursive. The journal begins August 12, 1942, and talks about why and how he joined the Army. It ends in 1945, in Saalfelden, Austria, during occupation duties at the end of the war. Much of the journal appears to be reconstructed in later years from recollections, notes, and conversations with other E Company men. Inside the journal are detailed descriptions of army life and combat, including references to maps and separate essays about everything from what it's like to have flat feet from the long marches while carrying heavy equipment ("Sheer torture. My arches were gone. I found a podiatrist who sold me a pair of steel arch supports.") to a probing query about motivations for war ("What are we fighting for? Very few men in combat mention patriotic motives. Thoughts of making it through the war and going home are foremost in their minds.").

The two journals, together with his drawings, leave one of the most complete eyewitness accounts of life in Easy Company. What follows is the story of Burton "Pat" Christenson.

Off the Roof

Burton "Pat" Christenson was born in Oakland, California, on August 24, 1922. Few people ever called him Burton. Most of his friends either called him Pat, a nickname he gave himself, or Chris, the shortened form of his last name. His middle name was Paul, so Pat may have been a derivative of that. Family members knew him as Pat. Sometimes he signed letters as Chris.

As a child, he was driven to create. He never studied art professionally except for a few classes during one semester of college, and never worked at art as his career, but it remained a lifelong passion. The gifted boy could draw, play piano, and sing—talents he nurtured his whole life. Well into his seventies, he invited fellow Easy Company members over to his house, including Bill Guarnere, Bob Rader, Tony Garcia, Bill Wingett, Woodrow Robbins, and Mike Ranney, and "they chased the ghosts of the war together," said his son, Chris. During these impromptu get-togethers, Pat played the piano, the men sang songs from the 1940s, and they drank. "The men were never shy about drinking," Chris added.

While in the service, Pat and fellow Easy Company members PFC Carl Sawosko and PFC Coburn Johnson sang together with a guitar. Johnson was wounded during the Normandy campaign and sent home. Sawosko was shot in the head in Bastogne and died. Pat described losing his friend Carl as one of his greatest losses.

Pat's nephew, Gary Van Linge, thirteen years younger, lived just down the street from Pat. "He was always my hero," said Gary. Before the war, Pat took up archery after watching the movie *Robin Hood* starring Errol Flynn. Gary contracted scarlet fever at age seven and was quite sick for some time. The young boy had a thick book about Robin Hood, and Uncle Pat frequently came to the house and read to the child. "I've been involved in archery ever since," Gary said.

Pat was a creative teen. He made airplane models out of balsa wood kits. Paper was stretched over the wood and glued, then water flicked on the paper to tighten it up. Pat was a master at it, a real artist, noted Gary. The models flew with propellers and rubber bands, and if Pat made a model that wasn't perfect, he lit it on fire and flew it that way.

Pat could be adventuresome. At age thirteen he jumped off the roof of his house with a large beach umbrella to see if it would break his fall. "I don't know how much it actually slowed his descent," Gary said, "because he never did that again."

Pat was always athletic and physically strong. He made his own weight set by pouring lead into flower pots and sticking pipes in the ends. He was always doing pushups. "He could walk on his hands like nobody I've ever seen," Gary said. "He could walk a hundred yards on his hands, no problem. He was a natural when it came to going into the Airborne."

Pat taught Gary how to box and made him fight every kid in the neighborhood. It was more a sporting event than malicious fighting, and everybody participated. "All the kids in the neighborhood loved him,"

Gary said, "especially when he became a paratrooper. He was a hero to us kids."

He graduated from Castlemont, a big high school in Oakland, then worked for the Pacific Telephone company for a short time before the war. He enlisted at age twenty. "He wanted to serve his nation," Chris said, "And I think he wanted the challenge. My dad was a very competitive man."

Pat's journals concur. He described how he and a friend from work talked constantly about "getting into the fighting part of the war." They went to an Army recruiter's office during their lunch break at the phone company where they saw a brochure for the Airborne that read, "Jump to the Fight."

They were convinced the paratroopers were the only way to go.

The Toughest Man at Toccoa

After enlisting, Pat was sent to Toccoa, Georgia, where he wrote that, at first, "the majority of men had little conception of Army life and what was expected of them." Mostly, "too many men in our ranks were unsuited for the Parachute Infantry," which prompted heavy washouts. Over time, cohesiveness formed in the unit as the men hardened into soldiers.

"Pat became a paratrooper because he wanted to be the best," Chris said. "He didn't just want to be the average ground-pounding grunt, not to take away from that, but he wanted to be in a special unit." Pat held the physical fitness record at Toccoa. That's stiff competition—to be the toughest man at Toccoa. The family has a letter from Dick Winters verifying this. In *Band of Brothers*, the series shows Pat being the goat of training, drinking water on a run when he wasn't supposed to and having to run up and down Mount Currahee again. "We've asked the men who were there if that ever happened," Gary noted. "They said, 'Not to Christenson.'"

His young nephew kept a close watch on Pat's experiences from basic training onward. When Pat was in jump school, he taped his nephew's picture inside his helmet while making his five qualifying jumps, then commandeered an extra set of jump wings, which he sent home to Gary.

"He told me I was a qualified jumper," Gary said. "With those wings I was the envy of my school. In those days, everybody was well into the war effort. The armed forces were honored by teachers and students alike."

In spite of the rigorous training, Pat kept a rueful sense of humor. After the unit was sent to Alderbourne, England, for further training, he wrote, "Our training revolved around how to fight every conceivable way, and often, large groups of men gathered at the local pub." He described the food they ate in England—Brussels sprouts, turnips, and "I think they slipped some horse meat to us from time to time."

Headquarters staff expected an enemy invasion on England's airfields, so Lieutenant Winters picked three E Company men to teach unarmed combat to nearby defense units. Pat and the others selected were only privates, so Winters told them to borrow shirts from fellow sergeants in case they were challenged by the trainees. The three E Company men traveled to a nearby air base and taught the defense unit hand-to-hand combat techniques for several days. It was a rough-and-tumble crew, but Pat didn't back down. He wrote:

> After a period of time, a group came to me and exclaimed, 'Sergeant, no one can get out of this guy's hold. If this stuff works show us how you'd get away from him.' There, standing in the middle of the group, was a great big 300-pounder with a smile from ear to ear.
>
> I deliberately paused, directed a cold stare at him, then approached quickly and said, 'Make your move.'
>
> As soon as I felt his arms around me I immediately collapsed my legs and threw my arms over my head. I slipped out of his grasp and found the back of his neck with my hands. His body was now bent over my back. I jerked hard on the back of his neck. His body, off balance, came flying over my shoulder and struck the ground with a violent thud. Swiftly, I drove my knee into his neck. I had never executed that move as well before or since.
>
> The crowd roared with approval. Then and there, to that group, I was untouchable.

Time to Fight

The company moved to a marshalling area near Exeter, England, then to Uppottery Airfield in preparation for the D-day invasion. Pat describes flying over to Normandy on the night of June 5, 1944. "The aircraft moved along at a smooth pace. The only noise heard was the drone of the engines."

He was in the same plane as Lieutenant Winters, who stood in the door, watching the approaching coast of France get larger. Pat was second in line to go out the door behind Winters. Everything was quiet for some time, then a few miles into the peninsula, Winters pointed to the aircraft ahead and said, "Look, Chris, they're catching hell up ahead of us." Pat wrote:

> The red and orange tracers were reaching for the forward aircraft. Tension began to mount, nerves became taut. A burst of flak to our right aroused those still mesmerized by the long flight. [We were] conscious now that our drop zone couldn't be too far away.
>
> The flak grew heavier. We stood now, ready to get the hell out of that bobbing and weaving C-47, the pilot doing his damndest to elude the fire. Antiaircraft now hammered incessantly.
>
> It was time to go. On went the green light. Go-go-go!
>
> As Winters left the plane, a heavy burst of 20 mm hit the tail of the plane. I thought for certain he had gone right into it. I was out the door behind him in another second.

The shock of the opening blast tore much of the gear from Pat, as it did with many of the men that night. The pilots were flying too fast and too low. Pat was a machine gunner and carried a machine gun tripod, which he lost, along with his carbine, his ammunition and musette bag.

> During the decent, a machine gun traversed the 18 men in my stick with long bursts of fire. Adrenaline pumped through my body. Explosions filled

the air. A C-47's engine was on fire, about 150 feet off to my right. [The plane] seemed to be disintegrating.

A bell was ringing in a town off to my left. I thought, 'Keep your composure, assess your situation, plan your moves quickly. Christ, I'm headed for that line of trees. I'm descending too rapidly. Concentrate on your landing.'

I could see an orchard beyond the trees. As I passed over the trees I drew my legs up to avoid hitting them. A moment of terror seized me: 70 feet below and 20 feet to my left was a German quad-mounted 20 mm antiaircraft gun. That moment it opened up, firing at the C-47s passing above.

The Germans were concentrating on shooting someone else and didn't look and see him. "It was really fortunate," Pat told his nephew later, "because they would have given me a burst, and that would have been it."

It wasn't until years later when Pat watched the movie *The Longest Day* that he understood what the ringing bell he had heard was all about. He was near the town of Ste. Mère-Église when he jumped, and had always speculated the Germans were ringing the bell as an alarm. Actually, it was the townspeople ringing the bell because their church was on fire.

Pat landed high in an apple tree and crashed down the trunk. He found himself in an apple orchard, his only weapon a .45 revolver he had bought from a British paratrooper for fifty bucks. He carried that .45 throughout the rest of the war. He jumped into a hedgerow for cover and stepped on a dead American pathfinder, a large blond man. "It scared the hell out of him," Gary noted, "because the dead guy let out a grunt as the air escaped from his diaphragm." It was a gruesome start to the war. The night's adventures were just beginning. Pat wrote:

I remained quiet and still, moving only my head. Suddenly my eyes caught movement 40 feet in front of me. A silhouette of a helmeted man approached me on all fours. I reached for my cricket and clicked it once, click-clack, the sign of a friend. The figure stopped. I waited for the counter sign. There was no response.

The silhouetted figure began to move toward me again. My handgun pointed in the center of his chest. I again gave him the click-clack. He immediately responded with a hand raised: 'For Christ-sake, don't shoot.'

Immediately I knew it wasn't a German. It was my assistant gunner, Woodrow Robbins.

'What the hell's wrong with you?' I asked. 'Why didn't you use your cricket?'

'I lost the cricket part of the cricket,' came his stammering reply, (the sound producing part of the device).

It was then about 1:50 a.m.

Pat soon picked up a German Mauser, model 98, a bolt action rifle, which he used for the first few days of the Normandy campaign, then picked up a Springfield rifle with a grenade launcher attached. The guy he got it from also had a pack full of rifle grenades, so Pat spent the rest of the Normandy campaign as a grenadier. He described the rest of the Normandy invasion to Gary simply as "one small skirmish after another." Pat turned from description to philosophy in his journal and wrote:

Of course there is fear in combat.

Some men think too heavily about their chances of getting hit, maimed or killed, and their fear turns into terror, so torturous that they become unable to function as combat soldiers.

Others fear personal guilt and public shame from [the possibility of] fleeing during a battle. The mind working too heavily and too often on these thoughts has broken some good men. Once you have disgraced yourself, the agony of this disgrace is never completely bearable.

Once you get a reputation as a good man in battle, you do your damndest not to tarnish it. Personal honor is valued. Fear of scorn is something you guard against. You have seen others fail and disgrace themselves. You want no part of it, but you realize it could happen to you, so you work at being good at your job and suppressing any thoughts that could hinder your effort.

You tell yourself you're young, strong, aggressive, and that getting hit or wounded will happen to others, not to you.

In his art journal, Pat described the interrogation methods used against captured prisoners, most likely first encountered during the Normandy invasion. Along with the description of interrogation he included a darkened pencil sketch of two men with a single candle between them. He wrote:

> Many methods were used to gain the necessary information from the prisoners we captured without torturing them. A little theatrical setting [was used] to create tension and terrifying thoughts in the P.O.W. The apprehension, just waiting to be interrogated, not being allowed to relieve their bowels or urinate, was torturous in itself. But these were our orders when we captured a German. Lewis Nixon, one of the original officers of E-Company, was an S-2 in the regiment during combat. If anyone could gain intelligence from a P.O.W., I'm certain [Nixon] ranked with the best.

The Pit of Your Gut

On September 17, 1944, Pat jumped with Easy Company into Holland for Operation Market-Garden. He noted that although they drew sporadic enemy fire, the jump was made on a Sunday afternoon in daylight, a "parade ground jump," easy and straightforward, and nothing like the nighttime Normandy jump.

Still, the jump wasn't without its fears. Pat had become a squad leader, and replacements had come into the unit. He turned introspective and commented on leadership styles:

> You are committed to make this jump. Your composure in the eyes of the new men will show. Let them see the efficiency of a leader emerge from that force if you're going to command the respect of your men. Above all, don't embarrass yourself by showing the least sign of fear, even though it's there in the pit of your gut.

Easy Company liberated the town of Eindhoven and continued on toward the town of Nuenen. Pat first carried a Thompson submachine gun in Holland, which he didn't like because of the extensive amount of ammunition one needed to carry along with it.

Of all his war experiences, he wrote most extensively about those near Nuenen:

Company E boarded the top of the tanks and headed toward Nuenan. E Company's first platoon was in the lead. First squad of that platoon loaded on the lead tank. I made sure my squad was all aboard, then I boarded. The men left an open spot for me in front right, next to the 75 mm cannon. My pals.

We moved out toward our objective. When we reached the outskirts of town, a man spotted a German half-track moving across a field on our right flank. He shouted his discovery to the tank commander. Our tank halted. The tank commander traversed his 75 mm and quickly knocked out the German vehicle. The great noise and vibration created by the cannon cleared the tank of men in seconds.

Because we were so close to entering the building area of the town, we decided to disperse into skirmish lines. There was a house on each side of the street, [each having] a front yard and back yard area, like typical American tract homes. Each property line had a hedge to separate the back yard area from one another. Bull Randleman's first squad was assigned to the right hand side of the street. The second and third squads to the left side. Bull said he would take the front yard area with the machine gun crew, and I would take the riflemen and sweep through the back yard area toward the heart of town. Tactically, this sounded right. The left side of the street was covered in the same manner by Martin's and Rader's squads.

We moved in unison slowly toward the heart of Neunan, suspiciously eyeing anything that could hide a kraut. Suddenly two Germans came out of a second story window. Quickly, they began to move across a roof. In a second, my Thompson was pointed their direction. I pulled the trigger. They were within 35 yards of me, but the gun did not fire.

There, in the heat of battle, Pat quickly remembered that there was one part in the Thompson easy to get in backwards. The part would fit in two ways, but the weapon would only fire if the part was in the correct position. He had taken the Thompson apart fifty times before he got in the plane, but recounted to Gary later that he obviously had got the part in backward. So Pat field-stripped his submachine gun right there and fixed the problem. He continued:

> This little incident strung the nerves a little tighter. We were moving at a hasty clip—this is what made the two Germans bolt from their concealment rather than fire at us: they knew we would be on them in seconds.

And then a squad leader's worst fears were realized:

> The last house had an open field next to it. I parted the foliage of the hedge that separated the field from the house. I must have been spotted by a German machine gunner. Before he could fire, I pushed through the hedge and dropped into a ditch just on the other side. Robert Van Klinken, one of my riflemen, was following me closely. [Van Klinken] peered through the same opening as I had, just as the German machine gunner depressed the trigger. Van Klinken was hit with three bullets.

Pat later speculated to Gary that the Germans must have zeroed their sights on him in the hedgerow when he went through, then fired at the next man, Van Klinken. Pat grabbed Van Klinken and pulled him through. Van Klinken was still groaning, but dying. The machine gun must have climbed slightly while firing—as they're prone to do, Pat told Gary—and Van Klinken had been hit in the groin, with two in the chest. The men were still under heavy fire.

> The rest of the riflemen were now in the same ditch as me, looking toward the area that the machine gun fire had come from. Richard Bray shouted to me that he had captured a German at the end of the ditch and wanted to know what he should do with him. I suggested he keep him covered until I could find out what the rest of the platoon was going to do.

British tanks moved behind Easy Company as they crouched in front of houses. Sergeant Johnny Martin spotted a German tank nearly hidden in a hedgerow, no more than one hundred yards away, but the British tanks continued to approach, unaware. The following part of the action is also covered extensively in the miniseries:

Martin ran over to the first approaching tank, stopped the British tank, and quickly explained to the tank commander the location of the enemy tank, just below and to the right of a power pole on his left flank. The enemy tank was waiting for a shot at the British tank.

The [British] tank commander continued to move forward. Martin again cautioned the tank commander that if he continued his forward movement, the German tank would soon see him.

The British tank commander exclaimed, 'I caunt see him, old boy, and if so, I caunt very well shoot at him.'

Martin shouted, 'Well, you'll see him in a minute,' and rapidly moved away from the tank.

The British tank finally exposed itself to the German tank. [The British commander stood] with his head and shoulders completely exposed in top turret. A sharp Bam! broke the silence. The British tank jumped and shook as the German cannon shot penetrated its armor, taking the legs off the driver. Then came the nauseating interruption of flame that seemed to always follow when a Sherman is hit. The rest of the tank crew came flying out of hatches I didn't know existed and ran toward us. The tank continued to move forward at a slow pace. By now it was an inferno.

What we did not know was that Bull Randleman was in a ditch next to it, and to keep from being incinerated he was forced to move in the direction of the enemy.

[Another British tank, following the first British tank] nudged along the same path, as if he had not seen the first tank get hit. The past scene did not influence his caution at all. Bam!, another shot. This time the [second] Sherman shuddered and stopped completely. Again, those who survived came tumbling out of the hatches.

A German machine gun cut loose to our direct front, biting into the dirt to my left. With so much confusion and bungling, I was oblivious to what was happening to the rest of my platoon. I could not see any one except four of my men. I cursed the confusion and waited, assuming Lieutenant Peacock would shout out some kind of order. Another burst of machine gun came from the enemy lines. Another shot from the enemy tank hit the house behind us. We had to make a move.

I shouted to my men to my right, ordering them to get up and move to the rear behind the house. Once behind the cover of the house I shouted to Carl Sawosko to help me carry Van Klinken to the safety of the house. But each time we exposed ourselves, the same machine gun that cut Van Klinken down burned in more bullets.

[Pvt. Philip] Longo, our first platoon medic, walked over to Van Klinken as if the war had ceased, and picked him up and carried him to the cover of the house. [Van Klinken's] face was ashen, he would soon be dead. The Germans must have seen Longo, but did not fire at him. This had happened before in the case of a medic, if that's what they thought he was.

Machine gun fire was hitting all around the house, and as an organized unit we ceased to exit. Lieutenant Peacock turned his head from side to side, not uttering a word. I said, 'Lieutenant, if we don't make a move, the krauts will soon come in on our flanks.'

'Chris, I'm not sure what to do,' [Peacock said].

'Let's withdraw—now!' I said.

He hesitated. 'Who's going to start the withdrawal?' (The Germans were firing a machine gun in the path of our only escape route.)

I said to the men around me to move to the rear in two's and keep spread out. The men began to move. All got clear of the house. Peacock dashed across the danger area and I was close behind him. We ran as fast as we could for several hundred yards when we finally ran into the rest of E Company. We mounted the rest of the British tanks and rode back to Eindhoven.

The rest of the story is also recounted in the miniseries, told there with slight changes. Pat's record noted that the next day a British scouting party moved into Nuenen and returned with Bull Randleman. Bull had a bullet hole through his shoulder. Bull told the men what happened to him in the meantime. Pushed into German lines and separated from his men, Bull found an empty barn. A young Dutch girl tried to bandage his wound, then left him alone. He fixed his bayonet to his rifle and waited. Soon a lone German entered the barn. Bull ran him through and hid his body with hay. Bull spent the rest of the night in the barn, waiting for morning. By dawn, the Germans had moved out and Bull was evacuated.

Gary noted how another good buddy of Pat's, Bill Dukeman, was killed by a rifle grenade a few days later. After the war, Easy Company member Joe Liebgott cut Gary's hair, and sometimes told Gary war stories while he sat in the barber's chair. Liebgott recounted to Gary that when Dukeman was killed, the men were taking cover in a ditch. The Germans were firing different weapons that burst overhead and dropped shrapnel on the men. One was a rifle grenade that burst and killed Dukeman. A piece of shrapnel went down through his back and through his heart. The deaths of Robert Van Klinken and Bill Dukemen shook up Pat greatly, Gary noted.

Pat later traded his Thompson for an M1 rifle, which he liked much better and used throughout the rest of the Holland campaign. The men fought on the line for seventy days in Holland. On October 3, 1944, Easy Company was relieved from their duty around Eindhoven and transported by truck to an area known as the Island, the area between the Waal and the Neder Rhine. The company engaged in various patrols and battles until November when the company was relieved and sent to Mourmelon, France.

In his art journal, Pat depicts and describes several scenes that take place along the dike. One pencil sketch shows a group of men being blown up. Underneath, he wrote:

Winters passed the order that everyone would open fire when my machine gun commenced firing. As my eyes adjusted to the darkness there seemed to be at least fifty krauts busy digging in and just milling about the top of the dike. I gave [PFC Dale] Hartley the order to fire, then the whole platoon opened up. Krauts were rolling down the dike toward us like bowling pins and running in all directions. From that very beginning we were hunting, shooting, and capturing Krauts, so the Germans we did not shoot either gave up or ran away. Our casualties were one killed and 15 wounded. The Germans must have lost more than 75 killed, wounded, and captured. That day we were victorious. Tomorrow it may be their turn.

He also drew a picture of two men in a foxhole in the middle of a storm, looking glumly toward the horizon, and described the weather:

And then there was the rain, the ever-constant rain. The raincoat must have been designed by the krauts. It kept the rain out, but soon your body would sweat, for the coat could not breathe. You cursed the rain and the coat. You became cold, then even colder, and when you were convinced that your body could stand no more, you found it could.

A Dismal, Depressing Place

On the eighteenth of December, 1944, Easy Company left their base camp in France and traveled by ten-ton trailer trucks in division convoy to Bastogne, Belgium. E Company was ordered to hold the line at Bastogne during the Battle of the Bulge, Hitler's last desperate bid to turn the tide of the war his direction. They arrived on the morning of the nineteenth and hiked the rest of the way into the town. Pat describes it as "a dismal, depressing place."

While marching with the rest of the battalion toward Bastogne, Easy Company was commanded to move from the rear to the point position of the column, the first and most exposed position. Pat turned again to leadership philosophy and recorded his observations of Dick Winters, once his company commander and platoon leader, now a battalion executive, immediately after the command came through.

Captain Winters was standing out in front looking completely, in all respects, as tough as usual, without even trying. I've never seen this man show a quarrelsome, pugnacious attitude. When you're as tough as he is, you don't have to act tough to prove it. I am sure Winters knew [the gravity] of the situation.

At Winters' command, Pat's squad assumed the scout position. Small-arms fire could be heard in the distance. Soon off the road and into the woods, the density of the woods made forward movement slow. "No opposition," Pat wrote, "but you've experienced enough in this game of war not to allow yourself to become careless or overconfident." The unit stopped at the base of a tree line. The men dug foxholes and prepared for the worst. By nightfall, they were completely entrenched. The first flurries of snow came on December 21. The weather grew increasingly cold. That same night a heavy snow fell with "unbearable freezing temperatures." Pat picked up the narrative again on December 23, 1944:

> The blackness of the early morning surrendered to the new dawn. It was cold and quiet, and snow had fallen intermittently [throughout] the night. The flicker of a small fire could be seen in the rear toward the first platoon CP [command post]. [The fire] was well under control, for there was no tell-tale smoke that a German artillery observer could see. [If there had been smoke,] that area would have been shelled or mortared immediately.
>
> The early morning hours passed with only the sound of sporadic small arms fire to our left flank and occasional mortar fire a great distance away.

Pat's recollections of Bastogne end there, but in his art journal he draws several pictures of his experiences in Belgium. One shows a man's leg exploding, being hit from mortar fire, the picture a tribute to Bill Guarnere and Joe Toye, who both lost legs in Bastogne. Another shows a jeep being hit by a mortar blast, which Pat saw happen and described. Other drawings depict patrols, tank battles, mortar fire, and hiking toward town on point.

Pat described Bastogne as "the worst artillery he had ever seen," Gary said. One time they let German tanks go right over their foxholes. Then they stood up and shot the infantry behind the tanks. By the time the tanks turned around, the allied men were gone.

Toward the end of his time in Bastogne, Pat's feet froze. He was evacuated and put in a hospital. Gary said, "I remember when he wrote home about it. The letter said he got to the hospital and the nurse wouldn't let him take a bath because of his frozen feet, (apparently they didn't want men recovering from trench feet to be immersed in water). But Pat just couldn't bear the thought of getting in that clean hospital bed, as filthy as he was. So he took a shower anyway, and the nurse chewed his ass out."

Pat recounted two other stories to Gary, the first of his wounding. The men were sleep-deprived, walking dead men almost. Pat was lying in a foxhole with his arm outside the hole. He heard shrapnel coming in but was too exhausted even to move his arm. Sure enough, he was hit in the arm. He didn't put in for a purple heart. "He figured that after Dukeman and Van Klinken got killed, what he received was nothing," Gary said.

Later, the men were at an intersection and a German officer came running out of the woods with a potato masher grenade, intent on throwing it. But the grenade went off in the German's hand, blowing it off. Streaming blood as he was, the German kept his wits and sprinted back into the woods. The men never did get him. They were all still ducking down due to the grenade blast.

A Life Lived in Liberty

Pat continued on with Easy Company until the end of the war. He was with his unit for occupation duties in Germany and Austria.

Then in fall 1945, Gary, now a ten-year-old boy, remembers hearing the good news. "We got a call from my grandmother. 'Pat's home,' she said. I could hear her over the phone. Instantly I was out the door running down the street to their house. My mother yelled at me to come get my jacket, but I wasn't turning back for anything."

Pat was a tech sergeant by war's end. Gary remembers being very impressed with all the stripes and decorations he had, the spit-shined jump boots. "He was a sharp soldier," Gary said. That first night home, Pat talked about the war, mostly just saying that he was glad it was over. Funny thing was, he looked up at the ceiling inside his parents' house and said, "Wonder if a mortar could go through this." Pat wanted to get on with life, same as the rest of the guys. A few evenings later the family held a big dinner celebration.

Pat went back to his job at the telephone company, but he never seemed to be fully content there. He wanted to be a professional artist or horticulturalist, his other passion. He was also big into physical fitness and, as a side business, started one of the first public gymnasiums in Oakland, building it in a greenhouse. Famed bodybuilder Jack Lalanne, also an Oakland resident, was a friend and frequented the club. Pat did professional landscaping on the side from 1967 to 1987, building immaculate Japanese gardens.

Pat married his wife, Mary Jo Bonham, in 1947. They had three sons, and bought a big home near Oakland with a huge yard where he created himself a sanctuary with a Japanese garden and wooden decking. He slept outside in summertime. Chris noted: "My father was probably like many of the fellows who came back. He was haunted by a lot of his war experiences. My room was adjacent to the back yard. I'd have the window open and remember hearing him in the night, many times. He had put stone pathways in the backyard, and I'd hear him walking on the pathways at two or three o'clock in morning. Afraid, I'd go to my mother. 'Your father's having funny feelings,' she said. That was how she put it. It might have been insomnia or nightmares, but I believe it was post-traumatic stress. Later in life I worked as a police officer. I retired in 2007 after a fairly significant injury, and I grew to recognize what post-traumatic stress looked like. My dad and I grew closer later in life, but he never really did explain what was going on in his head. My mother explained more later on. She said, "Your dad's reliving the war, having nightmares, he's thinking about the loss of his buddies, the significant people in his life."

Mostly, Pat lived for his family. He did whatever he needed to do to care for them. If he took a vacation, it wasn't for him, it was for the kids, Chris noted. He was an avid bow hunter and fisherman, but never at the family's expense. He never had an extravagant vehicle. Mostly he drove older, used cars. He lived a simple life, but he lived it to the fullest.

Pat spent lots of time creating his artwork, working on his or others' gardens, sometimes for pay, usually for free. He built a cabin at Lake Tahoe with his sister's husband. He loved the mountains and ocean. Chris described him as "a universal man. Some of us are good at some things, but Dad was good at many things."

Pat was a craftsman who built birdhouses and made elaborate wood carvings that were sold in gift shops in San Francisco and Sausalito. He picked up pieces of cedar and pine in the Sierras and carved everything from figurines of American Indians to Jesus.

The family was Catholic, not necessarily devout, Chris said, but they attended church for many years. Pat had an aunt who was a nun. Pat was a highly ethical man and believed in following the Golden Rule. He was always known as a gentleman, even around his war buddies.

Pat started out in the phone company climbing poles with those old straps and spikes. He could shimmy up like a bear. They called his section in the company "craft" because it took an artisan's and technician's mind to do it well. He worked his way up to management but hated his new role, so he quit and went back into the field, which floored his wife because it meant a cut in pay, Chris noted. But Pat was wired as a kinetic person. He had to be able to dig into his work with his hands. He wanted to get out there and get into the wires, not shuffle papers and people. On his seventieth birthday, just for fun, he went out and climbed a telephone pole with his old rig. He retired from the phone company in 1977 at age fifty-seven.

Pat was big on ethics and doing the right thing. Later in life he told his son that he had always been true to his mother. "They were married a long time," Chris said, "and I'm sure there were moments they felt less than thrilled with each other. But he never bailed. He never went astray on my mother."

After Mary Jo got sick in 1997, she passed away very quickly, dying of liver cancer within three months of diagnosis. "It was a shock to everyone," Chris said, "but it really took my father for a loop. He was absolutely destroyed." She was just sixty-nine when she died. "After she passed, my dad got good and drunk at the end of her funeral. He said, 'I've lost my wife of fifty years, I just don't care anymore.' Dad retreated into grief. It was reflected in his diary and in other papers. Dad lost his passion for life, for his artwork, for writing. He just stopped doing those things."

Then Pat started to have health problems of his own. First, he had an aneurism, a ministroke. "The train just derailed from that point on," Chris said. The stroke rewired his brain. He was slow and unresponsive, and was placed in a hospital in Salinas, near where his son, Pat, lived.

"Dad was a tough old sonuvabitch," Chris said. "The hospital called us from time to time, saying things like, 'Your dad has been very feisty lately.' A few times he even needed to be restrained because he'd start slugging if he didn't like what he was getting. He was just confused. For a short time he ended up in an Alzheimer's facility in Freemont. He didn't know where he was, or who he was, or what time period he was in. He had lost track of his perception of time, and said things like, 'Well, Malarkey's sitting over there. I just told him he had outpost duty.' I'd say, 'That's not Malarkey.' He'd say emphatically, 'Of course it is.' He was just rewired."

Then, surprisingly, the unthinkable happened. One day Chris visited him in the Alzheimer's facility and he said, clear as day, "Son, I've got to go home."

"Dad, what are you saying?" Chris said.

"I've got to get out of here," he said, "I'm fine."

And he was. Pat had defied the odds. His brain had healed. The family had him assessed, and he checked out fine.

The family wasn't eager to let him be on his own just yet. Two cousins who grew up with him in Oakland moved into his home with him, staying about ten months. Pat started exercising again. Most of his functioning returned, even to the point where he passed a DMV test and drove a car again. The physician didn't bark a bit.

Then, he got colon cancer, which they removed, and he was okay.

Then Pat fell in his backyard, broke his arm, and jacked up his hip. "There was only so much the old war bird could take," Chris said.

Pat's son, Tim, had the financial means by then to take care of his father very well. Tim arranged to have a caregiver live with him in his home around the clock. She took good care of Pat, and they had a good friendship.

Toward the end, Pat developed an ulceration on his back. Family members took him to the doctor and discovered he had lung cancer. It didn't come as a surprise. "He had been a chronic cigarette smoker since the war," Chris said. "That was just the mindset of that era. They received cigarettes in care packages back then."

The doctor said surgery was an option, but that Pat might end up on a ventilator.

"I don't want to go out like that," Pat said. "Let the cards fall where they may."

They didn't give him a timeline, but toward the end family members knew he was in massive pain. "You could tell by his mannerisms and expressions," Chris said. "He never complained. He drank wine and self-medicated instead."

He went into a coma with a high fever with short respirations. Then he was gone. He died December 15, 1999, in his own home. His three sons were with him when he passed.

Chris called Bill Guarnere to fill him in. In those days Bill kept track of everybody. Dick Winters wrote the family a letter, which says in part:

I always took pride in having my best-looking man out front carrying the guidon [a small flag carried for marking, signaling or identification] for reviews by dignitaries. And that man, or course, was always Pat, who, with his clean-cut good looks and wide shoulders proudly carried the Company E guidon.

When it came time for the big jump in Normandy, I wanted my best, most dependable man right behind me, that man was Pat again.

All of Company E men share the loss of a true comrade.

The last entry in Pat's art journal shows a Christmas card he drew in 1944, which he sent to his fellow soldiers in Easy Company. It depicts a helmeted soldier. Underneath is one of his poems:

So you think you're getting old, Pal, and time is running short.
Your hair is changing color and thinning, you report.
You've had your good and bad times since 1945.
So best count your blessings, that you are still alive.
And look upon the bright side,
    remember all the young men we left beneath the ground.
For one day we will see them where happiness abounds.
You can worry all you're worth.
When it's time to bite the bullet,
    there's a better place, than here on Earth.

Merry Christmas,
—Chris

8

WALTER "SMOKEY" GORDON

Interviews with Elizabeth "Bebe" Gordon, Linda Gordon,
and Cleta Tracy Gordon, daughters
With additional information from Walter Scott Gordon III, son,
Gay Gordon, daughter, and Cleta "Junie" Ellington, niece

Some people are consistent. Everything about them fits a mold, no surprises. Others, like our father, don't fit any mold. It's all guesswork when you try to figure them out, and half the time you'll be proved wrong. In fact, just when you think you've understood them, they throw you a curveball and do or say something that doesn't fit your understanding. This was our father. He lived through some extraordinary times and circumstances and was always a paradoxical figure, not only to us, but to all who knew him.

This is the story of Walter Scott "Smokey" Gordon.

Early Years

We know little about Dad's upbringing. He talked quite freely about his life but never dwelled on early years much. We know that his parents didn't marry until they were both thirty, which was unusual for their day, and they both had unusual names. Dad's father was named Walter but was referred to as BeeBoy or just Bee, nicknames from his childhood. Dad's mother was named for the heroine of a dime novel (the equivalent of a modern trashy paperback). Her mother had read the book and was struck by the heroine's style, but her father was dead against such a name from such a source. He wanted to call her Deborah instead, but his wife held out, so the baby who became our grandmother was called simply "the baby" until three years later when a new sibling's arrival forced the issue. They had to give Grandmother a real name then, and Cleta she became.

BeeBoy and Cleta grew up, met and married, and became a popular couple in Jackson, Mississippi, with many influential friends. BeeBoy became a spec builder and real estate developer and "got it when the gettin' was good," as they say down here. But his properties were leveraged on top of each other. When the Depression hit, the first of his properties fell and the rest came tumbling down. BeeBoy lost almost everything, and our grandparents went from being on top of the world to barely hanging on to their home.

Through good times and bad, our Gordon grandparents were sustained by their regard for one another, their friends, their wit, and something else: a cook. No matter how hard times were, BeeBoy never let go of Grandmother's cook. It may have been self-interest on BeeBoy's part, because Grandmother's entire culinary repertoire consisted of grits—not a difficult dish: just boil water, add grits, add salt, stir, and wait.

Like her fictional namesake, our Grandmother Cleta was spunky in her own right. She had gone to college up north in Chicago, then later transferred down south and continued her studies at Belmont College in Nashville, Tennessee. She became a teacher in Hattiesburg, Mississippi, and was fired from the school when she was spotted riding a horse astride. Everyone knew that all "ladies" had to ride sidesaddle. When students and parents learned of her dismissal, they threatened to fire the entire school board, and Grandmother was reinstated. She was an extraordinary teacher, and we know of at least three of her students who named their daughters Cleta in her honor.

Whatever else they may have been, Cleta and BeeBoy were not prepared for parenthood, especially not for two babies at the same time. The birth of our daddy and his twin sister (named Walter and Cleta) stunned them. Our daddy told us that BeeBoy would drive up to the house at the end of the day, and, if he could hear the wailing of babies, would simply put the car in reverse and drive away. He'd return only after he was certain his offspring were safely asleep.

Daddy was a bright young man, articulate, quick, and able to recall details of anything he had read. He had a wonderful vocabulary and studied Latin, yet, consistent with his paradoxical nature, did very poorly in school. Teachers always complained about his behavior. Knowing Daddy, we doubt his wit and joking manner were curtailed in the classroom.

The family was not especially religious, but Daddy, on his own, became a faithful Episcopalian, a lay reader and an altar boy. He knew the Bible like the back of his hand. In spite of the normal childhood squabbles, Daddy always adored his twin sister. He was extremely close to her and later her husband, and their three small children. Tragically, Cleta died in her early thirties of breast cancer, which was the turning point of Daddy's religious life. Following her death, anytime he was asked about his faith, he would reply, "Any God that could take away the most beautiful creation to walk this earth, I want nothing to do with."

He was always willing, however, to engage in discussions of religion. We have deeply religious relatives with whom Daddy could quote scripture chapter and verse. We wondered how a person who had lost his faith could know scripture so well and asked him. His reply was typical of this untypical man: "Don't you know that the Bible is the greatest book ever written?"

Enlistment

Daddy enrolled at Millsaps College for a number of semesters, but his mind was on foolishness, and his transcripts reflected it. He was flailing about aimlessly, when an opportunity to make something of himself came in the most unlikely of situations: the call to arms. Here is another contradiction in this contradictory life: this lackluster student and lazy philanderer became absolutely on fire to become, of all things, a disciplined soldier.

In those days, you didn't need to explain why you wanted to go off to a foreign land to serve your country. If you were healthy, over eighteen, and walking around town, you needed to explain why you *weren't* serving your country. But when Daddy first tried to enlist, he was rejected. He had flat feet and was color-blind.

When he told his father he wouldn't give up, BeeBoy offered insight. "One thing the military tries to do," he explained, "is displace you from your home turf so your homesickness won't tempt you to rush home at the first challenge. If you enlist down south, you will train up north and vice versa."

Armed with this information and determined to try again, Daddy hopped a train heading north and ended up at a recruiting station in Philadelphia. He had heard about a special unit being formed called the paratroopers who would get more pay. It sounded fun, but it never occurred to him that they were paid more because most people don't want to jump out of airplanes into enemy territory where other soldiers are on the ground, shooting at them.

So there he was, in South Philly, waiting in a line to enlist. As the men in line with him read out the eye test, Daddy memorized the letters and faked his way through the eye test. We never asked him how he faked the flat foot test, but our guess is that the Army never thought he would live long enough for flat feet to become an issue. Daddy trained initially at Camp Lejeune in North Carolina, then later at Camp Toccoa in Georgia.

Geographically speaking, BeeBoy was right on the money!

The War Years

The "Smokey" nickname came from a tobacco-chewing habit Daddy had in his war years with Easy Company. When we were growing up, Daddy always smoked either a pipe or a cigar. He was never one to consume alcohol, claiming that whatever he drank, he would drink with voracity. Water was his drink of choice, way before it was fashionable. He couldn't get enough of it. During training, he found he required more water than the average fellow and devised ways of gaining access to his comrades' canteens. In the field, he began to carry extra Hershey's bars, which proved to be just what a soldier considered a fair trade for a big swig of extra water.

Dad and Carwood Lipton often went on leave either alone or just the two of them. Many others preferred to go drinking and try their luck with girls. But Lipton and Dad wanted to tour museums and art galleries. This did not stem from a highbrow attitude but was a way to take in the local culture. They could be mischievous, too. Once, while the men were training in Aldbourne, Dad traveled to the city of Bath, England, with one of the men. On a museum tour it came time for lunch and the museum closed. Daddy and his buddy hid inside the building. As soon as they found themselves alone they stripped down, jumped into the water of the ancient Roman baths, splashed around like eggbeaters, then got dressed and resumed the tour after lunch was concluded and the museum opened again.

Daddy was in the 3rd Platoon, and this isn't much known about the Band of Brothers, but there's a real hierarchy among the men regarding which platoon they came from. Most of the needling is done in good nature. Once we asked Bill Guarnere why there weren't many pictures of him taken during the war. He was quick to reply, "I'll tell ya why, dammit, 'cause your dad and Gutty[1] were in the back posing for pictures like tourists, while 1st Platoon was on the front line getting their heads shot at."

Dad jumped on D-day and landed near an apple tree on a farm in Normandy with only half his machine gun. It was too heavy to jump with the whole. He was about six miles off course. Fortunately, John Eubanks, who carried the tripod to the machine gun, was the first man Dad met on the ground. Unfortunately, Eubanks had felt no need to be carrying around a tripod with no gun or gunner in sight, so he had promptly discarded it upon landing. Dad was able to prop the gun on low stone walls and shoot from that position.

Forrest Guth joined them shortly. The men had a couple of ways to identify friendly troops in the dark: one way was for both to sound their

---

1. The nickname for Corporal Forrest Guth, Gutty, or sometimes seen spelled Goodie, is pronounced like *duty*. He was one of the few paratroopers who carried a camera in Normandy.

toy crickets that they carried, and another was for one person to speak a word and the other to respond in a code that had been established earlier. As Dad, Guth, and Eubanks roamed the Normandy countryside, they heard a loud whisper coming from the dark. A soldier challenged them with the code word—"*Flash*." Before Dad or Gutty could even catch their breath, Eubanks blurted "*Lightning*," a logical answer, yes, but unfortunately not the right one. (The correct response that night was "*Thunder*.") Knowing what was sure to follow a wrong response, they hit the dirt as their comrade lobbed a grenade their way. Fortunately, they escaped injury. The unknown soldier scattered, and they never did learn his identity. Floyd Talbert joined them a short time later. Eventually they joined up with a group from the 502nd that had spotted some Germans under a barn near Ravenoville. Dad and some of the men had to take out a bunker there.

Dad was wounded while fighting in Normandy. They evacuated him to a hospital in England where he was put in a cast that ran from hip to toe. As different groups of military upper brass toured the hospital, they spoke to each wounded man, and if appropriate, pinned a Purple Heart to the man's pillow, where it was supposed to stay. Dad heard out each group as they talked about their appreciation of the military, about his service and valor, and on and on . . . then once they left he unpinned each award from his pillow and stashed it. After a few weeks he had a small cache of Purple Hearts. He knew they'd come in handy some day.

After eight weeks in the hospital, Dad returned to Easy Company. Floyd "Tab" Talbert had been mistakenly wounded by another Easy Company man's bayonet. He arrived back at the company about the same time Dad did, but Talbert hadn't got any awards because his wound hadn't come from an enemy. Tab was truly one of Dad's favorite people, and there was no one he loved to tease more than Tab. Dad and Paul Rogers, another of Dad's good friends, put together a makeshift award ceremony, complete with an infamous poem called "The Night of the Bayonette," and awarded Talbert his very own Purple Heart with much pomp and circumstance.

Dad was wounded for the final time in Bastogne on Christmas Eve, 1944. It was early morning and snow covered the rocky frozen ground.

His assistant was a new man and had dug their foxhole, but not deep enough. Daddy was taller for a paratrooper, about six-one, and stuck out of the foxhole. A sniper got him in the left shoulder. The bullet traveled across his body and came out his right shoulder. It nicked his spinal column, which left him paralyzed from the neck down.

Paul Rogers and Jim Alley heaved him out of his hole and hauled him into the woods where Doc Roe gave him morphine and plasma. Lipton rushed over to see what he could do to assist. As Lipton leaned over Dad, trying to get him to talk or respond, one of the men looked down and said, "Lip, you're standing on Smokey's hand." It was then that most of the men realized that Dad had no sensations from the neck down and that his injuries, this time, were very serious. It was a story that always caused Lipton's eyes to well up when telling.

Dad was taken to an aid station, then by ambulance to Sedan, then flown to England and on to a hospital in Wales. He was placed in a plaster cast from the top of his head to his waist with only his face left unplastered. But the cast was in the way, and the open wounds from the bullet holes couldn't be treated. Medical staff cut the cast off. Two holes were bored into the sides of Dad's skull. Steel tongs were inserted and clamped off, which held his head immobile, (the device was called Crutchfield Tongs). Pulleys provided traction and prevented any movement prompted by the rest of his body. Dad stayed in that position, flat on his back and staring at the ceiling, for six weeks.

One day while Dad was recuperating, Dr. Stadium, who was treating him at the time, turned to the nurse and said, "Keep an eye on this one, he's goldbricking." Daddy was infuriated. "Damn it!" he yelled, "If I could climb out of this bed, I'd show you what goldbricking is!" The doctor smiled as he walked out of the room. Daddy found out later the doctor was just trying to rile him up to help reconnect nerves and keep a fighting spirit in him. After the war Daddy learned of this doctor's whereabouts, which happened to be in New Orleans, and remained in touch with him for years. During his recovery Daddy's little finger started to move. He said it was really weird because hair had grown all over his hands and fingers. It reminded him of Sasquatch. Soon he was listed as "walking wounded."

Although Daddy started getting better, the Army chose not to release him. He was shipped to Atlanta and was there up until 1945 when the war ended in Europe. He was well enough to be sent home, but not dischargeable according to the Army. He speculated that they wanted to keep him around longer so that he'd continue to heal, releasing the Army of the responsibility of paying for a full disability. During this time his father kept asking him when he was coming home, but Dad couldn't give him an answer. Finally, after a routine examination, the attending physician informed Dad that he was well enough to be discharged from the hospital but would be sent to Fort Benning to serve for limited duty. Dad placed a call to his father to pass along this new information. BeeBoy became unglued and ordered Dad to relay a message back to this army doctor saying precisely, "If you send my son to any location other than home, I will personally drive him to the US Capitol building, march him down onto the Senate floor, strip him down to his skivvies, and let someone besides the Army make a determination!" It was not long after that when the doctor sallied into Daddy's room and said, "Son, you're going home."

Daddy was discharged from the military with 90 percent disability. For the rest of his life he suffered with chronic back and shoulder pain and always walked like a man well beyond his years. The worst part about his injury was that we could never give Dad a big hug around his neck or ride piggyback as children do because we were well aware of the pain he suffered. Whenever someone greeted him with a pat on the back, unaware of his disabilities, you could see a slight wince in his eye or face, yet he would never mention it.

Career and Marriage

Following the war the Army offered aptitude tests for the men to determine the best career for their particular talents. Daddy's turned out to be a bulldozer operator. He thought it best, however, to put his brain to use rather than his brawn.

Under the GI Bill, Dad enrolled at Cumberland Law School in Lebanon, Tennessee. Six months into law school he went home to Mississippi and passed the state bar exam. He returned to the university to officially earn his law degree but was actually a licensed attorney before graduating. He never practiced law, but instead became an oil broker, the liaison between the oil companies and the land owners to lease the rights to drill and own the oil below the surface.

Dad secured employment soon after graduating, but without a vehicle found it impossible to go to work. Vets with cash prompted huge lines at car dealerships across the country. Dad couldn't wait for a new car to roll off the line. About this time his letter writing began. He wrote to Henry Ford II explaining the predicament. The letter obviously got the attention of Mr. Ford, and Dad was phoned by the local dealership and told his automobile had been delivered and was awaiting payment and pick up. Dad got his car and was off to work.

In 1950, while on vacation in Acapulco, Dad's life changed forever. One day it was raining, and all outside activities came to a standstill. The hotel's social director circled everyone in the lobby and asked them to say who they were and where they were from. A nice rhythm was established as the speaker shifted from person to person around the circle.

A very tall and beautiful girl stood up and quietly spoke her name, "I'm Betty Ball Ludeau from Ville Platte, Louisiana," but before the next person could stand to speak, a male voice was heard from across the room, "Uh, would you mind repeating that name?" The girl was stunned as all eyes and ears were focused on her. She repeated the same. "Would you please spell that last name?" the man called out from afar. The girl was now overcome with embarrassment. That was how our Dad met our mama. He claimed it was love at first sight. At the very moment he laid eyes on her he declared to himself, "I'm gonna make that girl my wife." The courtship began.

Mama's father had died of a massive heart attack when he was only thiry-four and she was nine. She, her mother, and her brother fell into the care of her father's parents, who lived next door. Papa Ludeau was a man of means and had managed to acquire businesses, interests, and properties on which oil was found. Mama had been reared with the taste for a good life and never had any concerns of her own. Her mother, Eunice, was widowed young and lived a full life of travel and leisure. Once, for fun and enjoyment, Eunice signed up to be the official house mother for the Delta Kappa Epsilon fraternity at Louisiana State University. Mama, being in her early twenties then, managed to have an entire fraternity at her disposal as big brothers and she proceeded to dance her way through college.

During the courtship, Dad worked in Hammond, Louisiana, as a young oil man and he began to drive to Baton Rouge to see Mama. Since he wasn't a big dancer, nor did he have any interest in hanging out in "saloons," as he called them, they had little in common. As much as he persisted, she resisted. After a number of proposals she finally admitted to Dad why she was not fit for marriage. He would often retell the story of the moonlit evening when he again asked for her hand, and she responded with, "Walter, I can't marry you. I don't know how to cook!" The next words Dad said to Mama she could recall verbatim. "Betty, I'm not marrying you to be my cook, I'm marrying you to be my bride."

They were married June 14, 1951. Daddy lovingly referred to Mama as his "bride" throughout their marriage. Theirs was considered one of the most entertaining, independent, generous, joint-yet-separate unions that many have ever witnessed. Mama was his muse and the light of his life. He claimed that she was the most exciting and entertaining woman he had ever had the privilege to know. Whenever she would walk into a room or anywhere to join him, he would ask whoever was in earshot, "Isn't she the most beautiful women you've ever seen?" Throughout their entire marriage, not a day ever passed if Daddy was in Mama's company when he failed to say the following words, "Mama, have I told you how much I love you today? And tell me, what can I do to make you happy?" He absolutely loved her more than life itself.

Family Man

It should be said that as a parent, Daddy used military tactics in lieu of books by Dr. Spock. Dad had no hobbies. If asked, he responded in a gruff manner, "I work, that's all I know how to do, work!" He had no problem requiring the same of us. We can remember as toddlers being out in the yard alongside him as he raked the oversized magnolia leaves, picking them up one by one with our little hands and depositing them into a trashcan. He expected any job to be carried out precisely as directed, in a timely manner, and without argument or debate. Whenever given a task on our own it was our duty to report to him upon its completion. For confirmation and by rote his next question was always, "Are you ready for inspection?" If the task was not done right, we risked not only completely redoing the task but were subject to additional assignments.

We never wanted to appear idle when Dad came home from work. Whenever we heard his big Continental pull into the carport, the back door open, and the sound of heavy footsteps approaching, we bolted from in front of the television and either disappeared or began tidying up whatever needed attention. Needless to say, we were all instilled with a very strong work ethic and today will admit that Daddy gets full credit.

On many occasions, for a special treat, he took all five of us children out of school midweek to join him on a business trip to New Orleans, where we stayed downtown at the St. Charles Hotel. Our loving nanny, MowMow, packed our individual bags (usually large paper bags issued for groceries back then) and smiled as we drove off, knowing she was about to have a couple of days reprieve from all of us. Once we arrived, Dad lined us up like soldiers and gave us precise instructions. On his way to work, he dropped us off at the penny arcade in the French Quarter, each with five dollars to play nickel and dime machines. Lunch was spent around the corner at Krystal for hamburgers. At a predetermined time, he told us to find a man dressed like him, in a nice suit, and ask, "Sir, would you direct us to the streetcar headed to the St. Charles Hotel?" That evening we all dressed up and Dad took us to a fancy restaurant in the city. We would be considered babies by today's standards, but to Dad, five to eleven years of age was old enough to think and operate on our own. The one thing we all knew at the time and understood innately was to never get separated from each other in the city, and we never did.

Dad loved being a family man. At five o'clock his colleagues in the oil business knocked off work to go have drinks. But Dad wasn't a drinker. He'd say, "Why in the hell would I want to go drink with your sorry asses when I've got the most beautiful wife and gorgeous family waiting for me at home?"

When he was home, he was home, although he was on the road an awful lot. Since Mama didn't have any disciplinary control over us, sometimes our household could be compared to a monkey cage at a zoo. Many occasions when Dad returned home from work or from being out of town, whatever unpleasant events had occurred in his absence would work their way into that evening's dinner conversation. Whether we were innocent or not, it was irrelevant in Dad's eyes. Without any need for further investigation we were all deemed guilty and subject to punishment. He figured that even if he disciplined us when we didn't deserve it, there were plenty of times we had escaped punishment when, in fact, we did deserve it.

Dad kept a complex relationship with money. On one hand, it didn't mean anything to him. On the other, it was everything. As children and eventually teenagers, we had to pay money into what he called "The Kilowatt Box" if ever we were caught leaving a light on in our respective rooms. It didn't matter if we were over at a friend's house for a sleepover, or playing down the street, we would be summoned by him to return home to turn off the light. As teenagers, whoever was the last to come home in the evenings was responsible for turning off the front porch light. Dad was always the first to wake in the mornings, and if the porch light was still on when he stepped outside to retrieve his paper, he woke up whoever failed to do the job.

He would use money to manipulate and control our devotion. While we were off to college, he might mail a hundred dollar bill ripped in half with the enticement of coming home to get the other half. Or he might send a check but not sign it, promising to do so our next return home. We were often puzzled by these tactics as we gladly came home at every opportunity that availed itself.

The Citizen

Daddy had a tremendous sense of humor. Some of his practical jokes took months to develop. He wrote elaborate letters, sometimes as complete pranks. Once, he observed a prominent television reporter from New Orleans with her colleague out at lunch at his regular diner. The restaurant was all out of that day's special, which happened to be the only thing the reporter wanted. So she and her colleague left the restaurant without paying for two cups of tea. Dad assumed a pseudonym and posed as the restaurant's owner. He dashed off a lengthy, accusing letter, which said in part:

I ask you to remit the $1.40, which will settle your account. You will be happy to learn we did not count our spoons after your hasty departure.

The reporter wrote back an equally lengthy reply, a line of which reads,

It's mind-boggling you were so offended by our actions.

We have a letter written to Dad from the lieutenant governor of Mississippi, a good friend and former classmate from law school. We are unclear of the subject of the letter that Dad had first written that precipitated the reply, but the lieutenant governor jokingly wrote in part:

Dear Mr. Gordon.

I have been informed that you were wounded in the head in the last war. As a public official of the great state of Mississippi, I want to take this opportunity to say I am indeed sorry they didn't kill you.

Many of Dad's letters were written with a serious overtone. On the subject of "terror tactics now being used against the United States and our people," he wrote to President Ronald Reagan shortly after the Iranian hostage crisis was resolved, suggesting the president deport all college students from hostile countries who were studying in the United States.

> *I have observed students from Iran who are presently attending the University of Southwest Louisiana, and they were certainly vocal in their support of Iran when our fifty citizens were held in that country.*
>
> *Personally, I am weary of being the "nice guy" and having to suffer at the hands of these third-rate nations. While I do not see an answer to this horrible problem [of terrorism], I am satisfied words and threats are not the answer.*

A newspaper picture showed a mother distressed by her son's departure overseas for a stint in the military. The mother was "being comforted by a covey of ladies," as Dad wrote to the editor, and continued:

> *I am confident that some kind soul will see that [the serviceman] gets this unsettling picture of his mom. When he examines her obvious agony, his performance as a serviceman will no doubt be impaired.*
>
> *Perhaps if all moms would write cheerful letters and bake a few cookies, it would make the life of a serviceman more endurable. Some thought might be given to some volunteer work with the Red Cross. Anything would be better than weeping in concert.*
>
> *. . . I urge you to refrain from publishing any recitation of weakness which will be counterproductive for our servicemen. You failed to ask the usual insipid question, "How do you feel?" I will answer this question, she feels like hell, just as I do.*

Honor and Integrity

Daddy spent his last years in Mississippi. He was apart from our mother then, but they were in close contact and weekly traveled back and forth between Mississippi and Louisiana to spend time together. One of our sisters, Tracy, lived in Pass Christian with her husband and two children where Dad resided. Dad just adored his grandkids and spent a lot of time with Tracy and her family. They communicated on a daily basis.

One morning Dad didn't call Tracy, which was highly unusual. It was two days after his birthday. After ten a.m., the children's nanny, Miss Lillian, tried phoning Dad and found his phone busy. Dad always took his phone off the hook at night and was an early riser, so this was unusual. Miss Lillian loaded the children into her vehicle and drove over to check on Daddy and found his newspaper still on his front door step. She opened the door, as she possessed a key to his condo, and Tracy's five-year-old son, Charlie, raced into Dad's bedroom and attempted to wake him. Dad had suffered a stroke during the night. An ambulance was called and he was rushed to the hospital. The family all got in cars and boarded planes to get home immediately.

We were first told by the neurologist that Daddy had a good chance of pulling through, and our hopes were high that Daddy would quickly recover, but within hours of being admitted he suffered another stroke, this one massive. Daddy lasted three more days and died April 19, 1997, at age seventy-six.

His funeral wasn't a sad affair in the least. Everybody told jokes and laughed, recalling pranks he had pulled, things he had said, stories that had taken on lives of their own. You couldn't talk about Daddy without smiling. He had become a local legend.

Dad was cremated. His ashes were kept in an urn at our brother's home until our dear mother passed away in 2009. We knew that Dad would be happy nowhere but with Mama, so his ashes were placed in her coffin, which now rests in our family plot.

What would we want people to remember about our father? His honor and integrity. Both of our parents, despite their faults, lived their lives this way. Once, they were talking about selling their home. Mama was at a social function when she saw a neighbor who was also a real estate agent. She mentioned that they would soon be selling and would call this realtor when they were ready to list. Nothing more was said or formalized. Soon after that a separate party approached our parents, and the house sold without ever hitting the market. After the deal was final, Dad made out a check to their neighbor the realtor. When Mama asked Daddy the reason for the check, he responded with, "Mama, you told him you'd list it with him." Mama quickly understood and dispatched a check that day.

Ties to the Band of Brothers

Dad is sometimes credited as being the vital link between Stephen Ambrose and the Band of Brothers, but this is perhaps over-told. They weren't neighbors, as has been reported, but lived about fifteen minutes away from each other in Pass Christian, Mississippi.

In 1988 during the annual Easy Company reunion in New Orleans, Ambrose's assistant at the University of New Orleans heard there was a group of WWII veterans in town. The assistant dropped by the hotel and asked if he could speak to the men. Many of them happily complied and sat for brief interviews. Many recommended he should speak with Gordon, since he lived just an hour away. (Dad was out of the hotel when all this took place). The assistant gave Dad's contact information to Ambrose and from there a relationship ensued. Prior to Dad's initial meeting with Ambrose for the book, he arranged for Lipton, Guth, and Dick Winters to join him for a collaborative interview.

Dad and Ambrose became fast friends, but Dad never sought to take advantage of the friendship and always respected Ambrose as an author and historian. They had lunch once in a while or met occasionally for coffee. When any of the men came to the coast to visit, Dad called Ambrose and his wife Moira, and they all got together for a seafood boil of whatever was in season. Dad was always grateful to Ambrose for choosing Company E as his subject out of all the outstanding military groups that served in WWII. Dad did not live to see *Band of Brothers* become a media phenomenon, but we're confident he's pleased and proud to see his brothers be revered and honored as all men who have fought for our freedom should be.

9

HERMAN "HACK" HANSON

Interview with Karen Hanson Hyland, daughter

I was lucky, growing up, that my dad talked about the war. He didn't shy away from his experiences. He described the war as something he was fortunate to live through. Because of that, life was a party, he always said, and he was going to have a good time. That was his philosophy, anyway.

He talked most about the war during the years I was in high school. I'm the oldest child in the family, and after work he sat at the dinner table and talked while my mom cooked dinner. He talked mostly about Bastogne. Everybody was so cold and thin, he said. It was bitter cold. He needed to wrap his feet with paper—anything a man could find to wrap around his feet or stuff into his shoes to try and stay warm. He talked about trees exploding from the constant shelling—tree bursts, he called them—and how scary that was: pieces of trees as sharp as arrows flew at you. He talked about digging foxholes with the men and sleeping in a hole in the ground. He talked about how the guys were special and about how they were his brothers.

Easy Company veteran Frank Perconte was a childhood friend of Dad's, and he and his wife came over regularly after the war. They talked about a lot of things together, and almost always, somewhere during the conversation, the war would come up. I remember a few of those stories too, but I wish I had been a little bit older so I would have paid more attention to them. Isn't that always the way it goes?

Anyway, this is what I know of my dad's life.

One of the Older Men

My dad was born in Joliet, Illinois, on January 3, 1917, which made him one of the older Easy Company men. His family lived on Ottawa Street. His mother's name was Artillia, but everybody called her Tillie. She had emigrated from Germany and we have relatives still over in Germany to this day. My grandfather was born in Sweden and immigrated to America. So my dad was a first generation American.

How did my dad get the nickname Hack? Actually, he had two nicknames. Hack was his first nickname growing up. I'm not sure how it came about because there were a number of people who also called him Henry back then. After the war, most people called him Hank.

Dad was the middle child. His parents were very strict. Dad grew up as a hard worker and loved sports. Golf was his favorite and he also loved baseball. They played pickup games in the neighborhood constantly.

Frank Perconte moved into the neighborhood when he was about ten, to the same street as my dad, and from then on they were best buddies and basically did everything together. That neighborhood was very tight. Families went on picnics with other neighborhood families and played sports with each other. Both Frank and Dad loved to play practical jokes. Dad seemed to have the lighter temperament. He loved to tease, he had a real charmer personality, and was very sociable and had a lot of friends. He valued education and always wanted to live life to the fullest and be the best at whatever he did.

Dad and Frank both graduated high school and went to work at Gary Steelworks. They carpooled together, although Dad only went one way with Frank. Dad went to Roosevelt University in Chicago during the evenings and took the train home. He studied journalism in college and got his degree after the war through the University of Missouri. Unfortunately we don't have any of dad's writings, journals, or letters anymore. Where they lived was right near the Des Plaines River. Not too long after the war ended, the river flooded, swamping their house and destroying all his writings.

Shot Twice

Dad didn't think he was going to get drafted, being older, but serving his country was still something he wanted to do. After the war started, Frank and Dad were at the movies one day at the Rialto Square Theater, and that's where they saw one of those shorts that described the paratroopers. They decided to do that and enlisted together. Their serial numbers were consecutive, only one apart.

Dad craved adventure and thought that jumping out of an airplane would be a fun thing to try. He said he always enjoyed the actual experience of parachuting—not into combat, but simply the rush that came from jumping.

Dad and Frank were two of the first four privates in Easy Company along with Skinny Sisk and Carwood Lipton. When Frank and my dad enlisted, they both started out in 1st Platoon, but because they played so many pranks on the other guys, they ended up getting separated. My dad went to 2nd Platoon, and Frank stayed in the 1st.

Just before D-day, when Dad was in England, his father passed away. Dad talked about that with us—how hard it was to lose a parent and be so far away from family. He really wanted to go home but wasn't able to, so he got away for a while by himself and tried to grieve in private and make sense of it all.

He jumped on D-Day and for Operation Market-Garden in Holland and for the "third jump"—off the truck in Bastogne, as the men say. He found it astonishing that the Dutch were so grateful to be liberated.

He was right there in a foxhole in Bastogne when Joe Toye and Bill

Guarnere lost their legs in the shelling. The shelling was so bad, he said. Many of the men were so upset at what had occurred before their eyes. He and Carwood Lipton helped keep the men together and pulled guys back into their foxholes until the shelling was all over. He talked about that quite a bit.

Dad was shot twice. Both times, luckily, no major organs were hit, so he was able to be patched up and sent back in. He was present in every single battle and was one of the few guys who made it all the way through the war from the first day in Toccoa to the end. He had scars from his shrapnel wounds, and as a kid I was always intrigued with his scars. The skin was pulled together and folded over in a little flap. One scar was up in his chest area, the shoulder, close to his heart. The other was lower. The bullet went right through him, leaving both an entry and exit wound. The first time he was shot it happened at the tail end of Market-Garden. The second time he got injured was just as they were pulling out of Bastogne.

Dad talked about the concentration camps, about how he had a hard time reconciling that with his German nationality. He wondered how these things could be going on and be attributed to his people. He had a really hard time coming to grips with that.

Sergeant Chuck Grant was a really close friend of Dad's. In Berchtesgaden, Chuck was shot in the brain by a drunken replacement from another company, and I know Dad had a really hard time with that. He (along with several of the other men) beat up on the drunken GI, and Dad even pulled a gun on him. I know that's one of the incidents my family worried about. How was it going to be portrayed in the series?

In the book, it mentions that it was my dad who pulled the gun,[1] but the series attributes it to Ron Speirs. I think the way that scene was ultimately portrayed was handled well. It showed the confusion and anger of the moment. Here, the men had made it all the way through the war, but one of their friends was gravely injured in an accident that could have been prevented. Dad said the drunken replacement was taken to a regi-

---

1. *Band of Brothers*, 285.

mental guardhouse for discipline, and that's the last they ever heard of him. Fortunately, Sergeant Grant slowly recovered, although he had some problems talking and he was partially paralyzed. After the war he attended some of the reunions and lived until the 1980s.

Almost every family vacation, we went to visit one of my dad's war buddies. They were like extended family to us. When we were young we didn't quite understand the connection all these people had to us. We visited Popeye Winn, Joe Toye, Walter Gordon—those are the ones I remember visiting. We went to the reunions as kids, and then even after my dad died, my mom insisted that we go. Easy Company is like family to us. We know quite a few of the kids as well as the men. My mom helped plan one of the national conventions for the 101st in Chicago. The main hotel was being renovated, so my mom booked all the Company E guys in a different hotel across the street. The guys had such a good time like that, just being together so much as a group. Everybody just hung out in the hospitality room morning to night, swapping stories. That was really when they started having the separate company E reunions, and not worrying about being part of the larger 101st ones.

Dad never saw himself as doing anything special in the war. He was just doing his job with the guys around him, he always said.

Pancakes at Breakfast

When Dad came back after the war, he finished college, then began to look for a job. He was a little older than most of the returning GIs and found that he was put at a disadvantage because of his age. Sears, Roebuck had an entry-level job open, but it had a maximum age limit, and dad was older than the limit, so on the application he fudged and said he was seven years younger. He got the job. He worked for Sears, Roebuck his whole career, in their catalog division, and ended up being one of their vice presidents.

Dad worked in downtown Chicago. He held the very first meeting in the Sears Tower while they were still doing the excavation. He took a bunch of people down to the basement with hardhats and a card table and set up the meeting. Only the hole was dug then. But he did it for fun, to say that they had the first meeting there.

Shortly after the war he met my mom, Jean Newman. She came from Fremont, Nebraska, and had moved to Chicago with a couple of her girl-friends after they graduated from college. They wanted to try life in the big city for a little while. The other girlfriends moved back to Nebraska, but my mom stayed in Chicago where she worked at a printing company. Years later, she worked as a kindergarten assistant and then as a travel agent.

My parents lived in Chicago when they were first married, then moved to Oak Park for a few years, then after my sister was born we moved to Lombard. There were six kids in my family altogether. We kept moving out to the suburbs like everybody else. By the time my youngest sister came along we had moved out to Lisle.

Mom and Dad had a good marriage and got along well. Mom adored Dad, and vice versa. Mom was a member of the DuPage Symphony Or-chestra and played several different instruments. She was very smart and got A's all through high school, except for gym. She was one of those people who are so smart that they almost lack a little common sense, and my dad could always play a good joke on her. Mom wasn't quite as fun-loving as he, but they went out every Saturday night to dinner or to go dancing. Weekly, they had people over to the house for barbecues and to play cards. Mom and Dad were big bridge players. Cards were always a big part of family life and vacations—wherever we stopped, they always held bridge tournaments.

As kids, we just adored Dad. We couldn't wait for him to get home. He was a lot of fun. My favorite memories of him all involve little things, like him taking us out for ice cream. He loved to sing and would good naturedly torture me with his songs. He sang "*Sugar, Sugar,*" and "*Knock Three Times.*" On Sunday mornings he cooked breakfast for us, big pan-cakes shaped like the initials of our names. He made up silly little nick-names for all of us. He called me Karrie, or Karriebrook, because one of the clothing lines in the Sears catalog was named that. My sister's name is

Amy, and Dad called her Amy Pamey Button Bright. My brother Mark was Marker Parker. My brother Kurt was Dirty Kurty, because he liked to play with his Hot Wheels cars in the dirt. The nicknames sort of petered out with the younger ones, but Dad always teased us kids. When my little sister was young and had to go to the bathroom, Dad said, "You know, when we were in the war we didn't get much toilet paper—so you can only use one sheet." He drove us around to our activities in the family station wagon. I was in Job's Daughters, and Dad always took me and my friends to the meetings. Afterward he got us ice cream. I know all my girlfriends adored him. He was just that kind of person, very sociable, always the life of the party, although he could be firm when he needed to be. He expected much from himself, and he wanted all of us to do our best. We didn't want to let him down. It meant a lot to us to have Dad proud of us.

Exactly as He Wanted

Dad died far too young, on May 15, 1971. He was fifty-four.

It happened around four o'clock in the afternoon during the running of the Preakness Stakes. Dad always said that after watching so many of his buddies go so horribly, he wanted to go as quickly as he could when he died. He also joked that if he could choose any way to go, he'd want to go while on a golf course.

That's exactly how he died. It was a Saturday and he was part of a golf league with Sears. He had just finished playing a round of golf. He won that day and went to post his scores. He was walking into the clubhouse to go have a drink with the guys, sat down, and was gone.

It was just one of those things—as quick as that. The hospital said it was an acute coronary occlusion, that he was very healthy, and that if he had been to see the doctor a few days before they wouldn't have been able to find anything. My mother always thought it was a piece of shrapnel, still in his body, that moved into his heart, because he had so much of it still in him.

The golf course was just a few miles from our house. It was a beautiful sunny Saturday afternoon. We were all home. Plans were being made to go out that evening to a school function. My mom and my sister were upstairs in a room chatting. We heard sirens and didn't think anything of it. A little bit later, the men whom Dad had been playing golf with came to the door to get my mom and take her to the hospital. We didn't find out he was gone until she came back. We were devastated. I was only fifteen, a sophomore in high school. My youngest sister was just six.

Dad's funeral went on for three days. He lay in wake for two days, one out by us in Lisle, and another in Joliet. He had so many people who loved him. The ceremony was packed. He ended up being cremated and the ashes went into an urn. Mom made a little display case on the mantle beside all his medals. She said he always wanted to be there looking after us.

Ironically my brother, Mark, was a lot like my dad and also passed away young, in his early forties, of esophageal cancer. He also went much too soon.

Mom passed away four years ago. She had Chronic Obstructive Pulmonary Disease (COPD) and died of a heart attack. She liked to have a good time all the way to the end. She had no regrets about her life.

Dad's Success

So many of the men after the war seemed to struggle so much, but my dad seemed to survive so well—I've often wondered about that, about why. He loved to party. He loved his martinis just like all the rest of the guys. He came home each night and had a drink while Mom was cooking dinner. I guess the drinking just didn't catch up with him.

My parents had a really strong social network. They could stay up all night with their bridge tournaments. They went out all the time, every weekend, whether business or just socializing. I know it helped Dad to have many friends.

Dad seemed to have a different outlook compared to many of the other returning veterans. Some of the men kept their experiences bottled up, but Dad certainly didn't. He chose to talk. And he could talk about anything. It wasn't just the war, he talked about a lot of things. He loved politics, and loved debating politics. He loved going out and meeting with people, and he never kept his feelings inside. You always knew what he was thinking.

And he had Frank Perconte around—one good, lifelong friend. They always had a good time when they were together.

What is one thing I would want people to know about my dad? That he was a very special, extraordinary person who cared deeply about other people. Everyone he came in contact with, he brought them into his circle of friendship and family. He wanted to enjoy each moment of life. He was a man of integrity, passion, and conviction who lived for his family, friends, and wife. I wish more people were like that.

10

JOSEPH LIEBGOTT

**Interviews with Jim Liebgott, son,
and Rhonda Kersey, granddaughter**

He was a machine gunner at Brécourt Manor and awarded the Bronze Star for bravery. He cut a finger off a German he bayoneted near Carentan and took the man's ring. He had a reputation of being very rough on prisoners, and perhaps the most widely recounted story of Private Joe Liebgott is when Captain Dick Winters ordered him to take eleven prisoners back to the battalion Command Post.[1] Winters noticed how edgy Liebgott was and made him empty his rifle except for one bullet, saying, "If you drop a prisoner, the rest will jump you."

But Winters liked Liebgott and considered him a good combat soldier and loyal friend. Liebgott dragged Ed Tipper to safety after Tipper was severely wounded in Carentan. In Bastogne, Winters made Liebgott his runner for a short while, giving him a chance to rest up from the extreme tension of the front line. Liebgott played a key role in the attack on

---

1. Ambrose, *Band of Brothers*, 150 (note: Ambrose's book notes eleven prisoners, Winters's book notes seven, cf. Winters with Kingseed, *Beyond Band of Brothers*, 143).

Noville a short time later, and was one of just eleven men from the original forty from 1st Platoon still around after the Battle of the Bulge.

David Kenyon Webster described him this way: "120-pound Liebgott, ex–San Francisco cabby, was the skinniest and one of the funniest men in E Company. He had the added distinction of being one of the few Jews in the paratroops. Both he and [Thomas] McCreary, ancient men of thirty, were the company elders."[2]

There are just two problems with Webster's description, according to Liebgott's family. He was a barber by trade, not a cabby. Although he drove a taxi for a short time in San Francisco before the war, it was never his life's goal or profession, as has been perpetuated. That's a minor issue. The bigger issue is that Liebgott was not Jewish; he was a German Roman Catholic.

This is the rest of the story about the real Joseph Liebgott.

Barber with Purple Hearts

Liebgott was born in 1915 in Lansing, Michigan, where his father worked for the auto industry. The family soon migrated to Oakland, California, where his father became a barber. Liebgott had one brother and four sisters. He was the oldest, and was very protective of his younger sisters. The children all went to Catholic schools, where Liebgott played soccer and boxed.

The parents both spoke German, as did the children. During the war, he was one of the company's interpreters. He considered working as an interpreter in Europe after the war, but changed his mind.

After Liebgott graduated from high school, he drove a taxi in San Francisco for a short while, then went to barber college, which was his profession when he enlisted in the army at age twenty-six. He went into the paratroopers to make extra money and put a down payment on a house for his parents with the cash he made in the military. He always looked out for his folks.

---

2. Ambrose, *Band of Brothers*, 170.

Liebgott told few war stories to his children or relatives, but they know he was one of the original Toccoa men, and that just prior to the D-day jump he cut some of the men's hair into Mohawks. He was wounded three times and received three Purple Hearts, but refused one because he considered the wound "just a scratch," he said to his son later. He instructed military officials to give the award to other men who had been hurt worse than he. After the war, Liebgott received a partial disability for complications from wounds sustained during the war.

When he first came home from the war, he disappeared for two years. Family members found out later he was living near Yuma, California. His buddies tried to reach him a few times to invite him to reunions, but Liebgott's father told them "not to mess with him," said his son Jim.

"Nothing's really come out about those two years or what he was doing then," Jim said. "Dad was a barber, and he always told me that if you're a barber you can go to any city and find a job. So he just took off and worked for a while. I believe it was a period of readjustment for him where he was just trying to find his way."

Liebgott met and married a woman named Peggy in Los Angeles in 1949. They had eight children together. During his career as a barber, he owned a few of his own shops, but mostly worked for other employers. The family lived in Oakland and Santa Barbara, and he owned a shop in Culver City for a while.

Jim described the atmosphere in the home while growing up as "fun, particularly with eight kids on a barber salary. We didn't have a lot, but we always had shoes and clothes, and were always well fed." One of Jim's favorite memories is whenever his father took the family to the beach. "He had only one day off per week, and he took us to the Long Beach pike, an amusement park with a roller coaster and pinball games. There wasn't much money to go around, but we always had fun."

For a hobby, Liebgott liked betting on ponies at the racetrack. He was a two-dollar bettor and never made anything at it. It was always just for fun. He often flew down to the Caliente Racetrack in Tijuana with his buddies. The owner at one of the shops he worked in had an airplane, and every other Sunday they used to fly down to Mexico.

"Dad had good friends," Jim said, "but as far as I know he never contacted anyone from his service days. I never asked why, but I think that was part of the way he coped. He just wanted to put the war as far away from him as possible."

Devoted Grandfather

The Liebgotts divorced when Jim was about fourteen. Peggy remarried, but Liebgott didn't. After the divorce, Liebgott stayed in the same area as his family. Liebgott's granddaughter, Rhonda Kersey, doesn't remember her grandfather being married to her grandmother. "She was remarried by the time I knew her," Rhonda said. "Her new husband was really loud, but Grandpa Liebgott was just the opposite, really quiet. Yet when he was around us, he was always laughing quietly."

Rhonda described him this way: "His hands looked like a man who worked with his hands, sunspots all over. He absolutely loved his grandkids. He had false teeth that he flipped out of his mouth and smiled, threatening to kiss us with his gums. He was a tickler. He never held babies over his shoulder, but always forward in a sitting position, facing out against his stomach, because he wanted them to be able to see everything. As grandkids, he always made us laugh, and there was never any real discipline going on when Grandpa was with us. Sometimes he took us shopping for the whole day. He didn't have a lot of money—I'm pretty sure all he had was his veteran's benefits, but there was this idea as a kid that Grandpa always had money."

As a grandfather, Liebgott excelled in a number of ways. He made all of the bikes for the grandkids by scouring thrift stores for dilapidated bikes. He stripped the bikes down to the frame, fixed and assembled them as good as new. He let each grandchild pick the color of new paint for his or her bike. He did customizations as well. In the late 1970s, he made a bike for a grandson that was metallic orange with a huge banana seat. Everything on it was chrome. "My brother and I never had new bikes from a store," said Rhonda, "but we were the coolest kids on the block."

Liebgott had his quirks. "I always knew the specific foods we were going to eat at his house," Rhonda said. "He had bite-sized candy bars and store-brand soda pop. There was no drinking water at his house, even on the hottest days. It was always, 'Have a soda,' and 'Here, wash it down with another soda.' He made tuna sandwiches and a delicious cucumber-and-tomato marinade that tasted fantastic. We've tried to duplicate this recipe in later years but have never been able to do it quite right."

He always lived in rental houses, usually older, with "ugly white interior paint and big, bubbly lathe and plaster walls," Rhonda said. "He didn't do yard work, but didn't really need to because the grass was always dead and the yard just dirt."

Personally, he kept very clean. Inside his house, he always wore corduroy house shoes. He wore his shirt tucked in neatly; his pants were always pressed, and he always wore a belt. All his clothes were perfectly ironed. His hair was perfectly groomed. It was always hot in his house, even when it was summertime and warm outside. "He was a skinny older man," Rhonda said, "frail in some ways. He must have always been cold. I never saw him wear shorts, even at the beach."

In Liebgott's house, everything had its exact spot, as organized as an Army footlocker on inspection day. He was compulsive this way. In contrast to his meticulous personal grooming, his houses were always grimy. For instance, he kept an old, tiny, metal fan, like in a Dick Tracy movie, on his corner table by the front door. If ever the fan was moved, a perfect ring showed underneath in the dust. His hands were always greasy from working out in his garage, and everywhere his hands touched on the walls were black smudges. He never vacuumed, ever.

Liebgott was very thrifty and cut corners wherever he could. He never owned a set of dishes but ate out of empty Cool Whip bowls and margarine pans. He bought pots and pans and even secondhand pens and pencils from thrift stores. Each week he went to several grocery stores to get his shopping done because he only shopped where there were coupons. He created very little trash and even tore paper bags into squares before putting them in the trash. He kept very current with the *TV Guide*. Whenever a page in the *TV Guide* was finished, he ripped the page off and disposed of it. He watched *T.J. Hooker, Knight Rider*, and *Jeopardy*, but he didn't like *The A-Team* because it was interracial.

"Bigot is a strong word," Rhonda said, "but if there was a stronger word, Grandpa would have been it. He threw around the N-word like it was nothing. He watched the news a lot and blamed whatever went wrong in the country on various ethnic groups. When I started dating, I dated this guy from El Salvador. Oh my gosh, my grandpa just threw a fit. 'Does he even speak English?' he growled. If you've ever seen the Clint Eastwood movie *Gran Torino*, that's how my grandpa was."

Rhonda was a teenager when her grandfather's health turned. He had a hernia and got quite sick and dehydrated, the hernia turned gangrenous and he lost the use of a leg. From then on he was confined to a wheelchair, and "he hated it," Rhonda said. "It kept him from doing all the things he did before. He couldn't make bikes for the grandkids. He was a different person after that. He [was] determined to adjust to life in the wheelchair and be independent again, but he was very angry about it, very frustrated that he couldn't move around."

Liebgott never liked technology. Jim bought him a microwave because he couldn't reach the stove anymore from his wheelchair, but he didn't like using the new appliance. "He believed the microwaves would come out and get him," Rhonda said. "He'd wheel up to it, put the food in and set the timer, then wheel away really fast. If he didn't wheel away with both hands giving exactly the same amount of pressure on each tire, he'd bump into the cabinets and grouse about it."

Family Came First

Toward the end, Liebgott lived in a rental that was halfway between his son's work and home, so Jim often stopped there on his commute home. Father and son watched TV together, and sometimes a war movie was on and Liebgott commented about things he had seen and experienced during his combat days. "That was the most he ever talked openly about the war—whenever the TV was on," Jim said. Occasionally he talked about the war when he got mad. He said he had done some killing, things that most people never have to do."

In 1992 Liebgott developed a tumor in his neck near his jugular vein. It pushed against his windpipe and caused pain and complications. Jim took his father to the hospital on Father's Day. Liebgott died just after that, on June 28, 1992. He was seventy-seven.

"He had been very strict about us not having a funeral for him," Jim said. "It was just his time to go, he said, and he didn't want anybody to do any lifesaving techniques on him or anything before he passed. He had a good life, he said, and that was it. Life was over. He was an altar boy in the church, but as an adult never practiced a faith or his Catholicism, never went to church, and never made us kids go to church ever. He never talked about religion or why he had taken the path he did with it."

Liebgott instructed his family that he didn't want anybody saying any words over him. He just told them to "burn him." The family had him cremated. Jim's younger sister has the ashes, and a younger brother kept his war memorabilia, some letters, and the original Toccoa book.

Representatives from the Liebgott family went to an Easy Company reunion in 2003. "One of the big questions we had was why everybody thought he was Jewish," Jim said. "It said 'Roman Catholic' right on his dog tags. We asked a couple of the guys and they figured it was because he hated the Nazis so bad. It was just an assumption they made. But I don't know why my dad hated the Nazis so bad. He was known for being a bit of a bigot, maybe it was just the times he grew up in, maybe it was a reaction to his German heritage, I don't know."

How would the family want Joe Liebgott remembered?

"He was an honorable man and a good father," Jim said. "He always took care of his family, and his family always came first."

"I know he lived for us," Rhonda said. "Whenever we were around, we had his full attention."

11

ROBERT MARSH

Interview with Marilyn Tittle, daughter

When it comes to my dad, I don't know where to even start. What if my kids were writing a story about me? What would they say? I'm certainly not perfect. That's the spirit in which I talk about my dad.

In many ways, my father, Robert Marsh, was a good guy. He was a good soldier and a good worker throughout his life. He cared about people. He helped anybody he met. As time went on, most of his family members came to him for help. He took care of both his mother and father as well as three of his brothers in their old age. All that was admirable.

But I saw a different part of his life.

I saw a man who brought the war home with him. He was not the best of persons, not after the war. That's what he showed me, at least. That side of Robert Marsh affected me most.

Why do I tell you this? My father's story is about what war can do to a young man. It's about how war can turn an innocent young boy into a sad, hurting, lonely, and confused adult. The soldiers coming home from today's wars deserve to live much better and happier lives than many of the World War II soldiers ended up living. Hopefully, they'll read stories

like my father's and find the help they need, if they need it. If today's soldiers do that, then the stories that are told years from now will not sound
like mine.

I have another reason for telling you his story. I also want to honor
my father's memory. Despite the way the war changed him, I will always
love him. My family has a treasured photo of his youngest great grandchild, Alyssa Piatak, standing next to his gravestone. The epitaph we chose
for Dad reads: "Gone But Not Forgotten."

That's the truth. We all loved Robert Marsh dearly.

Man of the House

Robert Marsh was the youngest of seven children. His father had been
married previously and had lost his first wife and baby in childbirth. His
father was studying to be a doctor at the time, and when he couldn't save
them, he sort of lost it emotionally, decided he wasn't going to be a doctor,
and gave up on life. He married a different woman, my grandmother.
They had seven children, he worked odd jobs and became a drinker.

Their son Robert, my dad, quit school when he was in the eighth
grade so he could take care of his parents. They needed help even then.
Dad worked at a little store on Pennsylvania Avenue in Columbus called
Nick's Food Market, about a block from where he lived. The older brothers in the family did their own thing. The two girls got married and moved
out of state. Dad was the softy of the bunch and became the man of the
house. That good-person side of him, the caring part, was always in him.
It was certainly there from the start.

Dad enlisted at age seventeen. He lied about his age to get in. Two of
his older brothers had been drafted into the Army already. Dad was in the
Army a total of two years, eleven months, and eight days. We heard that
statistic quite often while growing up.

I was three months old when Dad went into the army, and three years
old when he got out. He was just seventeen when he was married, and
my mom, Jean, was eighteen. Dad had been long out of school by then.
They met through friends. He asked her out, but she didn't like him at

first. Mom was a quieter person and described Dad as an "out there" type of guy.

Dad joined Easy Company at Fort Bragg before the unit shipped out for England and further training prior to D-day. I have a letter written in 1981 from Easy Company member Burton Christenson, who notes:

> *Robert K. Marsh was a member of first platoon. During [D-day, he] injured both legs and was hospitalized in England. He returned to duty with his unit in England and succeeded in making every battle campaign the 101st Airborne Division participated in until the Germans surrendered May 8th, 1945.*
>
> *Marsh could have been evacuated because of his injuries and sent back to the United States.*
>
> *Sergeant Marsh was and is a credit to his country. A real man's man and a great soldier.*

I love that last line. It points to the man my father was at the core, a credit to his country and a great soldier. That's how I want people to remember him most.

The bad part is Dad always had a hard time believing those good things about himself. He was mentioned in *Band of Brothers* a few times, notably in Hagenau. The book notes how Sergeant Marsh was driving a German truck as Private John Janovic leaned on the truck's door. The truck hit a log and Janovic lost his balance. Tragically, he was thrown to the road and died from the concussion to his head soon after.[1] It was a very sad post-hostilities accident, and yes, my dad blamed himself. That's one story we heard about in bits and pieces throughout the years. Dad said he even killed his own. Others said Janovic's death was an accident. "Well, you don't make those kinds of accidents," my dad said.

When Dad got out of the Army, my mother and I were living with his parents. Dad wanted us all to stay with them for a while because it was easier to take care of them if we were all together. We stayed with my

---

1. Ambrose, *Band of Brothers*, 293–284

grandparents until my mother decided she didn't want us to be there anymore, then we got our own house. My brother and sister were born after that. There are six years between my brother and I, and eight between my sister and I.

Dad worked at the General Motors factory in Columbus for many years, then went into the tavern business with my mom and my uncle. That was a mistake because Dad drank from the time he returned from the war until the day he died. What he didn't drink at the bar he gave away for free, so the business didn't work from a lot of perspectives. My uncle eventually bought them out, and my dad went to work at other jobs.

Dad's work ethic was always one good thing about him. He never missed a day's work. He never took anything from anybody. If he felt he needed something or wanted something, he worked for it. That's what he always told us: "You work for what you want and don't expect anybody to give you anything." He always provided a home for us. And we never went hungry.

Though he worked all week, he drank all weekend. It was always just beer, never whiskey or anything. People seldom think that beer can be dangerous, but it is if you drink enough of it. Dad drank Pabst, and he could really put it away. An eighteen-pack was no problem for him. Friday nights, he wouldn't come home until late and he was drunk then; sometimes he wouldn't come home at all. On Saturdays when he woke up he started where he left off. He was drunk all day Saturday. On Sunday he sobered up for work on Monday, and then we better all walk the walk, because he wasn't in a very good mood when he was sobering up. That happened pretty much every weekend. That was life as I knew it.

He was very strict with me. If I didn't dry a dish correctly and he found a spot, it didn't matter what time it was at night, everything came out of the cabinets and I washed and dried them all again before I could go to sleep. I always tried to do whatever I could for him. I got him his beer or whatever he needed. But I never could please Dad.

He was very strict with my brother, also. If we did something wrong as kids, we had to stand in the corner at attention for up to an hour. We couldn't move, and if he caught us moving, our time started over. I don't know if you've ever had to stand one place for very long, but if you have an itch somewhere, or you need to move a foot—well, Dad better not catch you. It could be two minutes before your time was up, but if he caught you moving, your time started over. My brother got caught several times like that. I remember him literally falling down in the corner, asleep. Then my mom and dad would get into it, because Dad said he had to stand there, and Mom said, "That's enough."

Dad talked when he drank, and it was all about the war, but everything was in riddles. You never knew the specifics of what happened. He mumbled and shouted and cheered, often talking about the different guys in the company. It was all good, what he said about the other men. They were his heroes. I heard their names so often I thought those guys were related to me: Winters and Guarnere and Christenson and Lipton and Martin. They were my surrogate uncles. Christenson was a really good man in my father's eyes. After I was married and became pregnant, Dad wanted me to name the baby after Christenson, if it was a boy. But I ended up having three girls.

Dad talked frequently about how he should not even have come home from the war. In his mind, the best men were buried over there. A few people referred to him as a war hero, but we didn't dare use that word around the house. That was wrong. "I am not a hero!" he said. I know other vets who express similar things, but with Dad it wasn't so much about humility as it was about self-loathing. Everything he did was bad in his eyes. He talked highly of the other men, but whenever he talked about himself, he was the bad guy. He lived with so much guilt. It seemed like he was proud to know that he was one of those great men who fought for the country, but he was in denial about any of the good parts he did.

I remember saying to him once, "Dad, everybody had to do terrible things when they were over there. You could have been killed."

"I *should* have been killed," he said.

That was his take.

We never went on any family vacations. Dad wasn't big into creating fun memories. But he loved to cook. That made a good family memory. He was proud of a few dishes he made—spaghetti with pork chops, meatloaf—and they truly were great. After I got married we often went there for Sunday dinner with the whole family. That's the one time everything wasn't so much about the war. It was about his cooking then. But those few moments of peace didn't happen often enough.

When Dad drank, he sometimes talked about himself as if he wasn't in the room, detached, in third person: "*He killed people. Those hands killed a lot of people, and do you have any idea what it's like to have killed?*" The questions were all asked in anger. One of his friends got blown up in a foxhole, and he mumbled about that often: "*Do you have any idea what that was like? To have body parts all over me?*" The more he talked, the angrier he got.

When he was drunk, he set up an American flag in the middle of our dining room floor. If you came in the front door you couldn't walk through the house to get to the stairways to go to your room. You better not come near the flag unless you saluted it.

One time he was drunk and tore up our house badly. I was about ten years old and sure, I saw him in this rampage. He went from room to room breaking things. I hollered and screamed. My mom tried to get him to stop. I ran to a neighbor's house to call the police. They arrived, and Dad ran out the back door. I'll never forget the two officers' astonishment. They looked at the debris and let out a low whistle. "Wow, what happened here?" an officer asked.

"My husband," Mom said. "He was telling war stories."

"One man did all this?" the other asked.

Nothing was standing in our home except the refrigerator and stove. Every piece of furniture was tipped over, ripped, or broken. The mattress was off the bed. Chairs were on their sides. The dresser was knocked over. Our entire house was torn apart.

Dad talked about committing suicide. He attempted it once by trying to hang himself in the basement. He was drunk. When Mom went down to see what he was doing, he had a rope over the rafters and around his neck and was standing on a crate. Whether it was just a show, or if he would have actually done it, who knows? Mom didn't.

When I was a kid I never understood why Dad was like this. I don't fully understand it today. I've read books and I've talked to a few of the veterans. That's helped, but I think, wow, Dad really needed help. Nobody knew where to go or what to do. I sure wish we had.

Always in Misery

For years I begged Mom to leave Dad and get us out of there, but she kept saying that she wanted us kids to grow up first. Finally in 1964, they divorced. Mom had put up with enough. I was twenty-one and out of the house, but my brother and sister were still teenagers at home.

Dad remarried around 1980, but I don't think he ever got over my mother. He always talked about Mom, even in front of his new wife. When Dad remarried, he didn't seem as bad as he had been. He was this way through the last twenty years of his life. But he continued to drink, and it was still always about the war, and always about something bad he had done and couldn't forget, and he was always in misery.

Did he need to sense forgiveness? Probably. That, and he simply needed to talk. He needed to make the decision to seek help. He needed to reconnect with his friends, but he wouldn't, and we couldn't make it happen for him. Mom was a Methodist, and we went to church when we were young, but Dad never went. He believed in God, I know he did, but he didn't participate in anything like that. He didn't participate in much of anything.

His friends from the 101st had reunions, starting right after the war. Dad never went. He got mail all the time asking him to come, and he'd tell us he had heard from Winters or from Guarnere. But he never went into much detail about the letters, and if you asked him, he wanted to know why you wanted to know. "*Well, why do you care? What do you want to know for?*" That was his attitude.

In 2003, Dad was pretty sick by then, he told me about a reunion coming up. They all wanted him to come. He gave me the date and times.

"Dad, why don't we all go to this," I said. "I would love to meet these guys. I've heard about them all my life."

"Nah, I'm not going," he said.

"Why?" I asked. "It'll be a good thing."

"Well, maybe I'll think about it," he said.

I called and got in touch with the guy putting it on that year, Ed Shames, and he knew right off who Robert Marsh was and helped set up everything for us.

But when it came down to it, Dad refused to go. We went ahead and went without him, me and my husband and kids. For the first time at that reunion, I got to meet some of these guys I had heard so much about all my life. We talked a little bit about my dad. They didn't say a whole lot. I met Bill Guarnere. He's just a fantastic guy. We've kept in touch on and off since then. It made me cry to think he literally begged Dad to come to these reunions for so many years. I really think it would have helped my dad to have done that: to connect with the people who had gone through the same things he had gone through, to talk to them and deal with the war, rather than it being his own private thing his whole life.

I know that going to the reunion helped me, just being able to talk to the guys and see them up close. It helped just for what I lived through. And I didn't go through the war, obviously. But it helped me understand the war more.

I read Bill Guarnere's and Babe Heffron's book. I'm not much of a reader, but reading it really helped me, too. I needed to shut it every once in a while because of tears, just visualizing what the men—what my dad—went through.

Last Years with Dad

Dad wouldn't talk about any of his health issues with us. As he grew older, I went with him to the doctor whenever he let me. One of the first times, the doctor had my father take his shoes and socks off and pull up his pant legs to his knees. My father's feet and legs were black. I looked in shock.

"You've never seen this before?" the doctor said to me.

"No." I didn't know what to say, other than "What happened?"

The doctor looked at my dad and said, "Oh, so you hide yourself well."

Dad let his pant legs go back down. "It's from the war," was all he said.

Dad hated snow. He hated Christmastime. Those were some of the worst times over there, I guess. He had gotten frostbite on his legs and feet during Bastogne. The doctor told me that dad was still lucky that he had his feet.

After Dad retired, the government couldn't find his records and told him he had never been in the war. "*Never been in the war!*" You talk about someone who was mad then. Still, he didn't want us to know what he was feeling. "*Humph, I don't care,*" was his only response.

He didn't have any amount of money or insurance, so he started going back and forth to the VA. He had no other choice. They kept telling him there were no records, but finally they relented and started to give him medicine.

The government got things straightened out. I don't know what level of disability Dad finally received, but it was the least amount possible. That made him even madder. They started sending him checks, amounts such as $1.60 a month. It was an insult, Dad said. He wasn't cashing them, and he wasn't returning them because "it wasn't worth the trouble." We kept a photocopy of the highest disability check he ever received. It came in 1997, for fourteen dollars.

Dad found out he had an aneurism in his stomach and needed surgery. He didn't want to have it done. We all had to coax him. He ended up in Dayton at the VA hospital. They did the surgery, and that's when they found the cancer. Three days after the surgery, he got on a bus by himself and rode back to Columbus. He wouldn't stay at the VA hospital. He didn't want anything from them, he said. He chose not to do anything about the cancer.

My mom passed away in 2004. I spent a lot of time with her before she died. I loved her a lot and miss her a great deal.

In July 2005, things started getting really bad for Dad with the cancer, and he grew very frail. He soon became too sick to say or do much about anything. Hospice people came; they took him to Grant Hospital, here in Columbus, and got him settled. There was a mix-up between nurses and other family members about whether to give him medication or not, and when I arrived, my dad was in so much pain, I could hear him from down the hall. He was screaming, "Let me die, let me die, let me die."

He had signed me the power of attorney over his health. We got him some pain medication. I just wanted him to die in peace. Dad started relaxing. In a while he was calm. After several more hours his breathing was different. You could tell he was ready to go.

He passed away later that day, July 30, 2005. I was with him in the hospital room, sitting near him at the bottom of the bed. My sister was sitting beside him holding his hand. I watched him take his last breath. The first thing that came to mind was "My dad's no longer fighting a war."

Letting Go

I deeply miss my dad now that he is gone, but what I really miss is the man my dad could have been if not for the war. I'm just comforted with the fact that he is finally at peace, no longer fighting a war. I don't think my dad ever lived the kind of life he wanted to live. I think he gave his life for his country while he was still overseas, and when he came home, it wasn't really him. He fought the war from age eighteen to eighty-one, and he never let that war go.

He had always talked about being buried in Dayton National Cemetery for veterans. We got him a beautiful casket. It was for a soldier and had parachutes and flags on it. They held a military funeral for him with a twenty-one-gun salute and military honors. He had what he wanted. Those honors are what he deserved and needed to have. Getting my dad into Dayton National Cemetery brought a measure of peace for me. I felt like it ended the way Dad wanted it to end.

I do know he had a good side. He didn't want anybody to know about it, but he cared about all of us in his own way. When I think through his life, I see now that he was so young, yet he had to grow up so fast. At age fourteen he was working to help support his mom and dad. At seventeen, he was a soldier fighting to defend his country. At twenty-one, he was taking care of a wife and child as well as his parents. How I wish things could have been different. I can't imagine what he went through. We all handle things differently, and sometimes we don't understand how our actions affect other people. Maybe my dad didn't understand, either.

I think too much of that good man was left overseas. The big theme of my dad's life was that he should have sought help. Things could have been different. I believe that. Things can be different—I think anyone coming home from war needs to hear that.

12

ROBERT RADER

Interviews with Donald Rader, son,
Robin Rader, daughter, and Lucille Rader, widow

Robert Rader was mentioned in the original book but not portrayed in the miniseries. Nonetheless, he was an integral part of Easy Company. His family has always been proud of him and enjoys telling his story. Robert was one of the few vets who talked openly about the war to his family, though not in great detail. He stood tall his whole life, and his family thanks him for being a positive example. This is his story.

Seventy-Nine Cents a Day

Robert Rader was born October 9, 1923, in Manchester, a small town on the Ohio River. His mother had family who fought in the Revolutionary War, and they were given land along the river as payment. His father was in the All-American Division in WWI, fought in five major battles in Europe, and was wounded and gassed. After the war, he worked as a stone-cutter for cemetery markers, and times were very hard financially. They lived along a road and if someone's rooster got hit by a car, they were out there quick to retrieve it for the dinner pot. Robert's father was in poor health after the war and passed away in 1942, just before his son went into the service. He gave him the simple, sound advice, "Just do your job and come home."

Robert grew up during the Depression. He was one of six children. Still in school, he, along with his older brothers, enlisted in the Ohio National Guard, basically so they could get food and the rest of the food in the family could go to the youngsters. Robert was sixteen when he enlisted with the Guard. They made seventy-nine cents a day.

Pearl Harbor happened in 1941 while Robert was in the National Guard. Right after that, the Guard discovered he was underage and kicked him out. Fortunately, they gave him an honorable discharge. The certificate meant he didn't have to go into the war. He went back to high school and graduated in 1942, the first in his family.

Parachutes and Lardy Cakes

Robert and two hometown friends, Don Hoobler and William Howell, volunteered for the 101st. It was Hoobler's idea to join the paratroopers. The idea of the extra money appealed to the men. They also wanted to be the best.

Robert had grown up with Don Hoobler. They played baseball, swam in the Ohio River together, and stole watermelons from the other side to bring back. Robert always enjoyed sports. He was a skinny kid, six feet, two inches tall, and actually gained weight during the war. In high school he played football, basketball and baseball. His school was so small that if you didn't play football, you weren't allowed to play any other sports.

After the friends enlisted, they were sent to Camp Toccoa. Robert was with the 101st from beginning to end. Bill Guarnere gave him the nickname "Rook," but Robert wasn't a chess player. His family speculates it was loosely the Italian version of his last name.

The family has a picture of Robert, Hoobler, and Howell at Toccoa. They were country boys and called themselves the "three hillbillies." Others thought they talked funny with their Appalachian twangs. They palled around with a guy from Colorado named Bill Dukeman. Howell was blown out of a foxhole in Bastogne, wounded, but lived and made it home. Hoobler accidently shot himself in the leg with a souvenir Luger. The bullet hit a main artery and he bled to death. Robert talked about Hoobler's death every once in a while after the war. It shook him up quite badly. Robert's son, Donald, is named in honor of Don Hoobler, and his son's middle name is Dukeman, in honor of Bill Dukeman, who also died in the war. "It's always been an honor to me to share these men's names," Donald said, "I've never taken it for granted, what they gave for our country."

The men trained a lot. Robert told his family about the big spaghetti lunch they had at Toccoa, and how the men puked it up later because Captain Sobel made them run up Mt. Currahee right afterward. Robert also told his family that despite his dislike for the man, he respected Sobel too, because Captain Sobel helped make the men tough so they could survive the war.

Robert enjoyed parachute training, particularly jumping out of the high training tower. He liked it so much he did it more times than was required. He rose to the rank of staff sergeant and became the push master, the last person out of the plane. During one training jump, his chute didn't deploy properly. He was the last to jump, but the first to hit the ground. He got in trouble because whoever was in charge didn't believe he had problems with this chute.

On another practice jump, he was hit in the head by an ammunition holder, a large metal box. The piece of equipment had broken loose and was falling while the men were jumping, which wasn't uncommon. Robert suffered a detached retina, but was otherwise okay.

The men were transported across the Atlantic for more training in Aldbourne, England. Sometimes during a practice jump, men landed some distance from the rest of the unit, and needed to hike back to their unit on their own. When that happened, the men sometimes took advantage of the extra time and scrounged for lardy cakes along the way, a type of English donut made out of fried flour, butter, cinnamon and sugar. They dropped in at the local towns, picked up the cakes, and ate them in the woods on the way back.

Robert talked about free time in Aldbourne. Sometimes the men played basketball and baseball. They met a lot of townspeople this way. Years after the war, Robert visited Aldbourne and still knew a lot of people there. On their last practice jump, the majority of the people of Aldbourne came out to wish them good-bye.

Battered and Frozen

On the plane ride over to Normandy, a shell blasted through their plane's body and flew directly between Robert and Johnny Martin, so close they could feel the burn. They talked about it for years after. Later, they found out the plane they were in took 250 hits while they were flying to Normandy.

Robert made the jump from an elevation of under two hundred feet. The green light that indicated when they were to get out of the plane had been shot off. So they used a bell to tell the men when to jump. The co-pilot was wounded. He took shrapnel in the leg, and there was a miscommunication with the pilot, who thought all the men were already out of the plane. The pilot turned the plane around and started heading back to England with them all inside. That's when they all bailed out.

Robert wore a leg bag during the jump that flew off as soon as he was outside the plane. He lost his weapons in the jump, hit the ground hard, and hurt his back. He landed in a cow pasture next to a sharp pole. Later he was found to have three fractured vertebrae. Nothing was ever done for it and he continued on. The first person he ran into after landing was Burr Smith, who gave him a cricket, a .45, and a sack of grenades.

Robert had landed near Ste. Mère-Église. He and some men fought a minor firefight, not against the Germans themselves, but against some white Russians and Polish troops who were fighting on Germany's side because they hated Stalin more than the Nazis.

When the assault against Brécourt Manor happened, Robert and others were deployed between the 88s at the manor and the beach to help offer protection for the assault at the manor, making sure that no Germans stationed near the beach ran back to help during the fray.

Near Carentan, Robert's squad came across a bivouacked group of Hitler Youth, who engaged in a firefight with the men. Robert told his family the youths yelled in German, "I will die for the Führer." The men had no choice but to take them out, which really shook Robert up. After the firefight, he saw the bodies, both of the German troops and also the Americans that had been killed. Robert vowed at that moment to spend the rest of his life devoted to helping kids. Later he made good on that vow and became a schoolteacher. After a month of fighting in Normandy, the men went back to Aldbourne.

The next big jump was Market-Garden in Holland. They jumped in daylight Sunday, September 17, 1944, and were in constant contact with the enemy for seventy-nine days. At one point the men were hunkered down in a barn. A man was cleaning his .45. It discharged and hit Robert in his elbow. He went to the aid station, but they were unable to ship him out due to the enemy's presence. So they bandaged it up and he went back to the line. Shortly after, he was in a bayonet charge.

After Holland, the men went to Mourmelon. Somebody made up a vat of hot chocolate, but something was wrong with it, so whoever drank it got diarrhea. On the way up to Bastogne in the back of a truck, Robert said he was feeling very sick, still from the chocolate.

In Bastogne, the men were surrounded and underequipped, with a lack of winter clothing and ammunition. Robert's eyelids actually froze open once. His feet, legs, and hands grew so cold he could hardly feel any of his extremities. He took a bullet in the hip, but was so cold he didn't realize it until a CAT scan in 1987 showed he had been hit.

Robert and Hoobler volunteered for guard duty on Christmas Eve as a Christmas present to the rest of the guys. Hoobler was a corporal, and they usually didn't let two noncoms pull guard duty together because they were too far away from the line. Robert told his family that the night was very cold. The men lay in the snow in the dark and whispered about Christmas dinner back home and what their families were doing.

Near the fighting at Foy, Robert instructed his squad to dig their fox-holes out in a field, not near the trees. A couple of men in his squad thought he was crazy. They were going to get killed out in the open like that. But when the shells came in, they flew right over and straight into the trees. So his squad wasn't hurt.

From there, the men went to Hitler's Nest, and then to Austria by war's end. Robert was discharged in November 1945, and offered a Purple Heart, but he turned it down. "How could I receive it when so many others were wounded so badly?" he told his family. Robert had numerous scars, the elbow wound, various shrapnel wounds, the bullet in his hip, and various nicks and cuts from ordnances that went off near him. He was awarded other medals, including two Bronze Stars for bravery.

Strict but Fair

As mentioned, Robert was one of the few who gained weight during the war. When he came home it was at night, and, not wanting to wake his family, he slipped into the home unannounced and hit the sheets up in his room. The next morning, his mother didn't recognize him. A lot of soldiers were coming and going in those days, and she had been boarding many of them. When she learned it was her son, it was a grand celebration.

All during the war, Robert had saved his money and sent it home to his mother for the family to use. But she hadn't spent a dime of it, so when he returned home all his money was waiting for him.

He opted to use the GI Bill and matriculated at Morehead State College on a sports scholarship, but his legs were shot, still numb from Bastogne days. So he transferred to Cedarville College in Ohio and received his bachelor's in education. He played some baseball and basketball for Cedarville.

Cedarville is a Baptist school, but Robert wasn't religious at all. A group of his buddies went there, which is the only reason he went. By rule, the school was "dry," but Robert helped to rig up a pulley system to lift kegs of beer up to his third floor dorm room. During winter he put his beer on the room's window ledge to keep it cold. He and his buddies ate a lot of pickled eggs, and Robert regaled his family with stories of going to chapel and expelling the smelly results of beer and eggs. Evidently the college put up with his high jinks, for Robert graduated.

He became a teacher and later a coach. Following the lead of friends, he moved from Ohio to California around 1950 where he met Lucille, a California girl and nurse. She and Robert met on a blind date and were married on Valentine's Day, 1953. Friends helped Robert land a job at the California School for Boys, which led to a teaching job in San Miguel, then another job in the Paso Robles School District, where Robert taught for the last twenty-five years until he retired.

Two children were born to the family, a boy and a girl, Donald and Robin. For fun, the family took trips to Yellowstone, Mt. Rushmore, Canada, and Easy Company reunions. They were a frugal family, and every day when they were travelling they stopped at little roadside shops and bought Vienna sausages, Ritz crackers, and red delicious apples, Robert's favorite lunch.

They often visited Easy Company men. Bull Randleman's family was part of regular life. Mike Ranney came down from San Francisco to visit several times. Salve Matheson kept in touch. George Luz Sr. and Robert wrote letters back and forth. Bill Guarnere came to visit. Leo Matz, who vowed that if he made it out of the war alive would become a priest, was in Robert's squad and remained a good friend after the war. After he became a priest, he visited Robert several times, including right after Robert's second heart surgery.

In 1965, when Donald was seven years old, the family attended an Easy Company reunion at Fort Campbell. Young Donald got the chance to shoot an M-60, a machine gun so large he had to lay on the ground to shoot it. Robin was five years older, but, despite her pleas, wasn't allowed to shoot the gun.

Robert coached freshman and JV basketball, and was very proud of the cross country teams he coached. During the ten years he coached cross country, seven of his teams went to the California Interscholastic Federation Finals. He had two All-Americans run for him, brothers Eric and Ivan Huff. He was very proud of them.

People described Robert as a strict but fair teacher. He didn't stand for any nonsense. He developed a strong reputation among other teachers, and soon all the rowdy kids—the ones the other teachers couldn't control—were sent to him. He was known to get a kid's attention by throwing the eraser against a chalkboard. Some of his classroom management techniques would never fly these days. In one instance he actually picked up a rowdy boy and threw him out the door. To this day, his former students say a firm hand was exactly what they needed. When Robert started teaching educationally handicapped students, he softened considerably, and didn't do any eraser throwing then.

In the early days of his teaching career, he actually worked two jobs. He taught school during the week. On weekends he was the assistant manager at the Paso Robles Airport. He fueled planes when they came in and kept an eye on things. He didn't earn Social Security with the school district in those days, but he did with the airport job, and he wanted that for his family.

Robert was also on the town's volunteer fire department for about a decade. One night in 1963 a large hotel caught fire in town. Robert fought the fire all night, came home in the morning, took a shower, ate breakfast, and went to work at school for the day.

Lucille worked as a nurse, then when the kids came along she stayed home, (which is when Robert worked two jobs). When the kids grew older, Lucille went back to work. Robert picked up more coaching then, which he considered a second job. For a hobby, he occasionally played softball in town or went fishing, but mostly he worked and coached.

Robert seemed to adjust well to life after the war. Why? "His family helped keep him grounded, for sure," Donald said. "I think the contact with his buddies was also very helpful—writing letters, going to reunions. He enjoyed quality activities where he could disconnect from the stress of life and his memories and get refreshed."

Robin remembered him struggling with memories of the war. "During Christmas he could get strangely quiet for days at a time," Robin said. "I asked him about it and finally he told me that Christmastime always brought back memories of Don Hoobler's death. In spite of the memories, he chose to continue on. The war did affect him, yes, but he was always conscious to not withdraw from his responsibilities."

Honorable to the End

Robert retired in 1981. Despite his robust career, he suffered from poor health through most of his life, mostly due to the war. Over the years he had two heart surgeries with nine bypasses. He lost a kidney, and had an aortic aneurism and gallbladder problems. He had stomach ulcers, and doctors eventually cut away half his stomach. But Robert remained determined. Once, immediately after a surgery, he went golfing and hit a hole in one on the first hole.

When he retired, he enjoyed playing golf with his wife. They also walked a lot together, and travelled to Paris and Holland. He liked to fish. He wrote a lot of letters to his fellow Easy Company men, and he enjoyed keeping in touch with them. He always signed his letters to his war buddies: *"Robert J. Rader, here. Be good. Be careful. Sleep warm."* He loved watching sports on TV and even bought two TVs for the living room so he could watch two sporting events at the same time.

Toward the end, when he couldn't physically keep up with things, life became more daunting. Robert needed to be on dialysis, and when that happened he moved from sitting in his recliner to lying on the couch. It was a different lifestyle toward the end. But even then, he didn't retreat. He kept up with his letter writing and calling his friends, keeping his focus on staying in touch with people and staying as active as he could.

Robert was on dialysis one day a week for nearly two years. His one kidney was still working, but his heart was failing. Lucille and Robert could still travel then, as long as Robert watched his diet. Then his other kidney failed, and the dialysis was upped to three times a week. That was the beginning of the end. Robert started to lose weight and grew very thin, 123 pounds on his six-foot-two-inch frame. The last six months he had no body fat and was extremely frail. The heater in the house ran all the time. He kept watching sports and writing letters whenever he could. He had some better days than others. Somewhere during that time there was a frank discussion with family members, and Robert decided he didn't want anything to be prolonged. "No more," he said simply.

In the final weeks, Robert had no appetite at all. Lucille came up with innovative milkshakes, just trying to get some nutrition in him. Whatever he wanted to eat, if it sounded good to him, they let him eat it, even if the food had forbidden salt in it.

The last week, Lucille called the children, now grown, and said, "Your father didn't get out of his pajamas today." This was very unlike Robert, who always got dressed and got ready for each day. Within a few days he became septic and his blood pressure went down. The family admitted him to the hospital for comfort care.

On his final day, Lucille went home from the hospital early because she was so tired. Donald drove her home, so it was just daughter and father in the hospital room. Robin turned on a John Wayne movie, *Rio Bravo*, and Robert and she talked about movie trivia. He was concerned about his wife. "Is she okay?" he asked. It was very quiet. He remained alert and oriented until the very end. Then he closed his eyes and just went to sleep.

"The death was a relief in many senses," Lucille said. "You hated to see him in the condition he was in at the end. He had fought the fight."

Robert passed away on April 7, 1997. He's buried in a cemetery close to the family on the top of a hill under shade trees with good drainage and a good view. His VA marker reads, "Beloved husband and father." Every Memorial Day and Veteran's Day a ceremony is held at the cemetery with flags and speeches. His flag is flown along the cemetery's driveway.

A couple years ago, after Robert passed away, the citizens of Paso Robles, spearheaded by Frank Mecham, a former student of Dad's and then mayor, had a bridge redone and renamed the *Robert J. Rader Memorial Bridge*. The family still chokes up about that. A dedication ceremony was held in his honor. "It was such a great honor," Donald said. "It was a great weekend. I know Dad would have loved it. He would have had a blast."

At the bridge dedication, there were former colleagues from the fire department in attendance, former students, civic dignitaries, and lots of friends and family. Nine of the E Company men came down: Buck Compton, Shifty Powers, Bill Maynard, Rod Bain, Ed Joint, Bill Wingett, Don Malarkey, Jack McGrath, and Earl McClung. Local merchants donated hotel rooms for the veterans, and they were treated royally.

How would the family want Robert Rader to be remembered?

Donald puts it simply: "We all loved my dad and miss him very much. He was an honorable man to the end."

13

MIKE RANNEY

Interview with Drew Ranney Coble, daughter

My father, Mike Ranney, first penned the words that led to the title of this book. He was a prolific letter writer and often wrote to his former company commander, Dick Winters, who saved everything he received. After Dad died in 1988 at age sixty-six from a heart attack, Dick sent us a bound folder of all the letters Dad had ever sent him. Dad wrote about visiting Easy Company men, including Burr Smith, just before Burr passed away in January 1983. That's the letter where Dad wrote the now famous quote about not being a hero personally, but serving in a company of heroes.

Dad had a degree in journalism and was a strong writer. He wrote poems, stories, jokes, and even his own obituary before he passed. You'll find portions of Dad's letters elsewhere in this book, for instance in the essay about Salty Harris, a good friend of his. Dad also penned the Easy Company newsletter for years. He described the newsletters as "very sporadic, cranked out to keep the old flames of comradeship and friendship burning." Then, five years before Dad died, he wrote a lengthy memoir called, *The First 61 Years: The Recollections of Myron N. (Mike) Ranney*. It was never published other than him photocopying it and distributing it to family members, but it contains much information about his life and years spent with Easy Company, whose members he greatly loved and admired. In another letter to Dick Winters in 1980, Dad wrote, "I really have two families—my own, linked by blood, and Easy Company, tied together by a great and uncommon experience."

What follows is the story of my father's life as I remember him, and, mostly, as revealed through his own writings.

A Daily Adventure

Myron "Mike" Ranney was born at home in a blizzard in 1922 in a little town called Kensal, North Dakota, the only child of Lucy and Russell Ranney. The snowstorm made it impossible to travel to the nearest hospital, which was in another town. His dad was an itinerant newspaper editor and printer who moved around to various towns seeking work to feed his family during the 1920s and the Depression. His mom was a schoolteacher and summer waitress in the local hotel's restaurant. You get a sense of Dad's surroundings from his description:

> Sere and bleak, generally flat with a few small rolling hills along the water-courses that drained the land somewhat imperfectly. The weather was atrocious: hot in the summer and incredibly cold in the winter. Minus 40 degrees F was not unknown. Trees were scarce—scraggly cottonwoods along the streams and in the coulees and planted groves . . . to blunt the knifing winds of winter.

In his earliest days, Dad lived in town but spent every moment he could at his grandparents' farm. "There was an abundance of love for me there," he wrote. "Grandpa was a stern old bastard to his children, but pretty much a softy as far as his grandchildren were concerned. Grandma was an absolute jewel of a woman—tall, regal, happy."

His Uncle Herbert's place up the road was appealing at first, but Uncle Herbert pulled a trick on him which scarred the young boy and for which Dad never forgave him. Dad asked what was in a gallon jug filled with amber liquid. It stood on stairs leading to the basement.

"Vinegar," Uncle Herbert answered. "Want a taste?"

"Sure," Dad said. He couldn't remember ever tasting it before.

Uncle Herbert burst into laughter when Dad made a face and spit the liquid on the floor. "It wasn't vinegar," Uncle Herbert said. "It was piss."

Dad was appalled and humiliated and "felt little remorse or sadness when [Uncle Herbert] died unexpectedly a few years later of a ruptured appendix."

As a boy, Dad was gregarious and well liked, good in school, and a quick reader. He described school as "a daily adventure." He looked up to his father, and they enjoyed a close relationship, although his home life wasn't stable.

The family was poor. Not *poor* poor, but they certainly did not have much money in the family, or in the community. The Great Depression hit everyone hard. Dad described how the crops failed several years in a row, chickens died in the intense summer heat, and "great swirling clouds of grasshoppers ate everything in sight, even clothes hanging on the line." The bank foreclosed on his grandparents' farm. One summer his parents took him to a cousin's house, said they were going away for the weekend, and left him for half a year while his father tried a new business venture. There's a letter from the boy asking his mother to send him his baseball glove.

Dad went through junior high school in Jamestown. The family settled there for several years, then moved out west to Roseburg, Oregon, where his father had a new job in advertising. Dad started high school and became an athlete, proud and capable, playing football. He delivered newspapers every morning at five a.m. and made friends with one of the country's most distinguished gunsmiths, who taught him how to shoot. The family ran out of money again and moved back to the Dakotas where they boarded with relatives. In high school and summers, Dad participated in the Citizens' Military Training Corps, a predecessor program of ROTC. You didn't get paid other than five cents per mile travel allowance to get to and from the camp. He hitched rides, got reimbursed for mileage, and pocketed the difference. Dad made twenty-five dollars over the summer, a huge amount then. He tried boxing as a sport and became the camp's lightweight champion by a knockout.

Dad attended the University of North Dakota for one semester as a mining engineering major, then dropped out when his father became sick. He was needed at home to help run the family printing business. By the start of the next summer his father felt well enough to return to work, so Dad hitchhiked west and worked in a copper mine. He went back to university in the fall and continued scrambling along, doing odd jobs, playing football, and living in the football house for free, just trying to keep himself together financially.

Pearl Harbor was attacked and the world turned upside down. Dad wanted to join the Air Force and become a pilot, but his eyes weren't good enough. His father objected to any enlistment, believing he would be deferred if he stayed in college. Dad caught a bus to Fargo where he enlisted anyway. He was sent to Fort Snelling for processing while waiting to be assigned elsewhere. He met a recruiter who told him the paratroopers were the best damn outfit in the Army, plus you made an extra fifty bucks. "I was offered the two most powerful appeals: glory and greed," Dad wrote. "I signed on the dotted line right then and there."

In the Company

Four days after enlisting, Dad rode a train to Toccoa, Georgia, to the then-named Camp Toombs (later renamed Camp Toccoa), where the 506th Parachute Infantry Regiment was being formed. He described the town and the camp:

> Our train pulled into a little town stuck in the foothills of the Blue Ridge Mountains. Somewhat prophetically, I thought, there was a coffin factory alongside the tracks near the depot, and I was reminded that duties of a paratrooper involved jumping out of airplanes into battle. A truck waited for us and we piled in and headed for the camp five miles out of town.
>
> The camp was a collection of tarpaper shacks huddled along a hillside. It

had served as a summer camp for Georgia National Guard units. Looming over it was a mountain called Currahee. That blooming mountain was to play a central role in our training. All eight of us [on the truck] were dispatched to W company, the holding unit for recruits pending assignment to an individual company.

Dad was soon assigned to Company E led by "Captain Herbert M. Sobel: big-nosed, swarthy, tall, lanky, and called simply, The Black Swan." Dad was assigned his gear and quickly made a sergeant and squad leader because of his previous military training.

With Easy Company filled to its roster strength of about 145 officers and enlisted men, our full-scaled training began—nightmarish runs, journeys through the obstacle course, and the military training, endless long marches and night problems. Each day was a physical survival test beginning with the Currahee run to the top and back, round trip, 7 miles. Time en route, under one hour. Twice during the 13 weeks I twisted my ankle in the ruts on the road and spent about 10 days in an army hospital outside Toccoa.

We ran everywhere with and without full field packs and various personal and squad weapons. We ran as individuals and as units of various size. Mixed in with the physical training was regular basic training—weapons, close-order drill, squad, platoon, and company field problems, marksmanship, and shooting at the rifle range.

Throughout the basic training we interjected early parachute training, learning how to jump and land from modest heights without getting hurt, flinging ourselves out of airplane fuselages 30 feet in the air. It was a masterful training program to overcome the basic fear of jumping into space. The system worked.

Just before Thanksgiving 1942, the men marched from Toccoa to Atlanta, about 118 miles. It took three days.

We headed away from Camp Toccoa in a light rain. Our route took us over unpaved back roads of red Georgia clay, and we slipped and swore up and down the hills. As the blisters formed and we weakened, we shared packs and weapons. Late [the first] night we pulled into our camping spot, put up our pup tents, ate, then crawled into our tents and collapsed. We'd covered 40 miles and it was still raining.

That night it froze. I'll never forget the morning agony of trying to cram my swollen feet into those frozen GI shoes. Somehow I did, along with 600 other guys, and that day we covered another 40 miles, now with much attention on us. We had a good public information officer, Lt. Jim Morton, who had worked on one of the Atlanta papers. He was getting us national publicity for our march. The Japanese marched tremendous distances at record speeds, and now an American army unit was demonstrating that it could travel farther and faster than the Japanese. It was just the stuff the nation needed.

The night of the third day we straggled into the outskirts of Atlanta to the campus of Oglethorpe University, beat, exhausted, and the darlings of the city. We weren't too tired that night to put on our dress uniforms for a city seeking to honor fighting men. That night we couldn't buy a drink, meal, or anything else in Atlanta. I went into a liquor store and a stranger offered to pay for whatever I wanted. I took two bottles of bourbon and gave him my thanks. It was a helluva night.

The next morning somehow we got most of the company formed up and headed down Peachtree Boulevard for a civic reception in the heart of the city. Dozens of bands were interspersed between our platoons, and the music, the welcome, and the whole event lifted our spirits. We were able to swing into downtown Atlanta in good order as we marched on to the rail depot for Fort Benning.

Jump Training

Fort Benning and parachute school proved easier for the men after the tough training they'd already received. They ran everywhere and did push-ups all the time, but they proved fitter than their new drill instructors.

Five jumps were required to graduate and get their wings. The men learned how to pack their own chutes and practiced jumping from two hundred–foot towers. The first real jump came soon. Jumping was always optional, but a refusal to jump meant six months in the stockade. Dad described his first and following jumps:

> I flung myself out the door, the chute opened with a snap, and a second later I was tumbling on the ground. Actually it was a little more like a minute before I floated down from 800 feet.
>
> The rest of the jumps passed quickly. There was always just a little anxiety, and usually we looked up quickly after the opening shock to see if any of the chute's 26 panels were blown and if the chute was filled properly.

Dad received his wings and a ten-day pass home. He returned to his parents' house in Fargo, "swaggering through all the parties and nightlife in that part of the state." Quickly, the leave ended and he returned to Benning, then was transferred to Camp McCall where more training occurred.

Dad became a first sergeant for the 3rd platoon, but found it too administrative and asked to be transferred to 1st Platoon as platoon sergeant. The company went on maneuvers in Tennessee during summer 1943, then was transferred to Fort Bragg, North Carolina, for more concentrated training.

In September 1943, the 506th was transferred to Camp Shanks, New York, then boarded the *Samaria* for the voyage across the Atlantic.

> The *Samaria* was a miserable ship, crammed with bunks jammed into the old cabins. We slept in shifts. The food was absolutely atrocious, so vile that Salty [Harris] and I made a deal with the cooks of the Royal Marine gun crew, who had a mess on the boat deck, to feed us. It was a tremendous improvement over going down three decks into a mess hall that always smelled of boiled mutton.
>
> The voyage itself was uneventful, dull, long. The highlight of it for me were the endless crap games in the corridors, and the fact that someone threw over the side the bags containing all the gear and personal items of our unloved first sergeant [Bill] Evans, who had replaced me in that post. I spent most of my time on deck, and perhaps that helped me avoid seasickness.

We arrived in Liverpool on a bright, sunny day in late September. As we sailed up the Mersey River to dock, all of us were craning our necks to see as much as we could of that land. As I peered around to see everything, a dive-bombing seagull scored a direct hit on my cheek. Welcome to England!

The men were sent to the little village Aldbourne, about 80 miles due west of London. Dad slept in a stable in Aldbourne that had its own stove, which he described as "singularly comfortable accommodations."

He celebrated his twenty-first birthday nearby at the home of the Blakes, "a warm-hearted, gregarious family" who had known his father during WWI. A public swimming pool was nearby, and a seventeen-year-old neighbor girl offered to take him swimming. Dad dove in, thinking he would show this young English lass what a fine swimmer he was. She splashed past him with "a tremendous burst of speed" and handily beat him to the far end. Only then did she explain that she was the United Kingdom's freestyle swimming champ.

The role Dad played in the mutiny against Captain Sobel has been widely discussed.[1] We have a letter he wrote home in November 1943 to his mother that reads simply:

Dear Mom,

Due to circumstances, etc. and to expedite communication between you and I, my address is now Company "I." And don't ask me why! This company will be all right although it is a helluva change from the old after 14 months. The new Joes are very friendly and I'll be all right. No more news of note, so I'll close.

Love and Kisses,
Your son
Myron

---

1. For more information, see the essay about Salty Harris in this book.

In his new company, Dad was going to be trained as a pathfinder, but immediately before the Normandy invasion he contacted Dick Winters and said he really wanted to be back with E Company. About June 1, 1944, five days before the Normandy jump, Dad's orders came through and he was transferred back to Easy Company.

Normandy Invasion

Easy Company gathered its gear and was transported by trucks to an air-base under tight security. The men were shown maps and models of their invasion area and drop zones on the Cotentin Peninsula in Western France. A key objective was to take the city of Carentan, a major transportation center and link between the Omaha and Utah beach landing areas. Easy Company was scheduled to land a few miles north and west of the city.

> The evening of June 5 found us out at the plane again, loaded down with individual and squad weapons, ammo, grenades, morphine syrettes for wounds, and Benzedrine to keep us awake for the first critical 72 hours. This night the signal was "go." Most of us were so heavily loaded we had to be pushed and pulled up into our planes. In addition to my personal gear, I carried six rounds of bazooka ammunition in a parachute bag strapped in front of me.
>
> The planes took off, formed up, and headed south and west. During the flight, I got a glimpse of the thousands of ships in the invasion fleet dotting the moonlit sea. We swung east and I watched the tracers thrown up by Germans who occupied the British-owned channel islands of Jersey and Guernsey. I saw the dark mass of France as we crossed the [peninsula] before jump time. A minute later we were ordered to stand up and hook up, attaching our parachute connectors to the cable along the roof of the plane.
>
> I was end man on the stick [18 men], waiting to jump while standing on an elevated wooden platform between two 50-gallon drums of aviation gas carried as reserve fuel. Our plane started getting hit. Sounded like someone pounded on a great brass plate at high speed.
>
> [P.F.C. Roy] Cobb, the fellow immediately in front of me was hit and fell

on the floor groaning. While I was seeing how badly Cobb was hurt, the green light came on and Lt. Harry Welsh led our stick out the door. The plane was lurching as the pilot took evasive action against the fire from the ground. Our orders were to jump unless severely wounded. I had to unsnap my connector to the cable, move it around in front of Cobb's and head for the door of the plane. I could see the green light swinging in front of me. The conduit holding the light fixtures had been torn loose from the wall of the plane. I pushed it aside and dove out the door.

My chute opened with a solid, jarring, slamming pound, and I looked around. I could see some buildings on fire, one plane going down in flames, and a few tracers, but none very close to me. I landed hard in an orchard with my chute draped over an apple tree. I was all alone.

Dad wrote only sporadically about his involvement in the fight in Normandy. He planned to write an extensive description of the fight someday, but died before he got it done. We know from other sources he was involved in the assault against Brécourt Manor. He wrote of various men and how they died, including his good friend Salty. In his memoir he described the combat in Carentan simply as "very heavy fighting."

The men's invasion duties ended in mid-July 1944. They were marched to Utah beach, where they boarded a naval landing ship for return to England. Dad described it as a "delight" to find showers, oranges, and milk on the ship.

One Shot

The men jumped into Holland on September 17, 1944, for Operation Market-Garden. It was part of a joint effort and they were technically under British command. Under the attack plan, three airborne divisions—the American 82nd and 101st, and one British unit—were to drop into Holland and seize and hold the seventy-mile corridor from central Holland across the Rhine, while a heavy British armored attack would race up the corridor, cross the river, and charge into Berlin for an early end to the war. In the course of the attack, the airborne units would capture and hold all essential cities and bridges along the road.

The plan backfired, and all divisions took heavy losses, particularly the British at Arnhem. In spite of the death all around him, strangely, he wrote:

> In Holland I somehow began to feel invulnerable, as though no German bullet or shell could ever touch me. I could move easily through heavy small arms fire and never get hit. I began to feel almost immortal. Winters came to rely on me to handle more and more responsibilities: setting up gun positions, coordinating attacks.

Two weeks into the Holland campaign Dad was recommended for a battlefield commission. But Dad never became an officer. After the fighting in Eindhoven settled down, the regiment was transferred north along the corridor. They were set to replace a Canadian division, but the move was stalled because they were engaged and couldn't break off the fighting. The opportunity was used to brief all NCOs on the position they were to occupy. About twenty of the men sat on the ground listening to an intelligence officer spell out the situation with the help of a large map. Pat Christenson was seated next to Dad in the bright October sunshine. As the officer talked, Dad cleaned his .45 caliber pistol.

> I field-stripped the gun and carefully cleaned the individual parts before reassembling it, something I could do almost blindfolded. When the reassembly was finished, it ended with the slide of the automatic in the rear position. Without thinking, or perhaps distracted by the lecture, I inserted the magazine of bullets and pushed the slide release, and the slide slammed forward. Now the gun was loaded and cocked. Since a cocked gun isn't normally carried that way, I pulled the trigger to let the hammer down.
>
> There was a tremendous POW. I'd forgotten it was loaded. I [shot myself] just below the knee in my left leg. Immediately a great sense of shame overwhelmed me. Somehow I had let down all my buddies and Winters.

Christenson slipped some morphine into me before the pain even began to develop. Thank God I hadn't shot someone else; there were other troopers sitting on both sides of me and directly in front.

A jeep arrived almost immediately and transported Dad to an aid station, and from there to a medical center in Brussels, Belgium, where he spent a few days. Although he had nearly blown his leg off, he described how he felt crushed in spirit more than anything. He had left behind his buddies, who were just about to face fierce fighting on the Island just south of Nijmegen. Dad's war was over that day in Holland, October 2, 1944.

From Brussels, I was flown to a military hospital in England where they began repairing my leg. The bullet had penetrated my calf and then hit and broken my shinbone, which deflected it down into my ankle. The bullet had done a fair job of ripping up my leg.

There were several operations to put the shinbone back in place and to take out the bullet fragments. The doctors were puzzled because the fragments they were getting out didn't weigh up close to the 500 grains. It wasn't until the third or fourth operation that they located the main body of the bullet, which had broken up and was now lodged in my ankle. They'd been taking X-rays higher up, close to where the bullet had entered my calf. The recuperation would take some time and a full recovery much longer. I was sent home to be discharged.

Dad left England on December 1, 1944, on the hospital ship *St. Olaf*, which arrived in Charleston, South Carolina, seventeen days later. He was in a cast and on crutches, but able to move around. He spent Christmas 1944 next to the radio, listening to the news accounts of his buddies' fight in Bastogne.

In the new year he was assigned to an Army hospital in Topeka, Kansas, then transferred to Camp Carson, Colorado, (it had been converted to an army hospital then to handle overflow patients from the war) in February to finish his recuperation. He got involved in war bond drives and writing news releases for GIs for hometown newspapers. He gave speeches at defense plants and civic luncheons throughout Colorado. Mostly, he wrote, "there wasn't much to do." He was officially discharged on April 24, 1945, when Easy Company was on occupation duties in Austria. Dad still felt conflicted.

> For the first time in more than two and a half years there was no one ordering me to do something.
>
> That night I caught the train [from Colorado] to Fargo. As I stepped off, there were Dad and Mom and Jiggs [his dog] and Betty [an old girlfriend]. My friends and buddies were still fighting, or wounded, or lying under white crosses in Army cemeteries, but I was home. It was a little frightening.

A Remarkable Time

After the war, Dad returned to the University of North Dakota, joined the Theta Chi fraternity, and worked part time at a restaurant and bar. He wasn't a super-strong student at the time.

> Drinking was our primary occupation. Most of us had money from savings, or working, plus the allowance the government provided through educational programs for veterans. I had about $6,000 in the bank when I was discharged. Settling down and going to school wasn't quite where it was, just then. Visits to the bars seemed to continue with unceasing regularity. Without realizing it, I was probably in pretty bad shape.

One bright point in his first year back is when he met our mom, Julia Hutchinson, who was vivacious, super-smart, and a journalism major. They soon started dating, and Dad switched from engineering to journalism. They got married in the summer of 1946, one of many thousands of postwar couples who did, then returned for their final year of college.

> That particular period was a rather remarkable time to be alive, with its sense of renewal. The war was over, the enemies defeated. We still hoped for

a harmonious relationship with the Communist world, since the Cold War hadn't begun. The work of rebuilding nations was just in the planning stage, and most people, at least in this country, seemed to be devoting their entire energies to making up for the time lost during WWII.

The University bulged with returning servicemen, some still [wearing] bits and pieces of their uniforms. Campuses frantically put together housing for married students who were eager to start their families while they began or resumed their educations.

There was an almost paranoid scramble back to normalcy, and a demand for the goods of normal times—cars, gasoline, cigarettes, silk stockings, sugar—all these things that had been rationed or impossible to find during wartime.

Five daughters were born into the Ranney household: Kathy, Christine, me, Laura, and Beth. I think Dad missed never having a son. He was a real man's man and took us girls camping military-style with knapsacks and no pillows or pajamas. "Just roughin' it," as he called it. He had a lot of whining to put up with.

Dad was a good father in many ways. He was very charismatic, a great storyteller, and could be tremendously fun. He never enjoyed structured times. He hated crowds and detested going to places like Disneyland. He loved being outdoors with his family, just going on picnics, or finding a watering hole somewhere we could all jump in. On Friday nights we often went to a nearby park where Dad barbecued. We took wax paper potato chip bags and slid down the playground slides, and Dad pushed us on the swings.

He was always a big smoker. Turning off the bedroom lights, he performed fabulous light shows with his cigarettes, blowing smoke rings as we lay back in bed. When I was about eight, he made up a whole series of stories about a three-legged horse named One Two Three Stump, who had a wooden leg for his fourth leg. Dad made up a sound effect, sort of a hand smack, which he made whenever he said, *"One Two Three Stump."* This horse got into all manner of predicaments: his wooden stump got stuck in a gopher hole and a gopher chewed on it; the bees made a hive in his stump. The story continued for many nights and held us in great suspense.

When I was nine or ten I remember working on his car with him, holding the lights in the evenings. I liked being one on one with Dad. He talked a little then about the service.

All the daughters (along with twelve grandchildren now) ended up spread across the United States. Kathleen taught at the University of Alabama and is retired now, Christine teaches at Cornell in upstate New York, I'm a high school physics teacher and live in northern California along with Laura, who works in the accounting field, and Beth, who is a fifth grade teacher.

Ups and Downs

The Ranneys moved a ton, mostly due to Dad's career and his constant ambition. He never seemed satisfied. There was always something better around the next corner. Dad worked his way up on newspapers in Redfield, South Dakota; Sioux City, Iowa; Minneapolis, Minnesota; then finally at the *Chicago Tribune* where he was a sports reporter, then moved out to California in 1959 to work for a public relations firm, which paid more. He worked most of the rest of his career in public relations, either for a firm or out on his own. Dad was always thinking about making his company bigger and better. He handled some large corporate clients in San Francisco. For the last years of his career, he went back to journalism and worked with several smaller papers in California.

In many ways he led a challenging adult life. His father passed away in 1947 of a stroke, about a year after Dad and Mom got married, and was sorely missed. Then, when Dad worked as a newspaperman, journalists in those days had the reputation of being "hard-nosed, two-fisted drinkers, which I had to maintain," he wrote. He was ambitious and talented, and at one time was the youngest newspaper publisher in the state of South Dakota. He often worked nights at the various newspapers, not exactly prime family-man hours.

There were huge financial swings in the family. When I was growing up we were fairly well off. We had a nice house with two horses and an airplane. I remember playing with Susan Finn, Burr Smith's daughter, when we were kids. We attended an Easy Company reunion in Las Vegas. My dad had his plane then. For some reason none of my other sisters wanted to go, so Dad flew my mom and me out to the reunion where we stayed at the Stardust Hotel and Casino. Dad was a big spender in those days and set up the hospitality suite for the men. I had charging privileges and enjoyed all the Shirley Temples and lemonades I wanted. Susan and I had a great time running around the pool.

By the time Mom and Dad got divorced in 1971, all the money was gone. I was in high school then, and he and Mom had been married for twenty-four years. Dad didn't pay child support, and creditors and tax agents began to call Mom. She had been Phi Beta Kappa in university and could have done anything, but when they divorced she had no outside career to fall back on. After the divorce, Mom got a job as a teacher's aide, went to San Francisco State University at night to get her teacher's credentials, and also worked at Montgomery Ward at night. Having them both gone was very hard for the family. I think my two younger sisters took more of the brunt of it. I was not happy with my dad during that time.

Four years after their divorce, Mom and Dad remarried and moved to Minnesota because Dad had a new job offer. Things didn't work out as planned: the job never materialized, Dad got another job where he wasn't as happy, and Mom got a job at an optician's business in town. She moved my two younger sisters out there, and they were in a fairly stable high school experience for a time.

Two years later, Mom and Dad divorced again. They never could quite hang together. Dad did a quick deed sale on the house and moved back to California. Mom moved back a year later. Mom never regretted either of her marriages to him. She said she'd do it all again, and never said a bad word about him.

Dad never liked authority much. He was sure of himself and liked to be his own boss. When you're doing public relations, you bring ideas to your client. If the client likes it, fine, but if not, then you redo your presentation. Often Dad disagreed with clients, and he lost several this way.

Some of his financial challenges also stemmed from continuing health issues. In his mid-fifties he was diagnosed with diabetes, and the disease was already quite far along. He had suffered one downturn in finances by then, and then ended up at the VA hospital when he was diagnosed with blood clots, which really affected his ability to work. His business collapsed. He endured complications from his leg injury his whole life.

Dad never really had an upturn after being diagnosed with diabetes. He struggled along for the next fifteen years, not quite being able to provide for himself or his family, yet surprisingly optimistic. It was always about how he could swing the next deal. Sometimes the deals would last a while, and sometimes not.

Bright and Full of Promise

I think Dad grew sweeter in his old age. Though I wasn't happy with him for a few years, I made peace with him toward the end. He had five grandsons in a row and was quite pleased about that. In his later years, he had a very dear friend, Elaine. They took a wonderful trip to Africa several years before he died.

My dad had many flaws that showed up right about the time I didn't want them to, in my early teens when I was trying to figure out who I was. Those flaws seemed big at the time, but I'm a little wiser now and his flaws don't seem that big at all. I look at the positive side of his life. He was a truly caring man, although caring might not be the exact word. When I look at all his writings, how he spoke about the men of Easy Company, I can see that he truly cared for others.

In his later years he had several silent heart attacks, which can go on unnoticed for some time and cause a lot of damage. He was in and out of hospitals, but always kept a certain undeniable *joie de vivre*. He joked that the nurses didn't know his true age. He had an octuple bypass in April 1988 and recovered from the surgery, but never fully. Too much damage had been done. He passed away in September 1988, far too young.

I have chosen a very safe life on purpose, so I don't have many risks. I've been a high school teacher at the same school for thirty-two years.

But Dad was much more a risk-taker. I give much credit to him for that. He really put himself out there. That was his philosophy in life: drive hard and never settle for mediocrity. If you're going to be in the military, or a journalist, or a media representative, or a high school teacher—whatever you're going to do—be the absolute best at it.

The philosophy helped him stay positive and resilient through many rocky years. I think of a quote from another letter Dad wrote to Dick Winters, this one written a few years before Dad died. Dad's words sum up his life and personality well. He had experienced a number of financial, health, and relational setbacks by then, but still found the courage to write:

At the ripe age of 61, I find myself blessed with good friends, warm memories, more serenity than I've ever known, and hundreds of ambitious dreams for the future.

This past year has been a fine one for me. During the holidays I will be with all my children, and the prospects for the year ahead are bright and full of promise. What more could a man ask? Or what more might a person wish for friends, such as you?

Good luck, and sleep warm.

Myron N. (Mike) Ranney

14

LAVON REESE

Interview with Marcia Reese Rood, daughter
With additional information from Joe Watson, family friend

Daddy's been gone since 1975. He talked a lot about the war when I was growing up, but I didn't pay attention very closely to his stories. He talked only when he had been drinking, and mostly I was trying to avoid him then.

I'm not saying this quite right. Today, I understand so much more of what Daddy went through in the war. I just wish I understood it back then. I would have listened much more closely if I did.

He Didn't Have Anything

My father, LaVon P. Reese, was born in Kempton, Indiana, on February 10, 1921. He had two brothers and one sister. His mom worked in a hospital as a nurse's aide, but I don't know what his dad did because he died when I was way young. I was born in 1947.

People called my father Von or Reese. His middle name was Paul, after his dad, so I don't know how his parents came up with LaVon.

I know Daddy's upbringing was rough. The family didn't have much money and needed to work hard. I called his sister to get some pictures and she said, "Honey we didn't have a camera back then; we just didn't have anything."

I think that's why a lot of these guys went into the paratroopers— it was a chance at a good job. It's also why they could handle the war— because they were raised so tough.

Dad graduated from Kempton High School. He worked odd jobs after graduation until he went into the service.

That's about all I know about his earlier years. He didn't talk about them much, and I never asked him any questions.

Parachuting into Bastogne

General George S. Patton—now that's who Daddy talked about all the time. I don't remember anything specific about what he said, but it was always General Patton this or that. The war was hard on Daddy. I know he had to shoot some young guys, and that always bothered him.

Dad was one of the original Toccoa men. He mentioned that. I always knew he was in Easy Company, and that's been verified a number of ways. Stephen Ambrose mentioned him a few times in *Band of Brothers*, although we didn't know about the book until the movie came out. After Normandy, Dad was promoted from private to corporal.[1] He was with the men toward the end of the war in Germany where his main interest was chasing women.[2] In Austria, he boarded a girlfriend for a while in a private house.[3] Dick Winters wrote that Dad joined the ranks of the NCOs just before the Holland campaign.[4] Daddy's picture is on the front cover of Don Malarkey's book: it's a group of Easy Company guys, and he's in the back row, the third from the right.

In 2001, Floyd Talbert's brother phoned and filled us in, and we went

1. Ambrose, *Band of Brothers*, 112.
2. Ibid., 149–152.
3. Ibid., 278.
4. Winters with Kingseed, *Beyond Band of Brothers*, 120.

over to Normandy with HBO. Several of the men remembered my dad. They said he was always a good athlete.

In addition to his other duties, Daddy was also a pathfinder. I've got some information about that. The 506th actually had three guys in their ranks who were trained as pathfinders—Red Wright, Carl Fenstermaker, and my dad.

You think of the guys parachuting into Normandy or Holland, but Dad was one of the few men who actually parachuted into Bastogne. It happened on December 22, 1944, just days after the Germans broke through the Allied lines in the Ardennes. Two sticks of pathfinders from the 101st Airborne Division jumped into Bastogne. Their mission was to set up signal beacons to guide in planes to get new supplies to the men. The resupply mission succeeded, thanks to the efforts of my dad and the pathfinders.

Joe Watson is a cousin of my mother's. He and Daddy bailed hay during summers after the war. It would get hot up in the haymow, and they'd get to talking. Daddy told Joe he was pretty scared when they parachuted into Bastogne. He said the Germans threw everything they had at them, and their plane was just coming apart. He wanted to jump out before he was allowed.

Daddy told Joe about a situation up there at Hitler's lair. I guess the boys were celebrating and all, and they just lined up and all pissed in Hitler's bathtub. They just lined up and let 'er go. That's what Joe said anyway.

History and Sports

After the war Daddy went to college at Ball State, here in Muncie, Indiana. He married my mother, Bernice, right after the war in '46. My mother was a bookkeeper and worked in an office. They had an apartment in Muncie while Daddy was getting his degree. She helped support him when he was getting that.

My husband Lester says to remember that Floyd Talbert stood up for

Mom and Dad when they got married. I never met Floyd, but I guess that when they got back from the war he and Daddy remained friends for a lot of years. Daddy never went back to many of the reunions. I don't know why. I wish he was here now so I could ask him about these things.

Daddy became a high school history teacher and got a job in Kokomo, where he also taught health and physical education. He was a great athlete and coached high school basketball and baseball. History was always his favorite: anything to do with World War II, that's all he talked about. I'm proud he was able to get his college education. Oh Lord, he just loved history and sports. There's a couple guys around here that knew him, in fact he coached them, and they always talked about how good of a coach he was.

Daddy and Mom liked to have a good time. They fished, camped, and did a lot of swimming, boating, and skiing. Anything outdoors, that's what they loved. Daddy was very muscular and loved to show off his physique, especially when he was drinking. He played a lot of cards here at the Legion in Sharpsville. We talked to Dick Winters, and he remembered my dad. Winters said the men nicknamed him "Blackjack," because Daddy loved to play cards so much.

We lived on a farm near Kokomo. My parents didn't work the farm for their living. It was my grandfather's farm, and there were four houses on it. Grandpa had given Mom and Dad one of the houses to live in when they got married and Daddy got the job teaching school. This was my mom's folks—they had 220 acres, corn, beans, wheat, milk cows, and Daddy helped out from time to time when they needed work done. Their son ran the farm later on. A lot of my growing-up years were spent trying to avoid my parents. So when I got old enough, I came to town a lot with my girlfriends.

Whenever Daddy Drank

As far back as I recall, I remember Daddy drinking. He didn't let it get ahold of him at first. The drinking got bad about when I went into junior high, then it got better for a while, then it got worse again until he died.

There were about fifteen really rough years where the drinking took hold of him completely. He had trouble keeping a job then. As a teacher you need to watch that.

Mother probably could have done more to encourage him to stop. She got on him, but she liked to drink, too, and they liked to go out dancing at places where a lot of drinking was going on. Whenever Daddy drank, he sat up at night and started talking—I don't know when he ever slept—then Mother got on him, and he got mad at her, and they argued.

Daddy could get so mad, so mean, when he was drinking. Whenever he drank he reminisced about the war. He went and sat on the back porch with his rifle, mumbling and yelling and shooting into the woods behind our house. When I started dating Lester in high school, Daddy got to drinking one night really bad and searched for his rifle. Mother gave Lester the gun and said, "You get this out of the house." Lester did. Daddy never threatened us with his gun. I wouldn't want it to come across that way. But when somebody's drinking and holding a rifle, you never know what kind of damage he might do.

Daddy liked to pick fights and found it hard to keep friends because he argued so much. Once, we had friends over playing cards, and Daddy picked a fight with the guy. It got so bad we called the police. Do I remember what the fight was about? Oh grief, no. Undoubtedly it wasn't anything worth fighting over. Daddy was probably bragging about the war, and the guy probably made some negative comment because he wasn't there. That might have set Daddy off. I really don't remember. I was young and probably in the other room trying not to hear.

As a kid growing up in that kind of environment, mostly I was just worried about being embarrassed. When a person's drunk, he can act pretty silly. I was always worried to be out in public with Daddy when he had been drinking.

I think I'm coming across that he was bad to me, and it was never that way. When he was sober, he could be a great guy. It's just that I don't have a lot of memories of when he wasn't drunk. Daddy had his fun moments. I remember him playing ball in the yard with me.

I got a phone call here about two months ago from my nephew. He said, "You know, I remember your dad every year on New Year's Eve. He called right at midnight, at 12:01. I'd look at my dad and he'd say, 'Well I bet that's Von calling to tell us GERONIMO!' That's what he always said when he called up on New Year's Eve."

He Was Only Fifty-four

It's funny, when I graduated from high school in 1966, I wanted to become a hairdresser. But Daddy wanted me to become a teacher, like him. My dad's sister was a hairdresser, and she lived about an hour and a half away. From time to time I went there by bus and spent a week with her. Now I wish I'd become a teacher—that's the joke—I'd have made a little more money than I'm making now.

Lester and I got married right after we graduated. I was an only child, and there were nine kids in Lester's family, so that's what I married into. Mother couldn't have asked to have a better son-in-law. Lester and I have two children.

Right about when Lester and I got married, Daddy lost his job in Kokomo because of the drinking. So my parents moved to Indianapolis, about an hour from us, and Daddy got a job in another school system. Mother quit her job in Kokomo and moved with him.

Mom and Dad often came up from Indy on the weekends and took the children back home with them. That was always one good thing about Daddy. He sure loved his grandkids. He got out there and taught them how to ride bikes, or got down on the floor with them and rassled. He showed them how to do pushups and stand on their heads.

How did Daddy die? Well, he fell off the porch while drinking and needed to go to the hospital. Then he passed away the second day in the hospital, just real suddenly. The autopsy showed cirrhosis and artery blockage. Six or seven things were listed. Basically, they felt that the alcohol had taken his life too early. He was only fifty-four. My parents went to church some, but not a lot. I hope he went to Heaven. That's all I can say.

There was a funeral. I have to brag on my husband a bit here. Lester wanted Daddy to have a military funeral. But it was July 3 when he passed, just before the July 4 weekend, and we couldn't find any veterans around. Lester called everywhere. I told Lester not to worry about it, but he said, "Absolutely not, Marcia, your dad lived and breathed that war, and he is going to have a military service." So he got it all worked out, and I was so thankful that Lester pushed to get that done. He's a wonderful man.

After Daddy died, Mother remarried a fellow who came over from Czechoslovakia after World War II, another military guy. She found some happiness in that marriage. He was a drinker, not quite as bad as my dad was, but he died of cirrhosis, too. His death took longer and was harder. Mother got lung cancer and died in 1993. She and Daddy both smoked and drank and partied a lot. It took its toll.

A Purpose to It

I've been reading up on this some. As hard as it is to talk about bad memories, there's a purpose to it. These young guys coming back from the war today, they need to be encouraged to talk to someone if they're having problems. There are places that can help soldiers nowadays, but back then you weren't supposed to talk about anything.

When we were in Paris, I met Bill Guarnere. We got to talking and I said, "All the stories I hear about my daddy, it seemed like he really liked the women"—of course he wasn't married then—"and he liked to drink."

And Bill said, "Well, honey, that was the way we all were back then. We never knew if we were going to be alive the next day. We liked the women and we liked the booze."

It just seemed that Daddy let the drinking get such a hold of him. The war created the bad situation, but after the war, if guys didn't rein it in, it took over their lives.

From talking to the other veterans, it gave me so much more respect for what my dad went through and helped me understand it so much more. I feel really bad that I didn't understand more of it when he was alive. I was so upset with him most of the time.

I still respect my daddy. Sometimes I wonder why we didn't help him somehow. Why didn't we do more? Why didn't we handle this better? But it doesn't matter. It probably wouldn't have happened anyway.

What's the one thing I would want people to know about my father? Basically, that he was a good man. He fought and lived that war his whole life, and it tormented him to the end. That's a hard thing to fight against all those years. At least he came home and got an education. He worked with kids. And he loved history. He wanted to teach history to teach kids to tell them what our country is all about. He just let the alcohol get the best of him.

15

EUGENE "DOC" ROE

Interviews with Eugene Roe Jr., son, Marlene Langlois, daughter, and Chris Langlois, Derek Tircuit, and Kyle Tircuit, grandsons

Eugene "Doc" Roe Sr. was featured prominently in the HBO miniseries as the soft-spoken Cajun medic who cared for the men during the worst of times. Episode 6 was almost completely devoted to Doc Roe's struggles to treat the wounded in the snow and cold of Bastogne. The men were running desperately low of medical equipment, and Doc Roe moved from foxhole to foxhole, scrounging bandages and morphine syrettes. He also befriended a Belgian nurse in Bastogne, who was later killed during a German bombing raid.

Despite a lot of airtime in the miniseries, Stephen Ambrose mentioned Doc Roe only three times in the book. The most prominent mention is as follows:

Medics were the most popular, respected and appreciated men in the company. Their weapons were first aid kits; their place on the line was whenever a man called out when he was wounded. Lieutenant Jack Foley, who recommended Private Eugene Roe for the Silver Star after a devastating firefight in Bastogne, had special praise for him. "He was there when he was needed, and how he got 'there' you often wondered. If any man [who] struggled in the snow and the cold, in the many attacks through the open and through the woods, ever deserved such a medal, it was our medic, Gene Roe.[1]

Doc Roe seldom talked about the war to his family, but he was a colorful man in other ways. His grandson, Chris Langlois, remembers him simply by the affectionate nickname *Paw-Paw*. In contrast to Chris's other grandparents, who were more straitlaced and reserved, Chris's Paw-Paw was rougher and tougher. Doc Roe always wore cowboy boots, always smoked, and was always deeply tanned and weathered by the sun. He owned acreage and ran a heavy-duty construction business from it. The grandchildren were always welcome to come over and play in the dirt pits and on the backhoes, bulldozers, and tractors that lay scattered around his yard.

This is the story of the real Doc Roe.

Growing Up on the Bayou

Doc Roe's son, Eugene Roe Jr., shares the same name as his dad. What's that been like for him?

"Well, nobody said a thing about it until the series came out," Eugene Jr. said. "Then I started getting a lot of letters and calls from fans of the series. Mostly, it's been good."

Eugene Jr. noted that even though the series portrayed his father as a Louisiana gentleman, the portrayal wasn't as accurate as it might have been. "He was much rougher and poorer than that. He didn't have nearly as strong a Cajun accent as the movie portrayed, and although everybody in the movie called him Doc Roe, he wasn't a doctor by any means. He only had a sixth-grade education."

Why only sixth grade? "Well, that's just the way things were, growing up on the bayou back then," said Eugene Jr. "Dad contracted polio as a child, which slowed down his schooling a bit. But he got past that, and it

---

1. Ambrose, *Band of Brothers*, 181.

didn't have any lasting effects on him. Basically, he quit school because there wasn't that much emphasis on education where and how he grew up. His family expected him to go to work—which is what he did. Funny enough, he was pretty adamant about me going to school though."

Doc Roe grew up in Bayou Chene, a town that doesn't exist anymore. If you study the history of that town, noted Eugene Jr., it was a backwater community of about five hundred swampers, lumberjacks, trappers, farmers, fisherman, and moss pickers.

"That's the climate in which Dad grew up," Eugene Jr. said. "His daddy worked on boats. There were five children in his family—three boys and two girls. Even though they were poor, he had a fairly happy childhood and didn't speak of any bad memories from back then. When he went to school, he took a boat, a type of waterbus. That's how they all lived, close to the river like that."

After Doc Roe quit school, he worked on shrimp boats and miscellaneous jobs to help support the family. In the 1920s, oil drilling began in the area, and water from the Mississippi was rerouted to build a spillway that flooded the town. The government told the people they'd have to leave. When the levees came through, the Roe family moved to Morgan City, Louisiana, which is where Doc Roe grew up as a teenager. After he came back from the war, he moved to Baton Rouge.

In the series it says that Doc Roe's grandmother was a *traiteur*, a traditional Cajun faith healer, but that was contrived by Hollywood, noted the family.

To the Church on Time

The family was never told anything about his enlistment, but daughter Marlene Langlois noted the big wartime story was about how her father met her mother. When Easy Company was stationed in Aldbourne, Doc Roe met a striking British girl who told him her name was Maxine. They met in Swindon, where she was assigned to work in a munitions factory. With all the British men going off to war, the young women were needed to keep the town running.

Maxine wasn't very impressed with Doc Roe at first, but he was persistent. One weekend he followed her to her boarding house. When he knocked on the door and asked for Maxine, "There's no one named Maxine here," came the stern reply.

Doc Roe was flummoxed. He had watched her enter the house. She had to be there.

It turns out that Maxine had given him a fake name. It was popular for the British girls to not reveal their real names to the Yanks. Her real name was Vera.

Sometime later, when Vera and Doc Roe were married, they named one of their daughters Maxine, in honor of the joke. The other daughter, Marlene, was named after the popular WWII song "Lili Marlene."

Vera and Doc Roe courted during his stay in Aldbourne and wrote letters when he was stationed elsewhere. The family has a picture their dad gave their mother from that era. It's signed on the front, "All my love to the dearest person in the world, 'My Rat.' Your old Rip, Gene."

During their courtship in England, Doc Roe visited Dartmouth several times. Vera talked about how Doc brought gifts to her family: chocolate and cigarettes, prized possessions in wartime England. He also gave her a silver-plated pistol with pearl grips. On one side it had his picture; on the other it had hers. When she went home with the pistol, her brother made her throw it into the channel. Vera had eleven siblings, and times were financially hard for her family. They couldn't even take care of all their children, so a few of them boarded with other families.

A wedding was scheduled for a beautiful weekend in early June 1944. What bride wouldn't want a June wedding? Vera showed up at the church with her white dress on, but Doc Roe didn't show. Their wedding date had been set for June 6, the D-day invasion, and the groom was jumping into combat. None of the men knew the exact date of the invasion, and Doc Roe wasn't able to get word back to his fiancée when he found out.

They decided to plan for a new wedding date as soon as the war in Europe was over and he could get back to England for a time. V-E Day was May 8, 1945, and Doc Roe married Vera in July 1945. They wanted a quiet, quick wedding and went to a justice of the peace. A taxi driver was one of their witnesses along with somebody else they didn't know.

In the series it shows Doc Roe developing a friendship with the nurse in the hospital in Bastogne. The family noted that's mostly made up. The nurse was a real person named Renée LeMaire, and it was probable that Doc Roe ran across her while bringing wounded back and forth to Bastogne, but there's no indication he had any sort of relationship with her or shared chocolate bars as is shown in the series. The series is correct, however, when it shows that the hospital/church was bombed and she was killed. A Congolese nurse is also shown in the series. In real life she was named Augusta Chiwi and worked in an aid station several blocks away. She survived the bombings.

More War Stories

Grandson Kyle Tircuit remembered a few war stories his grandfather told him. Immediately before the men were shipped overseas, some of them stopped up a tub, filled it with peroxide, and bleached their hair as a prank. Doc Roe was one of them.

Kyle also remembers his grandpa telling him about a time he treated someone with a head wound in Bastogne. Supplies were low, and the wound was serious, so the ever-resourceful Doc Roe took mud and snow and packed the man's brains back in his head. He was able to buy enough time to get the man to help.

Easy Company veteran Earl McClung told the family a story about when the men were in Holland, positioned on the dike. A shell came in and hit the foxhole two ahead of McClung's. The soldiers in the foxhole didn't climb out or make any sounds. By the size of the blast, McClung figured they were torn up badly but probably not dead. He shouted for a medic. Doc Roe came running and jumped in the foxhole where the two men were. It turned out the two weren't hurt at all. McClung said, "I felt so guilty for putting Roe in a situation like that—running in the middle of an artillery barrage, when no one was hurt."

McClung told another story that happened in Holland. Someone was wounded on a flatland area, and a medic was tasked with running out and picking him up. Doc Roe asked McClung to go along as a stretcher-bearer. McClung said yes and picked up his rifle.

"You can't take that with you," Roe said. "We're going as medics."

"There's no way I'm going out there without my rifle," McClung said.

Roe nodded. "Oh yes you are." They went out, weaponless, and brought the wounded man back to safety.

Doc Roe was injured in the fighting in Holland for Operation Market-Garden. When he jumped from the plane, he landed on some barbed wire and cut his calf. He eventually received more than one Purple Heart, but the family is not sure of the circumstances around his other injuries.

When E Company went to Eagle's Nest, the men raided Hitler's wine cellars, and one of Doc Roe's unofficial duties was to drive a big delivery truck around with all the liquor in it. The generals and colonels commandeered the champagne and fine brandies. The enlisted men got the wine and beer.

The wedding present that E Company gave Doc Roe and Vera came from Berchtesgaden—a set of forks and knives from the Eagle's Nest. There were no spoons, just forks and knives, with fine etchings on them. Years later, Doc Roe was inducted into the Louisiana World War II Museum's Hall of Honor at Baton Rouge. The family donated the forks and knives to the museum to be put on display.

When the war was over, Doc Roe came home first. His new wife came over later on the *Queen Mary* and emigrated through Ellis Island.

When Doc Roe came home he brought a German Luger home as a souvenir. It had a swastika on it. His mother took one look at it and said, "We're not having any of that in the house." She threw it in the bayou.

Grandson Chris noted that his Paw-Paw seldom spoke of the war except to talk about the good times he had and the friends he had made. In 1992, Chris's parents brought him a copy of the book, signed by his grandfather. "I was twenty at the time," Chris said, "at Louisiana State University. The first thing I did was go to the appendix and look for his name. He was listed just three times. I remember closing the book and saying to myself, 'Well, I guess Paw-Paw didn't do much in the war.'"

But that thought changed completely in 2001 when Chris and his family went to Paris for the world premiere of the series. "Whenever I said I was with the Roe family, people's eyes lit up," Chris said. "Other veterans would shake my hand like I had done something important. They'd say, 'Your grandfather was a wonderful man, an angel, a hero.' You don't ever think about those tough men using a word like 'angel'—but that's the word they used to describe my grandfather. Several said they would never want to be a medic, because when the shelling began, they were at least able to duck in foxholes, but the medic was the guy who had to get up and run through the middle of it. I kick myself a million times for not sitting down with him when he was alive and begging him to tell me more about his experiences."

Doc Roe's Brilliance

With the war over, Doc Roe and his new wife settled in Baton Rouge, where three children were born. Doc Roe was a good father who pursued outdoor activities with his children such as hunting, fishing, and horseback riding. He always owned horses.

One of Marlene's first memories of her father is of his rough, hardened skin from having to work out in hot weather so much. He often laid asphalt in south Louisiana where the temperatures regularly climbed to 95 degrees. He was dark brown from working all day in the sun.

"We had the most normal life you could think of," Marlene said. "We spent a lot of time on the bayous on little boats, fishing and crabbing. He stayed close to his parents and brothers and sisters, and we often visited. It was a very family-oriented way to grow up."

Marlene noted that despite her dad's lack of education, he was a brilliant man. "He could take plans and build a parking lot," she said, "or figure out a blueprint faster than most engineers could. Those were skills he was just born with. He never had any formal training. It was always amazing that he could accomplish what he did."

Grandson Kyle runs a construction business today. One of the contractors he works with has a lowboy trailer, a heavy-duty one pulled by a big rig. The contractor and Doc Roe built the trailer together years ago. It's still on the road and going strong.

The Roe children remember few household rules growing up, other than being taught to be respectful, which their father always was, and that boys couldn't hit girls. "Of course, Eugene [Jr.] was the baby," Marlene said, "and with two older sisters, we aggravated him as only older sisters can do. But Daddy was always very strong about that—you do not hit your sisters no matter how much they irritate you."

In the series, Doc Roe was shown smoking Lucky Strikes. That was authentic. Doc Roe smoked a couple packs of Lucky Strikes daily until the day he died. He liked to drink whiskey, too. "Mother and Daddy always drank Seagram's Seven and Coke," Marlene said. "It was always my job to make their highballs at night. I have no idea why that job fell to me, but that was my job."

"He could be pretty traditional," Eugene Jr. said. "For instance, he never wanted me to take typing in high school. He thought that was only for girls. It was the same way with band class. Real guys played football, he said. Only sissies played in the band."

Eugene Jr. speculated that there were two times in his life he disappointed his father. Eugene Jr. did well in school (he was class valedictorian) and was given an opportunity to go to West Point on scholarship. The West Point opportunity was a real honor. Eugene Sr. had a great respect for the West Point grads he served with, and Eugene Jr. knew his father would have loved him to go to West Point. But a military career did not appeal to Eugene Jr., and he also wanted to stay closer to home.

The second time was after Eugene Jr. graduated from Louisiana State University, when he went to work for Exxon. "I think he really wanted me to take over his construction business," Eugene Jr. said. "I remember him saying, 'I don't understand why an educated man would ever want to work for someone else.' That was his view of independence—being able to stand on your own. He had worked himself up to running construction companies with the limited education he had. So he really valued a man starting and running his own business."

Eugene Jr. noted that his father was pleased with him in other ways. "He was proud as a peacock that I made valedictorian. And we grew up sort of on a farm and always had cows and horses. I won quite a few trophies in horse shows, and he was always really proud of those trophies. He'd brag about me in front of other people. That's how he showed it."

The construction business is known for its seasonal ups and downs. Doc Roe experienced both. Sometimes he had more work than he knew what to do with. Sometimes, it was a bust. He went through bankruptcy, but at other times the money flowed in. When it did, Doc Roe was always generous with it. His grandsons remember as boys receiving hundred dollar bills at Christmastime, which seemed a fortune to them. Paw-Paw often bought them toys, too—bulldozers and tractors—things he could relate to.

"It was always a real adventure to go to his house," said grandson Derek Tircuit. "He had dirt, chickens, dogs, and all this large equipment all over, backhoes and tractors. As a young boy, that was heaven. You could run around in the middle of nowhere and climb on stuff. It was an adventure. And we could do whatever we wanted to—that was Grandpa's attitude toward us. If you want to go climb on a tractor, that was fine with him."

The marriage between Vera and Doc Roe was mostly good, said the family, but pressures eventually took their toll. Vera went back to England to visit relatives every four or five years, but the lack of immediate family wore on her. "I remember traveling back to England several times with Mom," Marlene said. "Maxine, age eight, Eugene Jr., eighteen months, and I, age six, went once. We flew on the old Pan Am planes and had to fly to Greenland first, then change planes to continue to England. It was hard for Mom to go back to England. She had to steel herself when she was away from her family. Then she saw them again, then she had to steel herself again to leave, never knowing when and if she'd be able to go back, or who would be alive when she did. It was always a mixed thing for her to go home. Telephone conversations were more difficult back then also.

For many years there was no phone in the family home. We used to have to call England person-to-person and contact a nearby pub. Somebody in the pub would relay the message and go get the family member, who'd come back to the pub at the arranged time. That's how mother would talk to her family."

After twenty-seven years together, Doc Roe and Vera divorced. About five years later, Doc Roe remarried, but Vera never did. She kept her British citizenship, but never moved back to England. America was her new home now. Family ties were always cordial with Doc Roe's new wife, as she played no part in the divorce.

Remarkably Calm

Doc Roe was more of a teacher than perhaps he ever knew.

Kyle remembers once when he was thirteen, his grandfather bought a brand new pickup truck, a Ford F-250. Somebody came to the yard to get a load of dirt, and Grandpa told Kyle to go move his new truck. "I backed it right into a ditch and put a dent in the bumper," Kyle said. "I figured he'd be really mad, but he just came over, looked at it, and said, 'Oh well. It's just the first dent in the truck, there's probably plenty more to come.' That's always stayed with me."

The experience also made a big impression on grandson Derek, who was there when it happened. "You could cause serious mayhem at Grandpa's place, but it just didn't matter to him," Derek said. "He had this weird calm about him. When Kyle put the truck in the ditch, Grandpa got the backhoe and pulled it out. You think, if you're a kid and you wreck some adult's truck, it's a pretty big deal. But with Grandpa, it wasn't. There was no cussing or throwing things, no freaking out. He just hooked up a chain and got the job done. I attribute his strange peace to what he had been through—the war, the concentration camps—he had seen it all, and after the war every other experience paled by comparison. One of your buddies gets his legs blown off, that's a problem. But a dented truck, in the grand scheme of things, that's nothing."

In spite of his calm demeanor, nobody messed with Doc Roe either. "Paw-Paw had been working on a car," Kyle said. "It backfired and he was burned. While he was home recuperating, I went deer hunting on his property with some friends. I forgot to let my grandfather know we were on his land. He figured somebody was trespassing. When we finished hunting, Paw-Paw had closed and locked the gate on us. There he was on the front porch with gauze wrapped around his head and a shotgun in his hands, trying to figure out who was on his property. You didn't mess with Paw-Paw."

When Doc Roe retired from the construction business, he did side jobs, then bought a Western apparel and gear store, which later burned to the ground, then was rebuilt. Doc Roe took it all in stride.

"Probably the thing I remember most from him was his attitude that anything can be fixed, no matter how messed up it was," Kyle said. "It didn't matter if it was a stuck machine or a burnt store, his take was always, 'Don't worry about things. It's all going to be okay.' I've seen him go from being bankrupt to rolling in the money again. He chose to keep a positive attitude through both good times and bad."

Doc Roe didn't keep in touch with his Easy Company friends until later in life. After he retired, he enjoyed reconnecting with his old friends. "If you'd have asked him what part of his life he was proudest of, he would have said his service in the war," Chris said.

Established in their Blood

In the early 1990s, Doc Roe contracted lung cancer and fought it for several years. "His chemo treatments were certainly not pleasant," Marlene said. "He always bounced back, but then started going downhill and never really got up again. He was at home, under hospice. We were there with him at the end. He fell into a light coma and died peacefully, just stopped breathing."

Kyle characterizes the last few months as "long, agonizing, and painful" for his grandfather. "It was really hard to see him go down little by little. The day he died it was like he had his old strength back. He was headstrong, wanting to get up and go to work that day. But his feet had swollen up and he couldn't put his shoes on. That was tough."

Doc Roe died December 30, 1998. The funeral was very plain and ordinary, a small, private ceremony, a tape recording of "Taps," a flag-draped coffin.

Marlene noted that her father was never known to be religious, but after he had contracted cancer and knew he was going to die, a man came to visit him every once in a while who did Bible readings with him. "I think it helped Dad reconcile things with God," she said. "I certainly hope he was at peace when he died."

How would the family want Doc Roe remembered?

"He was just a good person," Marlene said. "He treated people well. And I think that his service in World War II was something he was especially proud of. That's what I'd want people to know about my dad."

Things really hit home for Derek one day in 2001 on the trip to Normandy, in, of all places, the buffet line at lunch. He tells the story in his words:

My fiancée went to the line first and I sat down at random at a table with an older man, one of the originals. "What are you doing here?" he said gruffly. I told him I was the grandson of Doc Roe. His countenance completely changed, and then he laughed. "You know, I always saw your grandfather at reunions and he'd say, 'You know, I don't remember you, but if you drop your pants and show me the bullet hole in your butt, I'll probably remember which one you were.'"

In France, there's always a bottle of wine on the table. I asked the man if I could pour him a glass. He said sure, and we kept talking. "You never knew how Doc Roe got there," he said, "but as soon as a guy was hit, Doc Roe was immediately where you needed him to be."

About three or four bottles into it, we were done with lunch, and it was time to get on the bus to Versailles. Neither one of us had eaten anything; we had talked and drank the whole time. Of course I passed out on the bus.

I was twenty-seven years old at the time. He matched drinks with me and was just fine.

My generation really is still learning what these men went through. I know I am. Here's the perspective I've learned over time. The fact that I can do what I do every day is because these guys busted their asses for me. The freedom I live with and enjoy was established in their blood. They didn't even know me, but they were paying a debt for generations to come. That's inspirational. That helps me remember it's not all about me. It makes me want to be a better man.

That's how I'd want people to remember my grandfather.

16

FLOYD "TAB" TALBERT

Interview with Robert Talbert, brother

First Sergeant Floyd "Tab" Talbert was born August 26, 1923, in Green-town, Indiana, a small community outside of Kokomo, where he grew up. He was the eldest of the seven of us children (five boys and two girls) born to Russell and Nellie Talbert. We had excellent parents. The bartering system became popular during the Depression, and our father often worked in return for goods such as coal. He was an electrician and did wiring jobs sometimes for a ton of coal. He planted large gardens (called "truck-patches"), and our mother canned, cold-packed, and dried food to set aside for the winter months. One task as a youngster was to assist our father in the gardens. We never went hungry and we never heard our parents complain.

Most children born in this era knew what it was to be taught to work hard at an early age. As the Talbert children grew, we all followed this tradition and were sought out by various area residents because of our reputation for being hard and conscientious workers. Tab did the usual lawn mowing and trimming that many young people did, bearing in mind that in those days the mowing equipment was not as sophisticated as today. You pushed the lawn mower with people-power and did the trimming with a pair of scissors. As Tab grew older he worked for various farmers during summers. This meant he had to rise early and either walk or ride a bike to the job site. Later, among other summer jobs, he was employed by a building contractor and did carpentry work and roofing. This was the era before child labor laws, and youths were often willing to work cheaply. It was not uncommon for young people to get involved in doing "man's work" on a regular basis. Tab worked hard and became a very muscular young man.

Tab was an excellent athlete. He played on the baseball team and became an outstanding basketball player. He played four years of varsity ball and was noted for his long set shots.

By Common Sense

After high school graduation, Tab worked for a short time at the Haynes Stellite Division of Union Carbide, located in Kokomo, Indiana. In August of 1942, he joined the Army and volunteered for the paratroopers. He went to Camp Toccoa, Georgia, and followed the rigorous training and then marched to Fort Benning, Georgia, for further parachute training.

Three of Tab's brothers also served in the military. Max was attached to the 17th Airborne Division, I (Bob) served with the 11th Airborne Division, and Kenneth served in the "Big Red One," named for the insignia of the First Infantry Division.

Many things have been written about Tab's experiences during the war. In the morning hours, right after the Normandy jump, he met up with four men from Easy Company, and they joined up with a larger group from the 502nd and battled the Germans near Ravenoville. Shortly after the battle of Carentan, Tab was bayoneted in the chest by Private George Smith after Tab woke him for sentry duty. It was a cold night, Tab had thrown on a German poncho to keep warm, and Smith mistook him for the enemy. Smokey Gordon and Paul Rogers immortalized the incident in a now-lost poem entitled "The Night of the Bayonet." Tab returned to Easy Company in England, just before Operation Market-Garden, and

fought until the end of the war with his unit. Near the end, he was promoted to company first sergeant. Ambrose describes him this way: "A ge-
nial man, Talbert was appreciated by the enlisted men because he ignored
red tape and did things by common sense rather than the book."[1]

I attended one of the Easy reunions and talked with Amos "Buck"
Taylor. He told me a story about Tab and Smokey Gordon. The guys were
always playing pranks on each other. Buck and Smokey were standing in
a line waiting for something, and Smokey had a machete in his hand. Tab
sneaked up behind him and goosed him. Smokey reacted by jumping and
swinging the knife and slicing Buck's leg between his thigh and his knee.
When Buck related this to me, he was wearing shorts and he pulled up the
leg of the shorts and showed me a scar he still carries.

Once while fighting in the bush, Tab spotted a German behind one of
the trees in the forest. He said the German had his back to the tree, and
Tab could see the shoulder of his uniform protruding from behind the
trunk. Tab shot him with his M1, and the German spun around from
behind the tree and attempted to retrieve his weapon. Tab shot him a
second time and he died. When the area cleared somewhat, Tab rolled the
German over and discovered he was very young, maybe fourteen or fifteen years old. He said it affected him deeply, but the battle picked up
again and he needed to keep going.

We discussed situations like this, and Tab said that when they were in
heated combat, the thing on the minds of most men was helping to protect
their buddies and how to survive themselves. He often quoted General
Patton by saying, "The object of war is not to die for your country, but to
make the other bastard die for his."

One of the Best

After Tab was discharged from service in 1945, he attended Indiana University. He accepted a different position with Union Carbide (Stellite Division) in Kokomo, Indiana, and became a purchasing agent. He bought

---

1. Ambrose, *Band of Brothers*, 241.

a small farm outside Kokomo and lived there while working at Stellite. He met and married Arlene Hunt and they had one daughter, Linda, who now resides in Indianapolis. Tab became a member of Huck Finn's Rhythmaires, a small dance band, and he played guitar with them after hours and on weekends. Tab had started playing the guitar while quite young and would spend hours plucking and picking at home. Sometimes his fingers would actually bleed from playing the guitar so much.

Tab loved to be outdoors. He loved to go hunting, fishing, or play golf. I used to fish with Tab often and we hunted and played golf together. We often went to his home, where I always asked him to get out his box of army pictures and data. We spent many hours looking at pictures. He talked about the men he fought with: Shifty Powers, Smokey Gordon, Carwood Lipton . . . and many more. He thought highly of all the men he served with and spoke with respect when talking about them. He worshipped Dick Winters and considered him not only his commanding officer but a friend. Winters also thought highly of Tab. He once said, "If I had to pick one man to go with me on a mission, it would be Talbert." In his book, Winters stated that he considered Tab to be the best soldier in the unit.[2] Our family is proud of that!

Tab left Union Carbide and acquired a farm near Alexandra, Indiana. After living there for some time, he moved to Marion, Indiana, where he became plant manager of the General Tire & Rubber Company. Later, he became involved in the automobile industry and became a salesman.

He moved to California and he and Arlene were divorced. He later met another woman and married her. They returned to Indiana where he was in car sales again. After some time there, his wife wished to return to California and they moved to Redding, California, near Lake Shasta. He loved that area because of the exposure to nature and the opportunities for his hobbies.

In 1969, Tab had a heart operation. They inserted a valve and he was advised to return and have it checked at intervals. He never went back. He continued to work and indulge in his hobbies. In addition to car sales, he

---

2. Winters with Kingseed, *Beyond Band of Brothers*, 278.

was involved in many other activities. He did carpenter and electrical work on ships in the harbors and went overseas to do such work at one time.

One of the war stories Tab never got tired of telling was how Ed Tipper basically came back from the dead, at least for his friend Tab. Easy Company member Ed Tipper had been seriously wounded at the battle of Carentan, and Tab was sure he did not survive. But Tipper was recuperating back in the States, and while doing so he visited our family several times. He normally stayed over a weekend. We were able to watch his recuperation process as he visited. He was always welcome, and my parents thought very much of him. I think he enjoyed my mother's cooking. My mother tried to tell Tab in her letters that Tipper was visiting the family. Tab swore that he saw Tipper's plight in Carentan and insisted that it could not be Tipper.

Later, when Tab and Tipper did get together, it was a great reunion. They went out on the town one night, met a couple of ladies, talked to them for a while in a lounge. Unfortunately, the ladies happened to be married. The husband of the lady Tab was with walked into the lounge and confronted them. Of course they ended up outside, and a fistfight ensued. Tipper wanted to get involved, but he simply could not afford to risk work they had performed during his rehab. Tipper told me that he was not needed anyway, that Tab readily took care of the man, and the fight was quickly over. There appeared to be a lot of fights during that time. Obviously there were a lot of vets around, and it seemed that they had to rid themselves of memories in that fashion.

The Record, Set Straight

Ambrose wrote in his book that at the end Tab became a drifter and a drinker, and even described him as a "mountain man."[3] Tab drank after his service years as many vets did, but he was never a drifter. I confronted Ambrose about this, and my brother, Max, also discussed it with him. He told us both that he was going on assumptions and perceptions from some

---

3. Ambrose, *Band of Brothers*, 297–298.

of the other men in Easy Company and said he would change that language in his next printing. He died and it was never changed.

Tab's daughter was deeply hurt when she read the book. We told her that we had talked to Ambrose and that he had acknowledged that he was merely going on the assumptions made by people he interviewed and was planning to change it. That seemed to satisfy her at the time.

Most of Tab's moves were due to changed employment. He settled in Redding, California, and lived there for approximately ten years prior to his death in 1982. In 1981 he was contacted and attended the Easy Company reunion that year. Because he showed up in his somewhat used hunting suit (knowing Tab, it could have been a joke), someone tagged him with the mountain man title. If he was in dire straits and needed help or clothing, my brother Max or I would have been happy to accommodate him (which we both did from time to time). He was never a drifter or a mountain man, but by his own admission, he drank. Looking back . . . whenever he and I fished, hunted or played golf, we often enjoyed some liquid refreshment afterward. If people thought he drank too much, then so did I, for I drank along with him, and I never considered myself a heavy drinker.

Tab told me often that he was living life his way and was enjoying it. He was capable and had the ability to do almost anything. After his heart surgery, he lived one day at a time. The day he died, he and his wife went fishing in his camper. At one point, he told his wife he was returning to the camper. She said she wanted to fish awhile longer. When she returned to the camper, she found Tab lying on the floor where he had passed away. He died while doing what he loved to do. Linda, his daughter, told me that he "had his house in order" when he died.

17

JOE TOYE

Interview with Steve Toye, son

My dad, Joe Toye, was one tough customer. At the *Band of Brothers* premiere in France, I talked to Donnie Wahlberg (who played Carwood Lipton in the series) and Frank John Hughes (who played Bill Guarnere). They had talked to a number of the vets while filming to learn their characters. They said the veterans had all described my dad as "the toughest of the tough," which is really something, considering that group of men. Babe Heffron summed it up in his interview with HBO: "As tough as a cob." I think those were his exact words. I saw Frank Perconte at a viewing of the body of Hack Hanson's son after he died. Just like my father, they're all a little hard of hearing at this age from having all those 88s and 105s blow up so close to their ears. I sat down next to Frank and introduced myself; we had met before. At the exact moment as he spoke to me, the room quieted down, so everyone heard Frank say, very loudly: "Your father was a tough sonuvabitch, but he never had to go around trying to prove it."

Growing up with my dad, he could make me or my brother or sister melt in a corner just by looking at us. A classic Joe Toye story is that back in the 1960s he was in a local fire hall and had a misunderstanding with his brother Fran. I guess all the men in the town used to hang out after work at the fire hall and drink. So Dad took off his leg and started swinging it around, bouncing on his good leg, using his artificial leg as a weapon. I don't know if he actually hit anyone with it, but that's the way Dad was—you had to quit fighting him or kill him, because he wouldn't back down.

Intense and Tough

Dad grew up rough. He was brought up in the coal regions during the Depression, the youngest of nine kids, a big Catholic family. His father died when Dad was thirteen. He had to drop out of seventh grade to work. So that upbringing stuck with him a long time.

I think Kirk Acevedo, who played my father in the miniseries, did a good job of portraying my father's intensity and toughness, but the initial casting bothered my family a bit. Kirk played our dad more like an Italian mafia guy from the Bronx instead of a hard-nosed Irishman from the Pennsylvania coal region. Dad was never portrayed in the series as a leader either, which was too bad because he was a squad sergeant and took leadership roles in many combat situations. To be clear, there are no sour grapes with HBO or Kirk Acevedo. My goodness, there were Easy Company men who fought from beginning to end and were never mentioned in the series. We're not complaining.

Dad enlisted like everybody wanted to do back after Pearl Harbor. He was originally in the medic corps, which reminds me of a hilarious story—he always thought of himself as a bit of a doctor and did some things to us kids over the years that really made us wince. Once I got a little infection in my eye. Dad did a job on it, squeezed it, whatever. The next day I looked like a cyclops. "Ah shit," he said, "I don't know what happened." He was a medic for the first bit of time in the service. He was stationed in Maryland then and looked on the bulletin board one day. It said: "Paratroopers wanted. Extra pay." So that was enough for him. He joined, and they sent him off to Toccoa.

We've got a newspaper clipping that talks about the 120-mile march the men took from Toccoa to Atlanta. Apparently the day before the march, Dad and a buddy were involved in some sort of indiscretion and ordered to clean the company's stoves as punishment. They worked all night. Then, during the three-day march, they were ordered to stay awake all night to keep the fires going. So for four days straight, Dad didn't get a wink of sleep. But he endured.

Don Malarkey told me about when another soldier in Easy Company had thrown back a few too many and was in the barracks sitting on the side of his bed crying. He had just received a Dear John letter. Malarkey asked the guy what the problem was and he freaked out, pulled out his jump knife, and stuck it an inch from Malarkey's gut. Two strapping arms came out of nowhere and lifted the guy from behind, spun him around, pinned him to the wall, and then grabbed him by the throat. My father glared at the guy and said, "Damn it! You ever threaten Malarkey again and I'll kill you!" Malarkey told me later, "It scared the living hell out of the guy. And, for a moment, me!"

Dad was one of Major Winters's favorites. Winters described him as "an American hero of the first order,"[1] and the second best soldier in the company after Floyd Talbert.[2] That's pretty lofty company. He must have been damn good.

Dad was with Winters's group when they took the guns at Brécourt Manor. A grenade sailed in and everybody took cover. The grenade rolled right between my dad's legs. Winters yelled, "Look out, Toye!" My dad rolled over, the grenade went off, and my dad "bounced up and down from the concussion."[3] Only the stock of his rifle was destroyed. Years later, Dad joked if it wasn't for Major Winters yelling, he'd be singing soprano.

If Winters needed a volunteer, my father was often first on his list.

1. Winters with Kingseed, *Beyond Band of Brothers*, 178.
2. Ibid., 278.
3. Ibid., 86.

Volunteering for these missions was often close to suicidal, but when called, there was no discussion or hesitation on my father's behalf. Once, Easy was pinned down in ditches outside of Neunan, Holland. Their British tank support was being annihilated. Winters needed to find out what he was up against. He looked around and spotted my father and said, "Joe, I need a live prisoner." My dad wordlessly left his squad, crept into no-man's land, then came back with a German from the 107th Panzer Brigade.[4] That was something my father talked about once or twice. When we asked him about it, he sort of scowled and said, "I don't even know what they did with him."

Babe Heffron tells about how in one incident in Holland, my father went out behind enemy lines on reconnaissance with Corporal James Campbell, and the next thing you know here comes my father running through this mushroom cloud with his body riddled with shrapnel and his uniform smoking. Babe ran up and said, "Where's Campbell?" My father said, "He's gone." Babe said, "What do you mean, he's gone—let's go get him." My father said, "No, you don't understand. He's *gone*." Campbell had taken a direct hit from an 88.

Dad was wounded four times: in Normandy, Holland, and twice at Bastogne. On January 2, 1945, Dad was hit by a piece of shrapnel from a bomb during a German air raid. He was sent to an aid station and came back to the line the same day, his arm in a sling. He didn't want to let down his buddies.

In Bastogne he got pretty bad trench foot but didn't want to get evacuated for it. He had already received three Purple Hearts, and he kind of shook it off. Years later when I joined the service, he gave me some advice, "Find out who the good NCOs are and listen to them. And make sure you always wear dry socks."

Just to set the record straight: In Bastogne, when he lost his leg in the

---

4. Story is recounted in unpublished Dick Winters eulogy for Joe Toye given September 7, 1995. See text of full speech at http://www.joetoye.com/index.php?option=com_content&task=view&id=13&Itemid=27, accessed October 2009.

midst of all that intense shelling, he was outside his foxhole, yes, but there was a good reason he wasn't in his foxhole yet. As a squad leader, he was directing his men to get in their foxholes first. In the movie, it showed him out there just walking around. But that's not the way it was.

In the series, it shows Dad asking Malarkey for a cigarette after being hit. "Geez," Dad says, "what's a guy have to do to get killed around here?" Apparently, that line happened word for word. Neither Dad nor Bill Guarnere (who was also seriously wounded while pulling my dad back to a foxhole) were screaming or yelling even though they were both hurt badly. They remained conscious and calm.

After the shelling, they took Dad to an aid station in Bastogne. He had already lost a lot of his leg from the shelling, so they cut off the remainder below the knee. From there, they sent him to England. By the time he got there, gangrene had set in, so they amputated again, this time above the knee. He was a great athlete before he went into the army, a boxer. When he lost his leg, all that was over.

He was in pretty bad shape. My mother says he was 175-180 pounds when he went into the service, and when he came back to the States he was about 110. He almost died. It wasn't just the leg. He had shrapnel in his body until the day he died. I remember seeing scars all over his back, his good leg, his hands. Because of his injuries he also had nerve damage and limited use of his right hand, which bothered him that he couldn't grip anything properly. So it wasn't just his leg. He was just messed up. At least he survived.

From England, they sent him to the hospitals in Atlantic City where he paired up with Guarnere for about a year, both recuperating. They flew around in their wheelchairs, raising hell all over the boardwalks and bars. That's where he met my mother in fact—Atlantic City.

I expect that if he was alive today, things would be much different. Just like Guarnere and Buck Compton and all the ones who are alive to explain their stories, his autobiography would have made one hell of a book.

Big Heart, Ice Covered

Mom and Dad were married in 1946. They moved to Reading, Pennsylvania, where my father had lived with his brother, a state policeman, just before Dad went into the army. After the army, they returned and settled a block down the street from my uncle.

In those days, it was harder for a guy with one leg to get around and to find work. Dad drew some disability because of his leg, but it wasn't enough to take care of the family. He had always wanted to make a career out of the military, but that wasn't possible anymore. Even so, he always worked full-time. When he first got out, he worked for a textile plant, then in the steel mills for Bethlehem Steel. He sharpened bits, so he was able to sit somewhere with a sharpening machine. He worked there for more than twenty years until he retired. He was in the union and retired when he was sixty, then worked part-time at miscellaneous things to keep busy.

My parents had four children. My sister, Anita, is the oldest, then Pete and me, then our youngest brother Jonathan, whose birth, I think, was the final straw for my father in many ways. He had been through so much hardship in his life.

My youngest brother was classified as mentally handicapped, but it was more than that. He couldn't walk, talk, feed himself, go to the bathroom. I'm drawing a blank on the proper terminology, but it was basically a vegetative state. There was nothing to do for my little brother long-term, so he had to be put into a home about an hour away when he was three years old.

I know it hit both my parents really hard. I was only six when my parents divorced in 1963, so I don't remember much. After the divorce, my mother and us kids moved from Reading to Philadelphia and lived with our grandparents for a while. Then my mother remarried and we lived in Philadelphia until we all grew up and went our separate ways.

Everybody knew Dad as this gruff, tough guy. He had a big heart but it was covered in this layer of ice so much of the time. If you lived with him long enough, you could get beyond that, but it was hard to see beyond his exterior. My stepmother said, "I never met a more Christian man than your father." He was a pretty religious guy and went to church every Sunday. He was even in a choir when he was young. But it was much more than that. My stepmother was talking about the actions he took because of his faith. That's what she meant.

Dad went to see my little brother every day. After Dad retired, he was up there all the time, feeding him, taking care of him, a couple hours a day, every day—that was Dad's life. "Steven," he used to say to me, "I just want to live long enough to bury Jonathan, and then I'll be happy."

Jonathan basically just expired. He didn't have much of a stomach left by the end. There wasn't anything anybody could do for him. He wasn't supposed to live much longer than childhood, but he was tough. He died at age thirty-two, three times as long as anyone thought he would live. There must have been a lot of the Toye blood in him. My mother, Eleanor, was always very strong as well.

Sure as hell, a year and a half after my brother died, Dad died, too.

Nightmares and Patriotism

Dad was a hell of a patriot. One time while growing up, it would have been the Vietnam era, 1971 or 1972, I was a young punk, didn't know what was going on, and said something that was negative about the war. Dad went off like a Roman candle. "You know," he barked, "if the damn president called me today I'd go over and fight." Honest to God, he would have. That's the type of guy he was. It wasn't just talk with Dad.

He never complained. Never about his treatment. Never about the VA. Never about the Army. Never about his life before or after the war. That's not the type of guy he was. He was always grateful for what he had.

They portrayed him in the series as a quiet, almost morose kind of guy, but growing up, I saw another side of him. He wasn't a backslapper, but he had a pretty good sense of humor. Babe and Malarkey both said that when the bullets started flying, my dad sang Irish songs.

After my parents divorced, Dad and I met about once a month, then for two weeks vacation each year. He always took us out fishing and hunting, those were some of my best times with him. He never hunted himself. He said, "I had enough of that to last a lifetime." But he taught us how.

Some hilarious stories happened with him. It was my first time pheasant hunting, and I didn't really know what I was doing. A pheasant ran across the ground. I had my shotgun on it. All of a sudden, right in my sights, is my father. He yelled and froze. I got my rifle off him in a hurry and he said, "Whoa, I tried to put my good leg in my pocket—I thought you were going to shoot it off."

My brother did some crazy stuff. Another time while pheasant hunting, one flew up and my brother shot over our heads to get it. My dad dove in the ditch. "Goddamn it, Peter, what's the matter with you," he yelled.

One time while out fishing, we hit Dad in the head with an oar and put a big gash in him. It wasn't on purpose. He just gave us this look, his glasses all mangled, and we all wanted to jump out of the boat and swim for home.

Once at the shooting range, my brother handed my dad his rifle, and he said, as he always did: "No, no, I don't want to shoot anymore. I had enough of that during the goddamn war." My brother kept bugging him, so finally dad took the rifle and shot it. It had a scope on it, and it had been a while since dad had fired anything. He put the scope right to his face and came up with a bloody circle around his eye. He just swore a lot.

There was a bit of the "Irish virus" in the family, I guess, and Dad liked to tip back a few. When he wasn't drinking, he was really a great guy, but, yes, the drinking was always there. Unfortunately, that generation didn't go look for help. That was their life out there in the coal regions. They'd work their arses off all week long for a dollar a day, then go down to the bar to drink, and all the women would need to come to the bar and get their men out of there before they peed it all away drinking. That was the upbringing where Dad came from. The damn war didn't help, of course. I can remember as a kid watching TV with my dad and he's asleep in the chair, moaning with nightmares. He never would admit the nightmares with his hardcore demeanor, but that's what it had to be. To us, Dad was always a pillar of strength. But you never know what's in somebody's heart and mind deep down. I know Dad carried a lot of the horrors of war with him.

It's not like he ever talked about his feelings. One time he talked to Malarkey about how bad he felt about dropping out of school in the seventh grade, about how he wished he had made it all the way through high school. That's the only time we ever heard about how he felt deep down.

For years I was my dad's drinking buddy, but then I quit drinking in 1986. Before that, Pete was out west and I was here with my family and so I stayed around and drank with Dad, but it was getting to me, too. I would have lost my wife and family over it, so I stopped.

When I quit, I guess Dad started thinking about it. The alcohol had caused him a number of problems over the years, the divorce, basically losing his family, the anger. His first reaction when I told him was, "Baaah, what! Are you weak?" But as time went along, he told my wife (he never told me directly), "You know, I'm really proud of Steve." He said he was too old to quit drinking. But I'm sure he thought about it.

A Life Worthwhile

As you get older, you reflect. Once, in his later years, Dad said he didn't feel like he had done much with his life. I said, "Dad—Jesus, Mary, and Joseph—what you did over there in a year, ninety-nine percent of the population can't say they did anything close to it, before, during, or after. He looked at me like, "Really?"

I mean, you think of it: take just any one of those stories about Dad. Those men helped save the world. I mean, I served in the military, too, but luckily it wasn't in a time of war. What I went through is miniscule compared to what Dad and those vets went through.

Dad remarried in the late 1960s. His new wife had four children from a previous marriage, the two older ones were moved out by then, but there was a younger boy and girl. Dad was good to them and used to umpire the boy's games.

In his later years, Dad did all kinds of things. He took classes up at community college—painting, cooking. Nobody would know that, but he was a great cook. He used to cook up in the coal regions, that was part of his job then, and it stuck with him. As adults, he cooked up steak and lobster for me, my wife Bonnie, and our kids. I tell you, that was the best I ever had.

For hobbies, Dad loved working out with weights. And he loved to walk—if you can believe it. There was a track in Reading close to the house, and Dad went down there a lot. Even toward the end, he walked a mile a day. He watched a lot of sports. Any game we had, he'd come out and watch. He fished and took us hunting in the mountains. In his later years, he drove from state to state to see his grandkids play sports.

Near the end of Dad's life I was living out in Michigan. He wasn't himself at all, edgy, saying his stomach hurt. He actually cut out drinking caffeinated coffee, which wasn't like him, as he always had a stomach of iron. He went in for a hernia operation and found that he was just riddled with cancer—pancreatic, which is one of the worst ones, basically a death sentence.

Unfortunately I was in a horrible job at the time—it's all kind of a blur—and Dad's passing happened so quickly. My stepfather had just died, and we were back staying in New Jersey, getting ready to go to his funeral. Next thing we knew we got a call from my sister saying Dad had passed. So we went to my stepfather's funeral and the next day we went to my father's. It was a really bad time of life. And his death happened so damn quick. That's one of the things that's always bothered me. I never had the chance to say good-bye. My brother said I was probably better off that way. He had seen him in the last few weeks, and Dad wasn't in the right frame of mind then. He was about ninety-five pounds. You could tell it was his last days.

Major Winters came to Dad's funeral and did the eulogy, which was very classy of him. Winters lived in Hershey, Pennsylvania, about an hour away from Dad, and they did a variety of things together over the years. Dad was grand marshal in a parade once, which he really didn't like doing, although it was good for him. The accolades he received, although he couldn't stand them, they made him feel like his life was worth it. I'm glad the book came out when he was still alive. That was a good tribute to the men. I just wish he was alive for the miniseries.

What's the one thing I'd want people to remember about Joe Toye?

He was a loyal, tough, patriotic, Christian man. He was old-school and grew up the hard way. He was flawed as a father and flawed as a husband, yes, but he did the best he could considering the cards he was dealt. He lost much in his life but never gave up. I have a lot of respect for him, and I think that anybody who knew him does, too.

PART III

OFFICERS

Leaders from the Front

18

FREDERICK "MOOSE" HEYLIGER

Interviews with Fred Heyliger Jr. and Jon Heyliger, sons
With additional information from Mary Heyliger, widow

The last photographs of Frederick "Moose" Heyliger show him looking like an aged Abraham Lincoln, a tall, wiry figure with a white, bushy beard and no mustache. That was his trademark look in his later years, said his family, but, in spite of the wooly wraparound, Moose was never Amish. He watched a lot of old movies after he retired, and that's where the look sprang from. As a younger man, he was always clean shaven, and no matter what the stage of his life, he was seldom seen without his pipe.

"He was a cross between John Wayne and Archie Bunker," said his youngest son, Jon Heyliger. "That's how I'd describe his personality. He loved being outdoors like John Wayne, and spent as much time there as he could. If he had one flaw, he could sometimes be a bit of a loudmouth like Archie Bunker, though I can't think of any instances where he outright offended anybody. He was a pretty straightforward type of guy. What you saw is what you got."

Fred Heyliger Jr., his eldest son, laughs good-naturedly at how quick-witted his father could be. Years ago they were at a Boy Scout meeting. Heyliger was the leader and told the boys to recite the creed. When they came to the part about being "morally straight," some kid piped up: "What does that mean?"

"It means you can't sleep on a spiral staircase," Heyliger said.

"That line captures his personality," Fred Jr. said. "He could be very funny, on the good side of things. But also, he could choose to not deal with serious issues. Avoidance was one way he coped with life. He simply sidestepped certain subjects."

Like war.

The war always seemed just under the surface for him—never visible but always there. Once when Fred Jr. was fifteen, a neighbor named Ray offered to take them all deer hunting. "If you want to go hunting with Ray, go ahead," Moose told his son. "I've got this old shotgun and you can have it, because I'm never going to shoot a gun again."

Moose seldom talked about the war with his family, although the boys remember him having nightmares about it. One of the first times Moose ever spoke openly was when his family went to Normandy in 2001 for the premiere of the HBO series. During the first showing (which was the second episode, about the Normandy landing), Moose watched the first five minutes of it, then said: "Get me out of here, it's time to go. I know everybody gets shot. I saw it once, and I don't need to see it again." His sons urged him to stay and finish the showing. Reluctantly, he stayed.

Afterward, as they walked with him across the parade ground in front of the memorial, Jon asked him: "Dad, what were you doing when all that fighting was going on?"

"I had my ass up against a barbwire fence and was trying to not get shot," Moose said. That was the end of the discussion.

Moose, in fact, played no small part in the war. He led Easy Company during a critical season toward the Holland campaign's end, and his command became sandwiched between two other leaders at opposite ends of the respect spectrum. He followed the much-revered Dick Winters, and was the forerunner to Norman Dike, whom the men disparagingly referred to as "Foxhole Norman."

Moose's leadership style leaned more toward Winters's approach. Ambrose, after interviewing Winters, described Moose this way: "A good CO. He visited the outposts at night. He went on patrols by himself. He saw to the men as best he could, [and] like the men in the foxholes, he never relaxed. He bore up under the responsibility well, took the strain, did his duty."[1]

Snowy Moose Tracks

Moose was born on June 23, 1916, which made him one of the older men in Easy Company. He was twenty-eight when he became company commander.

Moose came from a large Dutch family and had five brothers and a sister. The family settled in Concord, Massachusetts. His father was a lawyer for an insurance company and had an asparagus farm on the side. (His dad had moved the family to the farm because he thought a farm was a good place to raise boys.) Moose refused to eat asparagus as an adult, saying he had eaten enough as a child to last a lifetime. The kids used to sleep sideways, three to a bed when they were young, which reflected the family financial situation. They did better later on, shown in that Moose attended the private Lawrence Academy in Groton for the last two years of high school.

One winter day as a child, Moose was heading outside with his brothers and grabbed his oldest brother's boots by mistake. The boots were far too big for him, and as the boys walked across the snow, one of the other brothers said, "Hey—look at the moose tracks." The nickname stuck, and Fred Heyliger was called "Moose" from then on. As a young man he stood six feet tall and weighed about 210 pounds, one of the larger paratroopers.

Moose loved being outdoors. He set muskrat traps as a child and checked them before he went to school. On the spur of the moment, he and his brother Ted decided to go winter camping one weekend. They

---

1. Ambrose, *Band of Brothers*, 157.

grabbed sleeping bags and food and hiked to a beach where they spent the night. It was December, freezing. Ted said he was never so cold in all his life. But Moose loved it.

Moose was a military man prior to the war. He spent three years as a private in the National Guard with H Company, the 182nd Infantry. His character was described by military records as "excellent," and he qualified as a marksman in 1934. His term of service expired, and he was honorably discharged July 24, 1936.

Moose enrolled at the University of Michigan where his older brother, Vic, excelled as a hockey player. Before finishing college, Moose was drafted into the 51st Field Artillery Brigade and trained as a machine gunner at Camp Edwards for a year. In 1942 he completed Officer's Candidate School at Fort Knox, Kentucky, was commissioned as a Second Lieutenant, sent to Camp Chaffee in Portsmouth, and then to the 506th PIR at Toccoa. He was promoted to First Lieutenant in February 1943.

Moose's first choice, militarily, was always to go into the Air Force, but it never worked out for him. He explained to his sons that he "could get the planes up, but couldn't land the damn things." He also tried tanks before becoming a paratrooper, but didn't like them. He joked about the tank brigade by referring to an old Bill Mauldin cartoon. Two guys look at a tank and say to each other, "There's something about a moving foxhole that attracts the eye."

So Moose switched to the Airborne. He described the hike from Toccoa to Atlanta as a "miserable experience," and added, "If Colonel Sink hadn't been so drunk when he read that article about the Japanese paratroopers marching, we never woulda had to do it."

While in the service, he married his first wife, Evelyn. They had a son, Fred Jr., in 1943, born the day Moose sailed overseas on the *Samaria*. The couple later had one daughter, Diane.

In handwritten notes kept by his second wife, Mary, he described how he parachuted into Normandy and landed in a pasture about 1:30 a.m., June 6, 1944. "It was black as the insides of a cow," he wrote. He figured himself about three miles off his drop mark and hiked to Utah Beach, arriving there about 7 a.m. He met up with other men and they worked their way north toward Cherbourg. He took over guard duty for some soldiers from the 4th Division, then stayed with the 4th for about a week before rejoining his unit.

In September that year, Moose jumped into Holland for Operation Market-Garden, where he was in charge of the company's mortar platoon.

During the night of October 22, 1944, he was chosen to head a rescue expedition across the Rhine River with twenty-four E Company men. Using portable boats, Easy Company successfully rescued 138 British 6th Airborne troops, ten Dutch resistance fighters, and five American pilots trapped behind German lines on the other side of the river. Lifeboats were left on the shore of the river, and the next morning, "The Germans blew the boats to smithereens," he noted.

Reports from Colonel Robert Sink commended Moose for his "gallantry, outstanding planning, and execution of the operation with no injuries." The men from Easy Company on the patrol were commended for "bravery, aggressive spirit, prompt obedience of orders, and devotion to duty."

Moose went on patrol Halloween night, 1944, along with Captain Winters. The two men were checking on machine gun positions when Moose forgot the password and was shot twice by one of his own men. The experience is shown in the miniseries. Winters dove into the bushes and wasn't hit. "I still don't remember the password," Moose wrote years later.

"Dad never talked about his injury," Fred Jr. said. "Not a word. But he had a good-sized scar on his shoulder and the whole calf on the back of his right leg was virtually gone. Dad always wore shorts in the summer, and I remember seeing his scars as a kid. He wore ski boots, the old leather kind that attached into spring bindings. He said the whole bottom of his foot was numb, and that the ski boots were the best sole he could find to make sure that he didn't step on something and not know it. Plus, the ski boots were heavy and he said, 'I need the workout.'"

After he was shot, Moose was in a variety of hospitals for the next two and a half years in Scotland, New York, and Atlantic City, until his discharge from the service in 1947.

A Life Outside

After the war, he decided to return to college, this time to the University of Massachusetts. He attended on the GI Bill and graduated in 1950 with a degree in ornamental horticulture.

Moose was employed as a salesman for various landscape and agricultural chemical companies for more than forty years and didn't retire fully until after his eightieth birthday. At first, he was a warehouse manager for the Eastern States Farmers Exchange, where he sold feed and fertilizer, anything he could get that kept him close to the outdoors, where he always longed to be. Later he worked for the Diamond Crystal Salt Company, then for another company that sold agricultural chemicals and seed to golf courses, cemeteries, and park departments all over eastern New England. He took side jobs landscaping and frequently helped out neighbors with landscaping and gardening projects for free.

"His career goal was pretty basic," Fred Jr. said. "He wanted to experience the outdoors full-time. He never quite achieved that. Sales was always his primary occupation. The work in horticulture was always on the side."

"I think he was basically happy with his work," Jon said. "I took for granted how much knowledge he had. He grew the most amazing gardens and flowerbeds you'd ever seen in front of our house. He had me plant apple trees as a kid, and we grew corn. He was always weeding and watering. As a kid I got to sell some of the stuff we grew."

Fred Jr. describes his father as a somewhat distant parent, almost unsure how to raise his children. But there were good times, too. When he and his sister were very young, Fred remembers fondly their dad hooking up their Chevy coupe and a one-wheel trailer. The family headed out from their home in Acton, Massachusetts, and set out for Truckee, California, where Easy Company member Bob Brewer lived. The family camped all across the country, there and back.

For years, Moose was a Boy Scout leader and took his pack to the mountains annually for a snowball fight. He was the chairman of the town's recreation commission and worked to get the town to buy valuable recreational land to set aside for public use. Rare and unusual plants grew on the recreation land, and Moose knew both the common and Latin names of them all.

He was constantly in touch with nature. "He'd get a bunch of neighborhood kids together on a cold day," Fred Jr., said, "and say, 'let's go to Crane's Beach today, pack a lunch,' and we'd all suit up in our winter clothes and go to the beach. Dad could tell us all the names of the birds, and where they came from." He kept plastic bags in the car, because if he found a particularly colorful bird dead along the road, he stopped and picked it up. Whenever he found one, he identified it by name, an indigo bunting, or a cardinal, or a Baltimore oriole, or whatever, and said something like, "Well I know a guy up in Freeport who ties flies, and he can use these orange feathers."

Moose and his first wife separated in the early 1960s, when Fred Jr. was nineteen, and divorced a short time later. The parents moved about twenty miles apart. Moose married his second wife, Mary, in 1966. She had four children from a previous marriage. Moose had two. Jon was born as the result of the new marriage. Moose was forty-nine when Jon was born.

"He took on a lot," Jon said. "When he met my mother, she already had four kids, and I'm sure that's not an easy thing to walk into. He must have really loved her. He took us many places, like to the Cape in the winter so we could play on the sand dunes, or up skiing, or hiking up to Mount Monadnock. He knew a lot about birds, trees, different plants. He could tell you the constellations. It was nice for a kid to take in all that information. He had a lot to offer."

One time one of the younger boys found a turtle, boxed it, and took it home. Moose made him take the turtle back and set it free. Another time Jon and a friend were at a sandpit and spotted a couple of birds. The boys thought their mother had abandoned them, so they took them home. Moose made them take the birds back and set them free.

"He was always making us dig somewhere or prune something or clear land," Jon said, "which seemed like a drag as boys—other kids didn't have to work on weekends. When my parents bought their house in Shirley, it was just a residential lot with all these thorny trees with humongous spikes everywhere. All told, we must have spent a couple years cleaning up the fields and brush.

"But he could also be very thoughtful at times," Jon added. "One time we were camping, and my hands were really cold. He boiled some eggs and told me to put them in my pockets to keep my hands warm. It was all practical stuff with him. He never wanted you to have a bad time."

Other family experiences proved difficult. Diane, the daughter from the first marriage, died in 1977 of a cerebral aneurism. She worked as an exercise jockey at Calder Racetrack in Florida. One day she got off a horse, said, "I don't feel so good, I've got a headache," and collapsed.

"Dad tended to disappear if ever conflict arose," Fred Jr. said. "When my sister died, my mom got down there to Florida right away, then called me. I was living in South Bend by then, and I went down right away as well. The EKG showed a flat line, and doctors said we needed to decide whether to keep Diane on life support or not. My mother said, 'I can't make this decision by myself.' So I called my father in Massachusetts; by that time he was remarried. 'I can't deal with that,' he said. 'You better take care of it.' So the decision fell to me."

The Fall Migration

Moose became more involved with Easy Company in his later years. Once, after all the kids were grown-up, he decided to drive from Massachusetts to visit Rod Bain in Alaska. Mary was worried about him driving that far by himself, so Jon went with him. They saw Johnny Martin along the way. Martin lived in Phoenix, but he also had a place in Montana.

Moose visited Dick Winters several times in later years. "Dad liked to go down to Hawk Mountain in Pennsylvania and watch the fall migration," Fred Jr. said, "which wasn't far from Hershey, Pennsylvania, where

Dick lives. I know Dad also stayed in touch with Bob Brewer; we always knew him as Uncle Skim. When Dad retired, his big goal was to have an acre of land in every state, get a trailer, and visit all of them. He wasn't able to complete the goal, but he enjoyed dreaming about it."

In the early 1990s, Moose suffered some minor strokes, which made him a bit unsteady. Then in 1995 he slipped while walking into a restaurant, fell, and broke a hip, which put him in a wheelchair for the rest of his life.

Being unable to move about on his own affected him a great deal, his sons said, but there were a few bright moments in his later years. "I think he secretly enjoyed the notoriety that the HBO miniseries brought," Jon said. "He never would have sought out any notoriety, though. He certainly never did when we were growing up. But I think he enjoyed being known as one of the Band of Brothers when he was in the VA hospital in Bedford, where he was at the end."

Jon speaks fondly of being with his father at the HBO premiere in Normandy. "Mostly, we just sat outside the hotel and smoked cigarettes together," Jon said. "We toured Paris some, but it was harder for him to get around because of the wheelchair. We met some French kids, and when they found out Dad was a paratrooper and in Normandy, they had all kinds of questions for him. He kept his sense of humor, too. When we were coming back from Utah Beach in a van, all of us were exhausted, but Dad kept cracking jokes in the back of the van. 'My eyes aren't mates anymore,' he said, like, they were so tired they weren't functioning together."

The family went to Paris in June 2001. Then, late that October, Moose had another stroke, this one major.

"I came up from New York," Jon said, "and Dad was in the hospital. They had to keep clearing his lungs because they were filling with fluid. It was pretty brutal for him. He could still talk a bit, but there weren't any longwinded conversations between us. I knew he was in a lot of pain. I asked if he could see outside. He said yeah. We said things like that. I think it was good just that he knew we were there and made the effort. I was with him one night, and he asked me what was on TV. I said I was watching baseball. That was the last conversation he and I had. I needed to go back to the city to take care of some business. The next day when I got back to the hospital, they said he had taken a turn for the worse during the night. From that point on he never opened his eyes. Then they took him off the ventilator. We waited until he stopped breathing. Then he was gone. I couldn't believe it. I kept thinking he'd bounce back."

His wife Mary remembers him saying, "Hi, love," when she arrived at the hospital, and that his last word before he died was "home."

"Just before he died, I whispered in his ear that I loved him and that I was glad he came into our lives," Mary said. "I don't imagine he heard me, but I hope he did."

Remembering Frederick Heyliger

Frederick Heyliger died November 2, 2001. The funeral was simple and short, just family and friends. A minister came and said a few words. His family put his ashes in the ground. "He really wasn't a religious man," Jon said, "I never saw him go to church or anything. But I remember him saying to my brother Stephen that there are no atheists in a foxhole, so he had some sort of belief in God, although I never spoke to him about it. What I know is that he lived a good long life and did things most of us couldn't dream of doing." Fred Jr. added that his dad went to church Christmas and Easter "whether he needed to or not,"—his dad's words— and always made sure the parsonage had the lawn mowed and the gardens weeded.

The family held a small ceremony at Sleepy Hollow Cemetery in Concord, where the ashes were interred. "He's got a nice view of Author's Ridge," Fred Jr. said, where Emerson, Thoreau, Nathaniel Hawthorne, and Louisa May Alcott are buried.

The two brothers paid tribute to their dad in different ways. Here are their stories, told in their own words:

Jon:

I try to keep in touch with the people involved with the Easy Company reunions, although I'm not as much a part of the reunions as I'd like to be. I
went to a couple after Dad passed away, but without him there, it felt harder
to go.

The year right after he passed away, I went to the reunion and decided
to leave a day early. I started to drive home. I left in the afternoon and drove
into the night, but then decided I had to turn around. I ended up back at the
reunion at six in the morning; I just couldn't walk away yet. There was such
a hole, and the only thing I could do was be around the people who really
knew him.

When I came back, I met up with a couple of Rod Bain's daughters and
we went hiking together. There was a big dinner that night. His daughters
were always really nice to me. Someone gave me some photos of my dad. I
dunno—I guess the Easy Company family was just really there for me when
I was having such a hard time.

My father's passing still leaves a big hole in my life. It's been almost eight
years now since he's gone, but I'm still not over it. I doubt I ever will be
fully.

It's funny, the veterans I've met all seem to have this gentleness inside
them. Sometimes it's tough to believe these men were also soldiers and
needed to kill people. It's like the war years are some kind of separate life for
them. It's hard to believe they are the same people. I think it's sad that Dad's
generation is all passing away now. Folks today don't realize that people like
my dad ever really existed.

Fred Jr.:

What's one thing I'd want people to know about my father? Well, it sounds
kind of cheesy, but I'm sure that he always meant well. He didn't always do
well. But I know he always meant well.

Some years ago I came across his senior yearbook from Lawrence Academy in Groton, where he graduated. The comment in his description was: "You can always find Moose wandering over the Groton hills with a pair of binoculars around his neck and a bird book in his hand."

I think that describes my father at his best. He was a man who loved the outdoors and cared for all living things. He did his job during the war and was a good leader. He cared for his families the best he knew how.

Picture Moose Heyliger wandering over the Groton hills with binoculars and a bird book. That's how I'd want people to remember my dad.

★ 19 ★

C. CARWOOD LIPTON

Interview with Mike Lipton, son

A journalist from the *New York Times* wrote an extended obituary about my father just after Dad died on December 16, 2001, at age eighty-one. The miniseries had just come out that year, and the article described him as among the central figures in *Band of Brothers*.

My dad is generally considered to have been one of the primary contributors to Stephen Ambrose's book, even suggesting the title from a line from Shakespeare's *Henry V.* Donnie Wahlberg portrayed him in the series as "a low-key, dependable member of the company who emerges as a strong leader while a first sergeant in the Battle of Bulge."[1]

That statement from the *Times* summed up well my father's life. He was a good leader, consistently dependable, and later became one of the more recognizable members of the group.

---

1. Richard Goldstein, "C. Carwood Lipton, 81, Figure in 'Band of Brothers,' Dies," originally published December 24, 2001, http://www.nytimes.com/2001/12/24/us/c-carwood-lipton-81-figure-in-band-of-brothers-dies.html, accessed September 2009.

Flamethrowers and Rabbit Hunting

C. Carwood Lipton was born Jan. 30, 1920, in Huntington, West Virginia. There were actually three Clifford Carwood Liptons: my grandfather, my father, and my brother. My grandfather was known as Cliff, and my brother was always known as Cliff, so to distinguish himself, Dad went as Carwood.

My grandfather's name was actually *Clifton Carlwood Lupton*, but he changed it. Dad said it was because people called him "Mr. Lipton" whenever they saw his signature, which doesn't explain why he changed his first and middle name, too, but I'm not aware that he changed his name to disguise ethnicity or anything like that. They were Scottish, originally landed in North Carolina, and proud of their heritage.

Dad was a bit of a hell-raiser as a young boy, inquisitive and resourceful. He told us stories about the crazy stuff he and his brother did.

Once they went rabbit hunting. Dad didn't have a shotgun, but he found a piece of pipe that was just big enough to drop a shotgun shell into. The lip of the shell held it at the pipe's end. They went out hunting, and Dad hiked around with this piece of pipe on his shoulder with his brother behind him. A shell was loaded in the pipe. His brother carried a block of wood with a nail driven through it. The plan was that whenever they saw a rabbit, the brother would bang the block of wood against the shell, fire it, and shoot the rabbit. Fortunately, rabbits were scarce that day, and they never got a chance to actually fire it—probably would have killed them both.

The heat in their house came from open flames in those old ceramic grates. One winter day, his mother had company over, and the kids were told to make scarce. Dad and his brother went out onto the porch and looked for something to do. They found a piece of metal and pounded the end into a flange. Disconnecting the heating grate outside on the front porch, they hooked up the gas line into their device. Basically, they built themselves a flame thrower. Dad held it, and his brother lit the end. Flames shot all the way across the porch.

Years later, Dad described the experience: "We weren't sure how to shut it off, so I kept moving this thing around so the house wouldn't catch fire. I couldn't let it stay in one place for very long. My brother ran downstairs and turned off the gas main, because that was the only way we knew to stop the gas. Then my brother and I had to sneak around the house and relight all the pilot lights on the heaters. The company was still visiting with my mother, and it was winter. So once the heaters went out, you needed to get them lit again quickly."

Growing up wasn't all fun. My grandfather was killed in a car wreck when my dad was ten. Dad was the older brother and wound up as the man of the house. His mother worked. His parents had been interior decorators and had run their own decorating shop in Charleston, or perhaps it was in Huntington. Back in the 1920s they decorated the governor's mansion in Charleston. So my grandmother continued the decorating business and always kept boarders with rooms she rented out.

Dad continued on with his adventuresome ways. When the war hit, he wanted to join the Army Air Corp to be a fighter pilot—that was his first choice. But right out of high school he had worked at a nickel plant in Huntington and had gotten a chip in [one] eye from a metal lathe, so his eyesight wasn't good enough to be a pilot. The second most dangerous thing he could think of was being a paratrooper.

Dedicated Soldier

Dad was one of the few married paratroopers. He met my mother, Joanne Eckly, on a double date just before the war. They weren't with each other on the date, mind you, they were each with the other person. But they liked each other, and began dating after that. They were married in 1943.

Dad had joined the Army in 1942 as a private. He was one of the original Toccoa men, was promoted to company first sergeant within a year, and was one of the noncoms who participated in the mutiny against Captain Sobel in Aldbourne.[2] Dad never talked about the incident with

2. See the essay about Salty Harris.

Sobel. He mentioned that Sobel had gotten them lost on maneuvers, and that he was concerned about Sobel leading them into battle. That was about it.

He was known as a dedicated leader and jumped into Normandy with his men on D-day. He landed in a walled-in area in the city of Ste. Mère-Église, joined up with some members of the 82nd, and then with Guarnere, Malarkey, Toye, and Wynn, then shortly thereafter with Winters. He fought with the men when they disabled the guns at Brécourt Manor.

Dad didn't talk a lot about the war and the military when we were growing up. I think it was an experience he wanted to forget, but he wrote two pieces describing two battles he was in. The first, of Brécourt Manor. The second, of Carentan, where he was wounded. Portions of his writings are as follows:

Brécourt Manor

We had two officers, Lt. Winters in command and Lt. Compton; two platoon sergeants, Guarnere and I; and nine men, and we had two machine guns, a 60mm mortar, and our individual weapons.

The entire group was stopped by the sound of German artillery firing from a wooded hedgerow area off to the right of the road that we were on. Lt. Winters was called to Battalion and was ordered to take and destroy those guns with his company. None of us had been in combat before that day.

Winters had no time for a reconnaissance, but from his initial observation he decided that there were several guns, manned and defended by probably at least 60 men, and that the guns were well dug in and camouflaged and that there was probably a network of trenches and foxholes around them. We learned later that he was right in all these estimates, and that the German forces included a number of paratroopers from the German 6th Parachute Regiment.

A frontal attack against those positions by 13 men could not succeed, but Winters confidently outlined to us his plan to deceive and defeat the German forces and to destroy the guns.

His plan was to concentrate a double envelopment attack on one gun, the one on the German left flank, and after capturing it to hit the other guns, one by one, on their open left flanks. He sent Compton and Guarnere around to our left to hit the Germans on the first gun from their right front. He sent Ranney and me around to our right to put fire into the German positions from their left flank. He set up the two machine guns in position to put heavy continuous fire into the German positions from their front. He then organized and led the rest of our men in a direct assault along the hedgerow right into the German positions.

With fire into their positions from both flanks, heavy machine gun fire into their front, and Winters leading an assault right into their defenses the Germans apparently felt that they were being hit by a large force. Those defending the first gun broke and withdrew in disorganization to a far tree line, and that gun was in our hands.

Our attack continued to each gun in turn from its exposed left flank. Winters blew out the breeches of each gun as soon as we had it with blocks of TNT. In all, the Germans lost 15 men, 12 [more] were captured, and many wounded. In E Company we had one man killed and one wounded.

Carentan

I don't remember any officers in the 3rd platoon in Normandy. Lt. Schmitz did not make the jump, and Lt. Mathews was killed early in the fighting, so I had command of the platoon. I set up outpost positions in the fields toward Carentan and patrolled the area to our front, visiting the outposts with Talbert or Taylor each night we were there. There was no enemy activity against us, however, while we were there.

Our part in the attack began on June 11th, D plus 5, when we were ordered to move out with the rest of the Battalion to the highway and, attacking to the right of it, to outflank Carentan from the West and South. This attack would cut the two highways leading into Carentan from those directions and a railway.

We moved out to the highway after dark and began our approach march with other units of the Regiment leading. There had been major fighting over the route we were following. The area was strewn with bodies, American and German, weapons and equipment, difficult to see clearly in the dark. We knew nothing about what to expect ahead of us, but we were not at that time receiving enemy fire.

We moved in column, well spread out, with connecting files maintaining contact between units. We reached the railroad and, as I remember, stopped there for a while, beginning to set up a defense, then moved out again to occupy the road leading into Carentan from the South. We reached it after daylight and were told that we were to prevent any German reinforcements from being brought into Carentan along it. I don't know the disposition of the rest of the Company or the Battalion, but the 3rd platoon was astride a road, which could have been a smaller connecting road instead of the main highway.

I had one bazooka in the 3rd platoon and [Ed] Tipper was the bazooka-man. We were told to expect German armor, and the only place I could find to put Tipper and his bazooka was at the bend in the road down over a bank from where he would find it almost impossible to withdraw if we were over-run. As he and I looked at it I knew that he was seeing that it was a do-or-die situation, but that there was not another good position. I said, "Tipper, we're depending on you. Don't miss." He said, "I won't."

After a short time, though, less than an hour as I remember, we were again ordered to move, this time to attack and clear Carentan.

As we reached the outskirts of Carentan we started getting German rifle and machine gun fire. The houses in this area were somewhat like row houses except that there were enclosed stairways leading up to the second floors from the outside. I thought that we were getting sniper fire from one of the upstairs windows. Buck Taylor and I were working as a team at this point, checking and clearing the buildings and area as we went, so I told him that I would go up the stairway to that room and that after he had given me enough time to get to the top he should throw a grenade through the upstairs window. I would then jump into the room and finish off whoever was there.

I ran up the steps and stopped outside the door. I heard the grenade thump into the room through the window and its explosion. I threw open the door and leaped into the room, my rifle thrust forward ready to fire. I couldn't see a thing! The room was filled with dust and smoke from the explosion. If there had been a sniper there and he had been able to shield himself from the grenade he would have had me silhouetted in the door, but the room was empty.

We continued to check buildings and work our way toward the town center. The rifle and machine gun fire against us seemed to decrease somewhat as we moved farther in, but mortar and artillery fire increased. Men were getting hit.

Someone yelled that Tipper was hit across the street from me. I ran over. He was lying there conscious but hurt seriously. A medic was bandaging his face and his eye was obviously gone. He had major wounds in one arm and one leg. I told him he would be well taken care of and moved on.

I came to a major road intersection, nearer the town center. There was small arms and machine gun fire coming down the street from the right, across my front. Across on the other side of that street, on the continuation of the street I was standing on, were several E Company men. There were explosions up on the walls of the buildings on the left side of the street that they were on, and they looked to me like German 5cm mortar shells fired at a low trajectory so that they were coming in somewhat horizontally rather than dropping in vertically. I was on the right side of the street I was on, against a building on my right, and I did not think that the fire could get to me, but I started yelling to the men on the other side to move farther along. I thought that in the noise and confusion they might not realize that mortar fire was being directed at them.

In the middle of my yell a mortar shell dropping vertically, a 5cm I believe, landed about 8 feet in front of me, putting shell fragments in my left cheek, my right wrist, and my right leg at the crotch. I can still hear my rifle clattering to the street as it dropped out of my right hand when it was hit.

It didn't knock me off my feet, but I dropped to the street to check how badly I was hit. I put my left hand up to my cheek and felt quite a hole. At first my big concern was my right hand as blood was pumping out in spurts. Talbert was the first one to me, and my first words were, "Put a tourniquet on that arm." The tourniquet checked the bleeding.

I felt the pain in my crotch, and when I reached down my hand came away bloody. "Talbert, I may be hit bad," I said. He slit my pants leg up with a knife, took a look, and said, "You're okay." What a relief that was. The two shell fragments there had gone into the top of my leg and had missed everything important.

Talbert threw me over his shoulder and carried me into the barn nearby that was being set up as an aid station. There I was bandaged up and given a shot of morphine, which knocked me out completely. When I woke up it was dark. They put me in an ambulance with another man whose shoulder was practically gone. He died on the way to Utah Beach, where I went into a tented field hospital for the rest of the night.

The next morning I was taken on an amphibious truck out to LST 512. Its ramp was down, and when the truck reached it, it drove right up the ramp into the LST, which took me to Southampton, England. From there I was taken to a US Army hospital in England for a six-week stay before rejoining E Company at Aldbourne.

Dad had healed up enough to jump with the company into Holland for Operation Market-Garden.

During the battle of Bastogne, Dad basically became the unofficial leader of Easy Company when it was under the command of first lieutenant Norman Dike, widely considered by the men to lack strong leadership qualities.

In Hagenau, Dad was wounded again, this time in his neck and cheek by a mortar shell. He went to the aid station, got patched up, and rejoined his unit the same day. A day after that, Winters awarded him a battlefield commission to second lieutenant. Dad talked to us about that. Of his whole life, I know that that was his proudest moment.

Dad continued on to the end of the war with Easy Company. In Berchtesgaden, Dad became acquainted with Ferdinand Porsche, the famed Austro-Hungarian automotive engineer who created the Volkswagen Beetle and many of the Porsche automobiles as well as having designed several of the German tanks. He was in a POW camp nearby. Porsche could speak English, and they sometimes ate meals together.

We met a bunch of the guys over the years, Winters, Guth, Walter Gordon, the machine gunner—he was my dad's best friend.

A Lot of Drive

I think my father adjusted to life after the war okay. It didn't seem to bother him much. He saw his life as being more than a paratrooper. He had a lot of drive.

Dad attended Huntington College in West Virginia on the GI Bill, majoring in physics and minoring in industrial engineering. He started college before the war, stopped, then finished afterward, stopping for a while for financial reasons when my brother Cliff was born. Three sons were eventually born: Cliff in '46, Tom in '48, and me, born in 1950. I think my oldest brother was born nine months to the day after my father returned from overseas. Dad was the first in his family to finish university. He remained a great believer in higher education, and instilled in my brothers and me the importance of a good education.

Dad's first career job was as an industrial engineer with Owens Illinois, a Fortune 500 company that makes glass container products. He stayed there for thirty years, maybe thirty-five, and rose to the rank of vice president of the International division, back when a title like that actually meant something.

Even though he was really busy with his job, he took the time to be a family man. He was my baseball coach for a couple of years. We played golf together, Dad and I and my brother Tom. Dad went to work early in the morning, then came home from work; we ate dinner as a family, then he spread out his work on the table and worked well into the night, reading reports and doing homework for the company. This instilled a good work ethic into us as kids.

He had both a wood shop and a metal shop in his basement. His hobbies were myriad, but he loved to do metal finishing and woodworking. He made furniture and machine parts. He liked anything mechanical. When he was in his early eighties, he rebuilt a player piano just for fun. The dining room furniture that's still in the family today was my great-grandparents' furniture that my father refinished. It's gorgeous stuff.

My father's job took us a lot of places. The family moved to Spain in '66. Cliff was already out of the house by then. Tom had just graduated from high school, so he spent just a summer there, then went back to the States to go to college. I had two years of high school to go. My parents spent seven years there, then moved to London for several years, then to South Africa for several months on loan to a company down there, then to Geneva, and spent the last twelve years of his career living there in Switzerland. Essentially, his job was to sell American glass-container technical assistance to European companies. So he travelled all over Europe and North Africa visiting companies that Owens Illinois had contracts with.

My mother was a housewife, raised us boys, and volunteered with the Red Cross. Sadly, she died in 1975, very young, at age fifty, of a heart attack. My mom kept everyone together. My parents were living in Switzerland when my mom died, and my brothers and I were living in various places in the States. Keeping everyone together after that was not my dad's forte.

Dad remarried in 1976. His second wife's name was Marie Hope Mahoney. When Dad retired in 1983, they settled in Toledo, Ohio, and later in Southern Pines, North Carolina.

The Elephant's Typewriter

We knew Dad had a lung ailment and had studied up on it. I think, in his case, it came from the environment he worked in all those years. He had spent a lot of time around the glass bottle machines where there are particles of hot molten glass in the air. I think that damaged his lungs.

I had blown my ACL out from playing softball and had surgery to repair it. I was well on my way to recovery, but then I was carrying something downstairs to the basement, missed the bottom step, fell and broke my kneecap in half. That happened two weeks before Dad died of pulmonary fibrosis in 2001. I was laid out and unfortunately wasn't able to attend his funeral. I really missed being able to do that, but it couldn't be avoided.

What are some of my favorite memories of my dad?

Sure, he ran the household like he ran a platoon. As a kid you definitely wanted to stay in line. If my brothers or I got called out on the carpet for anything, and if we replied to any question, "Yes, Dad," he would correct us with, "Yes, Dad, sir." He was definitely the boss.

But he definitely could be a lot of fun, too. He told us stories about cowboys, about a horse named "Old Paint," from back in his cowboy days, and another story he made up called "The Little Boy Who Didn't Like Ice Cream." This story always included the world's smartest elephant, who traveled around the jungle with a huge typewriter carried around by "coolies." (Obviously the term "coolies" is not politically correct now, but things were different back then, and that's the word Dad always used to refer to manual laborers from Asia.) People continually came up to this elephant and asked him yes or no questions. The bearers sprung into action and assembled a huge typewriter, and the elephant would type out his one word reply. Y-E-S or N-O. Then they disassembled the typewriter and continued their wild trek through the jungle. The story went on and on. We absolutely loved it. I should mention that the typewriter was a complete keyboard, despite that every question could be answered yes or no. We used to point out that this elephant did not even need a typewriter, he could just stomp a foot once for yes and twice for no, for instance. But then the whole story would have lost its appeal, Dad said with a grin.

That's how I'd want people to remember my father, C. Carwood Lipton: A strong, capable leader who had a great sense of humor. He could really keep us all in stitches. I wish he was still with us today.

20

RON SPEIRS

Interview with Marv Bethea, stepson

My stepfather, Lieutenant Ronald Speirs, was the stuff of legends. His nicknames included "Sparky," "Bloody," and "Killer." The stories abound: he shot one of his own sergeants between the eyes for getting drunk; he peaceably handed out cigarettes to twenty German prisoners, then mowed them down with his submachine gun; he sprinted crosstown through a veritable shooting gallery at Foy—the Germans didn't even shoot at him at first because they couldn't believe what they were seeing. The really astounding story at Foy is that after he hooked up with I Company on the other side of town, now under heavy fire, he sprinted back.

Are the legends true?

The facts that have emerged in later years hopefully speak louder than the rumors. Ron led the attack and destroyed the fourth and final German artillery piece at Brécourt Manor during the Normandy invasion. Later, with Easy Company wrongly positioned and staying put as sitting ducks behind a haystack during the attack on Foy, Lieutenant Speirs was ordered to relieve Lieutenant Norman Dike of his command. Speirs, then the commander of Dog Company, ran to Dike, blurted out, "I'm taking over," and Easy Company surged into Foy and took the town. Ron continued as the leader of Easy Company through the end of the war and ended up being company commander longer than any of his predecessors, including Dick Winters.

Of all the accounts and explanations surrounding the stories, one thing is clear about Ron: he took his responsibilities very seriously and cared deeply about the welfare of the men with whom he served. This is evidenced in the well-documented and eyewitness reports of his service during WWII.

Personally, we know there was more to Ron's life than what we read about in Stephen Ambrose's book or see in the HBO miniseries. What follows is the story of the real Ronald Speirs as we knew him.

How I Knew Him

After my biological father died in 1984, my mother, Elsie, met Ron Speirs at a singles' square dance. I lived in Montana at the time, and Mom lived in California. Mom and Ron were married in November 1987 and stayed together until he died in 2007, so they had twenty good years together.

I didn't meet Ron until the wedding. Mom said she didn't even know he had been in the military until they had been dating for several weeks—Ron just didn't talk about it much.

After they were married, we did not live geographically close, so I didn't get much of a chance to know Ron until several years later when he and Mom started spending more time here in Montana. I've got a brother and sister and they all have kids. I'm remarried, and my wife and I have six kids between us, so there was always a bunch of children running around. I can't overemphasize what a fantastic grandfather and great-grandfather Ron became to all our children. They'd tug on him, wanting him to take them on walks, and he was always patient and went out of his way to do whatever he could for them. Ron became grandpa to the whole crew, and he lived that role very well. It's funny how having grandkids can really bring out the best in people.

Although our family was aware that Ron had received some medals and had quite an extensive military career, we had little knowledge of the details. We accepted his explanation of a failing memory. Throughout his extensive career in the military, he had spent time in Korea, Spandau prison, Southeast Asia, and the Pentagon, and his memories tended to blend together toward the end. For some time, we understood and honored the possibility that many of his experiences during WWII were buried forever in his subconscious.

Although aware of the book *Band of Brothers*, our family did not pay much attention to the HBO production until Ron and Mom travelled to France for the premiere in June 2001. I had read parts of the book previously and remember being concerned about how Ron was portrayed and about how some of his alleged actions would be interpreted and portrayed in the series. When asked how he felt about this concern, Ron replied, "I'm eighty-one years old, what can they do to me now?"

He wouldn't have gone to that big shindig in France, except that Mom told him she was going to go whether he went or not. A tremendous photograph is often seen on WWII forums online of him and Dick Winters embracing with their yellow jackets on—that's the first time they had seen each other in more than fifty-five years since the war. The shot was captured at this event in France.

After the HBO premiere, Ron seemed to be more open to sharing some of his recollections. Shortly after Mom and Ron returned, our oldest daughter's wedding was held, and her new brother-in-law was soon heading out to West Point as a new cadet. The brother-in-law was very interested in meeting Ron, so Ron agreed to visit with him. I asked if I could tape the discussion, and Ron hesitantly agreed. During this one-hour conversation, I learned more about Ron's career than I had in the previous fourteen years. He seemed willing to share with this young man, about to embark on a military career, some of the details of his experiences, even ones we previously thought were lost to a failing memory.

The Life of Ronald Speirs

That said, we don't know much about his earlier years. We know he was born in Scotland on April 20, 1920, the same birth date as Hitler, which he joked about. His father was a Scottish engineer who immigrated to the US with his family during the Great Depression in search of employment. Ron grew up in Boston and took close order drill during high school, attended Citizens Military Training Camps during summer vacations, and graduated from high school in 1938.

He was initially drafted, but deferred involvement for two months to finish extension courses, then went into active duty at Camp Shelby, Mississippi. He volunteered for the Airborne and was sent to Camp Toccoa and soon became a platoon leader for D Company.

While the regiment was stationed in England just prior to the Normandy invasion, Ron was sent to Winchester to set up a camp for an infantry division coming from Africa. There, he met an English widow, a member of the Auxiliary Territorial Service, the women's branch of the British army. They married and had a son together, or perhaps vice versa. Several places in the miniseries he's shown looting German silverware and valuables to send back for his wife and baby.

The woman's husband had been reported dead. Actually, he had been in a POW camp and showed up alive toward the end of the war. That obviously put everybody in a very difficult situation. The decision was made for the woman to stay with her first husband. We don't know who made the decision—the woman, Ron, or all of them in conjunction. Ron never talked much about that, though he recognized the boy as his son and kept in contact with him from then onward. We have a letter from Ron to Dick Winters in the early 1990s where he wrote:

My son Robert, born in England during the war, is now an infantry major with the Royal Green Jackets Regiment. His English mother died some years ago. Last summer I visited Robert at his 200-year-old house in England. His three beautiful children are my pride and joy.

Albert Blithe—
he didn't die in 1948 after all.
Courtesy Chris Langlois

Pat Christenson,
resident artist of the Band of Brothers.
Courtesy the Christenson family

Bill Evans (in uniform) surrounded by his loving family,
as evidenced by this photo taken in 1943.
Courtesy Kelly Mears

Tony Garcia (left)
and Les Hashey,
young replacements
in Mourmelon, 1944.
Courtesy the Garcia family

Walter Gordon with his much
beloved twin sister, Cleta,
who died of cancer
as a young adult.
Courtesy the Gordon family

Terrence "Salty" Harris in England just after he was busted to PFC for his part in the Sobel mutiny and kicked out of Easy Company. Note the censored Screaming Eagle Patch on his shoulder.
Courtesy Brady Turner

Hack Hanson in training. He was a lifelong friend of Frank Perconte.
Courtesy the Hanson family

A strong and capable leader, Captain Frederick "Moose" Heyliger.
Courtesy the Heyliger family

First platoon man,
Paul "Frenchy" Lamoureux,
age twenty.
Courtesy Jerry Lamoureux

George Lavenson's dream
was to open a canoeing camp
someday.
*Courtesy Joel Lavenson
and Jake Powers*

[FAR LEFT] C. Carwood Lipton, who received a battlefield commission.
Courtesy Derek Tircuit

[LEFT] Robert Marsh in 1945. He was a married father when he enlisted.
Courtesy Marilyn Tittle

Captain Ron Speirs, a capable leader.
Courtesy the Speirs family

Joe Liebgott (foreground), with Doc Roe and Pat Christenson in Eindhoven.
Courtesy Hans Wesenhajen and Joe Muccia

Patrick O'Keefe, always an excellent family man,
shown after the war with his young son Kevin.
Courtesy the O'Keefe family

Skip Muck—the soldier everybody loved—climbing the ropes in training.
He was later killed in Bastogne.
Courtesy Eileen O'Hara

Newsman George Potter (right) after the war interviewing
a member of the Blue Angels, c. 1959.
Courtesy Daniel Potter

Alex Penkala, a good friend of Skip Muck's,
who was also killed in Bastogne.
Courtesy Rudolph Tatay

A young Bob Rader, who has a bridge named after him in California today.
Courtesy the Rader family

LaVon Reese with his wife, Berniece, and baby daughter, Marcia, in 1948.
LaVon became a school teacher and coach after the war.
Courtesy Marcia Reese Rood

The affable Mike Ranney with his dog Jiggs.
Courtesy Drew Coble Ranney

Four Easy Company members just prior to their first parachute jump:
Ken Baldwin (front); Floyd "Tab" Talbert and LaVon Reese (center);
and Smokey Gordon (back).
Courtesy Robert Talbert

Eugene "Doc" Roe. Note how he
signed the photo to his fiancé.
Courtesy the Roe family

Joe Toye, the toughest man in
Easy Company, shown after the
war with a girlfriend.
Courtesy the Toye family

Robert Van Klinken,
always loved and remembered.
*Courtesy the Van Klinken family
and Joe Muccia*

Gordy and Toni Carson on their
wedding day in Kaprun, Austria.
She is wearing his jump wings
as a broach.
Courtesy the Carson family

"Mortar and Artillery Fire,"
pencil sketch
by Pat Christenson.
Courtesy the Christenson family

Self-portrait of Pat Christenson,
copied from a photograph taken
before the last practice jump.
The next jump was D-Day.
Courtesy the Christenson family

Easy Company in ranks.
Courtesy Susan Finn

Easy Company on the march.
Courtesy Susan Finn

Mike and Julia Ranney with the first three of their daughters,
Kathy, Christine, and Drew, c. 1955.
Courtesy Drew Ranney Coble

Moose Heyliger and his granddaughter, Katie, in fall 2001.
Courtesy the Heyliger family

Fellow Easy Company members who came to the Robert J. Rader Memorial Bridge dedication in 2006. Back row (LEFT TO RIGHT): the Rader family with Don Malarkey, Bill Wingett, and Earl McClung. Middle row (LEFT TO RIGHT): Buck Compton, Shifty Powers, Bill Maynard, and Ed Joint. Front row (LEFT TO RIGHT): Jack McGrath and Rod Bain.   *Courtesy the Rader family*

Tony Garcia in 1959.
Courtesy the Garcia family

Pat O'Keefe and daughter Kris, at the Emmys.
Courtesy the O'Keefe family

Robert Marsh's youngest great-grandchild, Alyssa Piatak,
standing next to his gravestone. The epitaph reads: "Gone But Not Forgotten."
Courtesy Marilyn Tittle

Ron was married several more times throughout his life, although I'm not quite sure how many times before he married my mother. She was his last wife.

We've asked him about the wartime valuables he looted, if his first wife kept them or what exactly was the arrangement, and Ron said, "Well, I don't know where any of that stuff is, because I certainly didn't bring home any of it with me." Yes, he came home with a few smaller souvenirs—a Luger, a few coins, or whatever—but certainly no booty. No one knows what happened to that.

Ron had jumped into Normandy with D Company, where his platoon suffered high causalities. He was wounded in the face and knee by a German potato masher hand grenade, evacuated to a hospital, then rejoined his unit in England just prior to the Holland jump.

In Holland, Ron was the battalion S-2 Intelligence officer for Colonel Robert Strayer. While on reconnaissance, Ron paddled across the Neder Rhine alone at night. The enemy opened fire on him and he dove into the water with a German bullet in his butt. He finished recrossing the river by swimming and was found bleeding and exhausted on the south shore. In spite of his wound, he brought back critical information and later received the Silver Star for that adventure. He was evacuated by hospital train to England for recovery. I remember him talking about that. "Of all the places to get wounded, that was the best place to get shot," he said.

He rejoined the 506th in France just prior to the Battle of the Bulge. He wrote Ambrose a letter about the experience in Bastogne, pragmatically describing being in foxholes with German corpses nearby:

> *There had been an attack through the trees before we arrived and they caught a number of Germans. The bodies were frozen, so there was no stench. I turned one over, an artillery forward observer, and found an excellent pair of binoculars around his neck. The trees in the Ardennes are planted in rows, so in one direction the visibility was good, while in the other direction, there was a blank wall of trees.*
>
> *We had one firefight where a platoon sergeant was killed next to me—not sure if he was in D or E Co. I had just knelt down with Smith*

standing next to me when a German machine gun cut loose. It sprayed directly over my head, catching Smith in the chest. He fell in my arms, but was dead. There was nothing I could do for him.

A letter Ron wrote to Dick Winters in 1998 discussed the same incident:

For some reason I knelt down at the instant the German machine gun opened up, cutting across the chest of my platoon sergeant standing beside me. He fell in my arms without a word, probably feeling nothing. Those are the guys I think about 50 years later—why them and not me?

He wrote Ambrose about a poignant incident that happened in Belgium:

There was German artillery shelling—close enough to make us look for shelter. It was a stone farmhouse and looked pretty solid. To our surprise, when three or four of us got into the cellar, a whole Belgian family was there. They didn't seem too alarmed, so we stayed for perhaps an hour or two. With my poor French, the conversation was limited, but there was a lot of smiling and sharing of American candy and rations with the children. I have often wondered what happened to them.

After the war, Ron stayed in the service. He joined the 187th Airborne Regimental Combat Team in Korea where he commanded a rifle company for the combat parachute jump at Pyongyang, the capital of North Korea.

Later, at Fort Bragg, North Carolina, he served as military secretary to the 18th Airborne Corps Commander Major General Joseph Cleland.

In 1956, Ron attended a Russian language course in Monterey, California, and was assigned to Potsdam, East Germany, as a liaison officer with the Soviet Army. He became the U.S. governor of Spandau Prison in Berlin in 1958. The prison housed Nazi war criminals including Rudolf Hess, Hitler's deputy in the Nazi party.

In 1962, Ron served as a training officer in Laos, Southeast Asia, on a U.S. mission with the Royal Lao Army.

His final assignment in the Army was as a plans officer in the Pentagon. He retired as a lieutenant colonel in 1964.

Ron didn't talk about his experiences in Korea at all. About Berlin, he said very little. He mentioned how he met with Hess almost daily. It sounded to me like they had a mutual respect for each other, enemies of some regard. Other than that, numerous questions remain about his career. What assignments did he carry out in his position of liaison officer to the Russians? What missions was he involved in during his time in Laos? What other assignments was he involved in during his other days of service?

The explanation for why Ron hesitated to discuss these experiences is also now lost, although my guess is that it had to do with a combination of several factors: many of his experiences were quite unpleasant and painful to recall; his strict adherence to orders of confidentiality, even long after his service was completed; and certainly in his later days his memory was fading. He also didn't understand what all the attention was about. As he said many times, he was only doing his job.

Debunking Rumors

Knowing Ron's personality, it wouldn't surprise me if he wasn't liked much by the men who served under him. The veterans have told me he was certainly respected and feared, and a very strong leader. But he could be a real stickler for discipline and following orders, and I think his men probably didn't like him much because of that.

I've mulled over what I know about Ron's personality and put it through the grid of what's known about his wartime experiences. He was tremendously conscientious about doing the right thing. That character trait guided his life more than courage. Ron has been described in battle as fearless, but I have a feeling that, although his actions proved fearless in the end, Ron might have been simply too conscientious to not follow orders. Like the incident of running across Foy and back—I believe his attitude was, "Well, somebody had to do it." Ron couldn't ask anybody else to do it, so he did it himself.

I believe the other trait that drove his wartime experiences was his acceptance that he was going to be killed. He understood he wasn't going to make it out alive, but he was going to go down fighting. He recognized that, for whatever reason, God was watching out for him, and there was no way he was going to make it through unless God was protecting him. I wouldn't say he was a Bible-thumper, but I'm quite sure he considered himself to be a Christian. Mom and Ron went to church.

In the miniseries, it shows Ron (played by Matthew Settle) talking to Albert Blithe, who had hid in a ditch because of fear. Ron says the now infamous quote about how everyone is scared, and that Blithe only hid because he still had hope. He tells Blithe that he needs to function as if he was already dead—the sooner he does, the sooner he can be an effective soldier. We don't know if that was Ron's actual outlook or not, but in a letter he wrote in 1992 to Winters when drafts of the original book were going back and forth, Ron wrote, "Yes, I have the book and have just finished reading it. The memories came flooding back. How did we ever make it through the war? I did not expect to survive."

Regarding the story of Ron shooting his own man for being drunk: we have a copy of a letter Winters wrote to Ambrose in 1993 saying, "The story tellers have glamorized that tale for years." Winters described how the sergeant in question was shot because he twice ignored a command given by Ron to halt an advance toward Ste. Côme-du-Mont. The incident took place under heavy fighting when the men were extremely exhausted. Regimental headquarters had ordered the men to halt because they were planning an extensive artillery attack on the city. The artillery attack was to be gradually adjusted in increments of one hundred yards every four minutes. They wanted the men to follow the attack in. Continuing forward would undoubtedly have endangered many lives. After Ron shot the sergeant, he immediately reported the incident to his company commander, Jerre S. Gross, who was unfortunately killed the next day in the assault on Ste. Côme-du-Mont. Winters wrote:

Was the Sgt. belligerent to the order to halt the advance, or was he drunk/exhausted and not able to comprehend his order to halt the attack and then follow the rolling barrage?

The Sgt. ignored the order and pushed his men forward—Speirs shot him. In doing so he probably saved the lives of the rest of the squad. The squad members at that time were his witnesses.

Speirs does not deny shooting the man, but the reason goes far beyond shooting him just because he was drunk.

From recollections that other veterans have told me, things went even beyond that. This sergeant either drew on Ron, or started to draw on him, so Ron had no choice but to fire his weapon and kill him. This one individual was putting many lives at risk. You have to make a split-second decision, and Ron did.

Regarding the rumor of Ron shooting prisoners on D-day, that story is perhaps the most apocryphal, for no eyewitnesses have ever stepped forward to confirm the event. But how many other incidences like that actually happened? You can imagine that the men jumped right into the middle of hostile territory. Once they caught enemy soldiers, their unofficial orders were to take no prisoners, so what do you do with them? You can't bring them with you because you're in the midst of battle. Do you turn them loose so they can turn around and kill you? I hate to think what I would have done in that situation. My guess is that, if that's what happened, then that's what Ron did—he had a strong commitment to following orders. He thought, somebody's got to do this, and I'm in charge, so I've got to do it.

With Old Friends

How should Ron Speirs be remembered? Toward the end of the war, Ron wrote Forrest Guth a lengthy letter on June 11, 1945, after Guth had won a lottery to be sent home to the States. This to me indicates how much he cared for each of his men individually. It's four pages long, full of chatty news, and doesn't say much other than, "You're not missing anything."

Guth wrote to Ron on June 11, 2006, the exact date sixty-one years later. Arguably the best line from Guth's letter refers to the original letter sent by Ron. "The letter helped me to endure the loneliness of not being with my old friends," wrote Guth.

The last years of Ron's life were extremely difficult, to see this man who had been such a warrior and leader of men deteriorate like he did. I don't know if he was ever formally diagnosed with Alzheimer's, but my biological father died of Alzheimer's, and I'm pretty sure that's what Ron had, too. To see his deterioration was extremely painful for the whole family. We were pretty much on call 24–7 in the last days until he passed.

Ron will be remembered by many people for his actual as well as his rumored deeds during WWII.

To our family, he will simply be remembered as a loving husband, father, stepdad, grandfather, and great-grandfather. We miss him greatly.

PART IV

EASY COMPANY'S FALLEN

THOSE WHO GAVE THEIR LAST FULL MEASURE OF DEVOTION

21

BILL EVANS

Interview with Kelly Mears, great-niece,
With information from Margie Evans Kavanaugh, sister,
Melba Evans, sister-in-law, Stan Evans, nephew,
Ann Evans Biundo and Joan Carroll Varsek, nieces

My great-uncle, William Stanton Evans, wasn't liked very much when he was in the Army. I realize that from what I've read, and also from what's been said about him. Even my grandmother admitted that his personality could be grating at times.

Still, he was family. He was *our* family. And he had people who loved him—namely us. He was the brother of my grandfather, Larry Evans. My dad was born a couple of months after D-day and was named Stanton in his honor.

I never met my great-uncle, as he was gone long before I was born, but I've felt a strange kinship with him over the years. I grew up hearing stories about him, about how he was an accountant who worked at the Houston Ship Channel before the war and could have been deferred from active duty if he had wanted out. My grandmother said he volunteered for the service so his brothers, who had children, might not have to go to war. I knew he was a paratrooper in WWII and was killed on D-day when the plane he was in was shot down, but I never knew that he was part of an elite group of soldiers until the movie *Band of Brothers* came out.

A while back it dawned on me that if I ever wanted to know more about my great-uncle, there was no time to lose. Today's veterans aren't getting any younger. I knew very little about military history, but began looking for information about him in earnest. I talked with family members, pored through pictures and journals, contacted other Easy Company members who knew him, and tracked down various archival documents from courthouses, university records, and the military.

This is what I found.

The Roustabout Accountant

William Stanton Evans was born July 16, 1910, in San Antonio, Texas, the fourth of nine children (six boys and three girls). While the family usually called him Stanton, he preferred to be called Bill, which is how he was known in the Army. I call him Stanton throughout this essay to reflect the name he was most called by family members.

His parents, Thomas (Tim) Evans and Grace Purcell, were Irish Catholics who spent much of their childhoods in Mexico, since both their fathers were construction engineers for railroads being built from Texas into Mexico. His parents met in San Antonio and married in Monterrey, Mexico, in 1905. After they married, the family lived in Mexico City and San Antonio and often traveled between the locations. All the children, including Stanton, were born in San Antonio, except the youngest.

Tim, their father, was well educated and a stern father. His daughter Margie described him as "intellectual, a good speaker, proud of his family, very religious, impatient, and unforgiving." She described her mother as "loving, kind, generous, and patient." Margie was twelve years younger than Stanton and remembers him as a big brother she could go to. "He was handsome, always warm, and encouraged you to do what you wanted to do in life," she said. After high school Margie joined a convent and became a Dominican nun.

Mike Evans, Stanton's nephew, interviewed Stanton's brother, Walter, in the 1980s, who recounted some colorful stories of the Evans family early years:

Around 1914, Tim (the father) moved his family to Mexico City and went to work for a brokerage firm (E.E. Denight) based in Laredo, Texas. His agency represented Dodge, Cadillac, Jefferson, and other automobile companies. All autos sold in Mexico went through this agency. When Americans were forced to leave Mexico during the revolution, he and his family came out on an embassy train. Soldiers came with them on flatbed cars to protect them. During the trip, much fighting occurred. Many times they needed to dive to the floor as bullets came through the train car. Tim took the family back to Texas to live on a ranch in Premont, owned by his sister.

Grace (the mother) often told a story about their life while living in Mexico after the revolution began. It seems that the revolutionaries were hunting down and killing people of the church, especially priests. She and her husband lived in an old adobe house with the high walls and flat roof. Many times they put a ladder up to the roof, hid the priests and children on the roof first, then followed them up, pulling the ladder behind them. It is not known how many priests they hid or for how long, but it is clear that if they had been caught they would have been killed.

Stanton was ten years old in 1920 when the family moved to Houston. By then, his father had been hired to establish the Foreign Trade Department for the Houston Chamber of Commerce. His father eventually served as consul to nine Latin American countries and was instrumental in making Houston a major port. They were one of the first families to settle in the city of Southside Place, an enclave then on the western outskirts, but now close to downtown Houston. Tim was its first mayor, and served three terms.

In Houston, Stanton and his brothers often played at a neighborhood park. It had a big pool, tennis courts, and lots of room for ball games. The family ate dinner together every night, and table manners were stressed. After dinner, dishes, and homework, the children were permitted to relax in the living room with their parents. They were a close-knit family, and remained so even as the children grew up.

The Evans boys were all athletes. Stanton was a skilled diver and swimmer, and taught diving and swimming at the neighborhood pool when he was older. Melba Evans, who married one of Stanton's brothers, remembered the fun times they all had going to dinner, or just staying in, playing cards and shooting the bull.

Stanton and his five brothers all went to St. Thomas, a Catholic high school in Houston, where he was on the football team. I talked to the archivist at St. Thomas, who confirmed that Stanton graduated in 1928. The archivist sent me copies of some of his report cards, and I'd say my great-uncle was not a scholar. He also needed to take summer school to graduate. He and his brother Walter were a year apart in age, but for some reason, they were in the same class at St. Thomas. Stanton's first job as a young man was delivering milk.

Records show a one-year gap between high school graduation and Stanton's enrollment in Texas A&M University, known then as the Agricultural and Mechanical College of Texas. The A&M Office of Admissions and Records confirmed that he attended from July 18, 1929, to June 20, 1930, with a major in petroleum production engineering. I asked them to double-check the major, because it was Stanton's brother Walter who later worked in the petro-chemical industry. They confirmed that Walter's major was liberal arts and that he attended from 1928–1929. I think perhaps the records may have been mixed up somehow, but that's what they sent.

Stanton's attendance at A&M counted as prior military service, giving him the experience to become a first sergeant right after enlisting in 1942.

After college, he worked for Harris County in the purchasing department, where he worked for most of the 1930s. He was listed as such in at least two of the city directories. His sister-in-law, Melba Evans, remembered him later being a CPA for Harris County. She said that when war first broke out, he got a job with the Houston Shipbuilding Company doing accounting work.

Documents from the Harris County District Court show that Stanton married LaVon Ruth Hyett on June 20, 1935, in Houston. She was born January 5, 1915, and lived in the same area of Houston as he did. Her family was listed in the 1930 census in West University, which is the neighborhood next to Southside Place.

Apparently LaVon was not well-liked by the Evans family, but Margie, Stanton's sister, doesn't remember why. We have a family photograph from 1938 that includes Stanton and LaVon together. Stanton and LaVon had no children, and their divorce was finalized on June 11, 1940. I received copies of the divorce papers, and suffice to say, it was pretty messy. I don't think it would serve much purpose to air Stanton's dirty laundry after so many years, and I wouldn't want to hurt any of our or LaVon's family. The Texas Death Index and Social Security Death Index show that LaVon later remarried a man by the last name of Montgomery. She died August 15, 1987, in Houston.

My dad mentioned that Stanton was considered something of a "roustabout," and often got into fights at bars. Stanton's brother Walter recounted to his daughter, Ann, that if you went to a bar and a fight broke out, go look for Stanton and get him out, because he probably started it. Stanton's dental records note that he was missing eight teeth on the left side of his face, which might make sense if he was in a lot of fights with right-handed guys.

Plane 66

My grandmother, Melba Evans, and Stanton's niece, Mary Carroll Rigoni (whose sixteenth birthday was on D-day), both confirmed that Stanton decided to join the Army because his younger brothers had joined, and he wasn't going to stay home while they were fighting in the war. He was working for the Todd Houston Shipbuilding Corporation (its proper name) in 1941–1942, and was eligible for a deferment from military service, since they were building Liberty ships, vital to the war effort. He was older when he enlisted—thirty-two.

Melba added that Stanton also volunteered for the Army because he was single and didn't want his brothers who had children to be among those drafted. She said he was a brilliant man and very partial to his nieces and nephews. She called him "a tough little guy." (The Evans boys were all kind of short; Stanton's enlistment record lists him as five-foot-seven). Melba said that he looked forward to finishing his Army service and going back to work at the Harris County courthouse and a normal life.

His sister Margie noted that before being shipped out Stanton made a point of visiting everyone in his family, including his sister Genevieve and her family in Illinois. Margie said the visits were very important to him. Genevieve's daughter, Mary, said that they have old home movies of that visit. When Stanton arrived, he was all taped up from a recent bar-room brawl. She remembers him watering the cabbage in their victory garden with his drink.

Stephen Ambrose writes about how Sergeant William Stanton Evans was one of the first NCOs to come up through the ranks while the men were still training at Camp Toccoa. You had to be tough and a capable leader to make it as an NCO, so I know my great-uncle had a lot of the right stuff in him. He was considered a favorite of the controversial Captain Herbert Sobel, which might have made the men not like him much, and Ambrose notes that "Sobel and Evans played men off against one another, granting a privilege here, denying one there."[1] Once, Sobel and my great-uncle snuck through the company of men as they slept, stealing their rifles to teach them a lesson. They called the company together the next morning, but to their great embarrassment, they had gotten lost and collected rifles from Fox Company instead. Another time, he and Sobel inspected the barracks, looking for contraband, which didn't help make friends. My great-uncle refused to participate in the NCO mutiny against Sobel.

Some men from the company apparently did like and respect him. Winters writes how Sergeant Leo Boyle married a girl while in Aldbourne, and my great-uncle served as his best man.[2] Marci Carson wrote to say she found my great-uncle's name in the journal of her father-in-law, Sergeant Gordon Carson, listed as one of his buddies.

---

1. Ambrose, *Band of Brothers*, 24.
2. Winters with Kingseed, *Beyond Band of Brothers*, 119.

On D-day, Stanton flew to Normandy in a plane with the rest of the company headquarters men, including Thomas Meehan, then the Easy Company commander. It was the lead plane. Winters notes that the plane was hit with antiaircraft fire near the drop zone. Bullets came up through the plane's undersides and threw sparks out the top. After being hit, the plane's landing lights came on, as if it was going to land, then it did a slow wingover to the right as it approached the ground. It appeared they were going to make it, but then the plane hit a hedgerow and exploded, killing everybody on board.[3]

Easy Company member Pat Christenson wrote about the experience in his journal:

D-Day, June 6, 1944. Company E Headquarters plane was carrying a lot of explosives and when hit by antiaircraft fire a chain reaction may have taken place causing the plane to disintegrate killing everyone in the airplane. The airplane was piloted by Harold A. Cappelluto, its identification No. 66.

Forty-four years later the dog tags of 1st Sergeant William Evans and PFC William T. McGonigal were found in Normandy, France, by a farmer.

Family members don't remember the specifics of when or how the family was notified about the plane crash, but the news came as a shock. My grandmother, Melba, Stanton's sister-in-law, was pregnant at the time, and when they heard the news, it was so upsetting that she went into labor prematurely. Fortunately, the contractions stopped, and her baby, my dad, was born a few months later. He was the one named in honor of his uncle. Records show that the family was notified that Stanton was missing in action soon after D-day, and a telegram confirming his death arrived on November 11, 1944.

Margie said that, of the three Evans sons in the service, their mother feared the most for Stanton, in part because being a paratrooper was so new back then. Margie said her father took his son's death hard, but that

---

3. Ibid., 78–79.

his mother took it really bad. His mother kept thinking her son was still alive someplace and would turn up again one day. It took her years to accept his death.

I received Stanton's Army Individual Deceased Personnel File and it mentioned only that his personal effects were returned. His effects consisted of an envelope with letters, photographs, and a billfold. The rest of the file consisted of dental records and numerous correspondences back and forth between Stanton's father and the Army about the return of his remains. Apparently, Army regulations stipulated that all bodies involved in group burials be returned to the U.S. and buried in whichever National Cemetery was most central to all the families involved. Since the plane held soldiers from all over the country, the bodies from Plane 66 were buried in St. Louis, considered a central location of the United States.

To Help His Men

How would I want people to remember him?

I asked this question of my grandmother and Stanton's sister. Melba said simply that he was a good guy and was always willing to help anybody.

Margie, his sister, said she would want people to know that she loved him very much, and that he was someone who really wanted to serve his country and do the right thing. She said he was probably mean as hell, but was that way only to help his men.

Sergeant William Stanton Evans was my great-uncle, a cherished part of our family. I wish I had known him. I thank him for his role in preserving our freedom.

22

TERRENCE "SALTY" HARRIS

Interview with Brady Turner, nephew

I never met my uncle. Growing up, we always knew that my mom, Annette Harris Turner, had a brother in WWII, that he was a paratrooper, and that he was killed in Normandy. For years, that's about all I ever knew about Terrence "Salty" Harris.

After my mom passed away, I thought, "Well shoot, it's a shame if I never find out more information about my uncle." So I started to search for his name. It's about all I had to go on at first. His name led me to information about the Colville American Cemetery and Memorial in Normandy. It listed his unit. I sent an e-mail to Tom Potter, son of George Potter, one of the original Band of Brothers, and information started pouring in. It was jaw-dropping. Letters and e-mails and notes came back, parts of journals and diaries. I live in Alaska and traveled down to California to poke around in my parents' old cedar chest. My uncle had also grown up in Santa Monica. I found this old photo album I had never seen before. It had pictures of Mom at UC-Berkeley, where she attended in the war years, of her brother in a paratrooper uniform, and of him in Europe. There were letters, too, which provided a wealth of information. I ended up flying out to the Atlanta Easy Company reunion. A few of the vets brought photos of Salty Harris that they passed around.

This is what I found out about my uncle's life:

The Sobel Mutiny

My uncle had been in Annapolis, the United States Naval Academy, prior to the Army, but resigned from Annapolis under the pressure of accumulated demerits. Starting off as a Navy man is how he got the nickname Salty.

After the Naval Academy, he was refused admission to the Air Force and flight training because of his Annapolis record. He made several trips to Australia as a merchant seaman before enlisting in the army and volunteering for parachute duty.

As a paratrooper, he was one of the original Toccoa men. When they were first putting Easy Company together, my uncle was a private, then quickly became one of their earliest staff sergeants. He was a noncom in the 3rd Platoon and was known as a good sergeant.

He ran his platoon in the army on naval terms—he told his men to go "starboard" instead of right, or to "swab the deck" instead of "mop the floors." Apparently he was quite a character. Shifty Powers told me that they used to ship these guys by railroad to a training area, and Salty got incredible joy out of tormenting his men by repeatedly singing Navy songs. I'm not sure what the songs were, but apparently he sung them over and over until the men were all sick of them.

The big story about Salty is how he was one of the instigators in leading the mutiny against company commander Captain Herbert Sobel. Mike Ranney was one of Salty's closest friends and also involved in the mutiny. In his journal, Ranney describes Salty as "a broad-faced delightful Irishman with whom I had many adventures." Ranney also writes extensively about the mutiny:

> Salty Harris and I had been concerned for some time about the capabilities of Captain Sobel, the Black Swan. He was a well-meaning man, but not quite the sort to instill much confidence about combat. Naïve innocents that

we were, Salty and I organized a mutiny. Essentially, we got all the non-commissioned officers to threaten to resign unless Sobel was removed. The only exception in our ranks was the first sergeant, [Bill] Evans. Several of the company's officers were aware of the plan and gave tacit, if not overt, approval. In fact, Lt. Dick Winters, our company executive officer, sat in on our final planning meeting. I was in charge.

The next morning, Salty and I were arrested by military police and taken under guard to the regimental headquarters. Colonel Sink outlined the situation tersely and succinctly:

> "I don't know who in the hell you two bastards think you are, but you obviously don't realize the seriousness of the situation you have created. I could have you shot for mutiny in a war zone. But this regiment is going into combat and I don't want any disturbances just now. Plus, you both have had good records and we may be able to salvage something of the investment we have in your training. So I'm just going to bust both of you in the rank of private, transfer you out of Easy Company in separate directions, and keep an eye on you so that you can't cause any more problems."

Salty was transferred to A Company in the First Battalion. I went to I Company in the Third Battalion. We were separated immediately and not permitted to return to the Easy Company area to get our bags, which caught up with us a few days later.

Ranney explains how, after the transfer, he was recruited by Lieutenant Walter Moore for special assignment. Lieutenant Moore had been the men's platoon commander right at the start of training in Toccoa. Ranney agreed to the assignment and was shipped to special duty to an airbase near Nottingham, where he reconnected with my uncle. There, Moore explained the assignment more fully. Ranney continues:

The airborne command had decided that existing navigation systems weren't entirely adequate to assure that airborne parachute units could be landed in the right spots. We were going to invade France and probably jump at night. Our special group was to jump slightly ahead of the rest of the airborne units, put up special navigational aids (electronic homing beacons), so that the planes carrying the main body of troops could hone in on those beacons. The task was considered essential to the success of the invasion. We were called Pathfinders. And, oh yes, Salty was already there along with Carl Fenstermaker and Dick Wright of Easy Company. I headed for the barracks to see Salty. We were together again.

There were about 80 men and officers in the Pathfinder group from throughout the 101st division. Most were malcontents or busted non-coms. [Charlie] Malley [from F Company], ended up as first sergeant of the detachment, Salty as leader of a sub-unit, and I became supply sergeant.

Ranney was later able to transfer back into Easy Company before the Normandy jump, but my uncle stayed with the pathfinders for D-day. Being a pathfinder was not an easy job. It meant being out in front of the pack and facing most of the German army head-on and alone, thus being in a dangerous and costly position. When he jumped as a pathfinder, it wasn't just security detail either, or setting up lights on the ground. Along with Holophane lights and brightly colored panels to help guide in the vast armadas of C-47s carrying paratroopers and gliders to their drop zones, one pathfinder in each stick also carried radar transmitters called Eureka beacons, top-secret technology back then, that were to be guarded at all cost. A radio receiver in the aircraft honed in on the beacon on the ground. Only one guy in each stick jumped with a beacon, and in his stick, that was entrusted to Salty Harris. So he was an important guy. I got that information from the Ranney family, and it's also listed in a book by George Koskimaki.

Killed Instantly

My uncle's gravestone in Europe reads that he was killed June 18, 1944. But that is probably a little late. The battle for Carentan happened between the tenth and fourteenth of June. Burr Smith and Mike Ranney both indicate in letters that my uncle was killed in the same action in which he was wounded, which would have placed his death slightly earlier than recorded.

Ranney writes to my mother on July 25, 1944:

Dear Annette:

. . . You've probably gotten by now a crudely written letter concerning Salty. You see, Annette, I guess I liked him better than I ever have anyone else—he was that kind of a guy. He was the sort of a leader whose men would do anything for him. I'm not, and because of that I guess I make him my example. I tried to do as he did. And I'm trying now.

. . . If he could have known what was ahead, he'd have asked that you take it in stride and go on just the same. Maybe all this sounds strange to you, but I think that's what he'd want. Annette, there's a bunch of guys in this company who feel as you do—"it just doesn't seem possible he's really gone," but it won't stop them from doing their job, don't let it stop you.

Ranney writes my mom again, a short time later, apparently after receiving a letter back from her:

Dear Annette:

. . . I found out all possible information.

Salty was killed instantly by a sniper within our lines during the fighting near Carentan in Normandy. I'm sorry I haven't been able as yet to find out where he's buried. As soon as I do, I'll let you know. At the time, he was with [a different] company—so I wasn't with him.

. . . Take this the way he would want you to, Annette. He believed in a fate—most of us do now—the kind of fate that has little regard for race, color, or creed. If he could have known what was in store, it wouldn't have changed his actions. It came the way he'd want it to—he didn't suffer.

Burr Smith writes to my mother on September 7, 1944, from a field hospital in England. This is one of the letters I found in my parents' trunk. Burr's letter is written on that really thin paper they used back then.

Dear Annette,

I don't know if Salty ever mentioned me in his letters to you or not, but I've been his friend for nearly two years, ever since the first day at Toccoa. At any rate, I feel that I should drop you a line to let you know how sorry I am. . . . If it was in my power to do so, I'd have taken his place, and I say that in all sincerity. I was wounded the same day he was hit, and I didn't know [he was dead] until I was released from the hospital. You'll never know how I felt when Red Wright told me.

The last time I saw T.C. he came trudging down a dusty lane—all smiles—and I was so glad to see him that I cried—actually cried with relief to see him. I thought he was gone D-Day, and to see him was heaven on earth.

. . . I hope I haven't made you feel worse. We all miss him like mad. [He was] one of the grandest people God ever placed on this rotten earth. . . . The only course open is to pledge myself to the cause of making sure that the things he died for are not forgotten.

There's a picture that's circulated on the Internet that shows fellow E Company veteran Forrest Guth visiting my uncle's grave over in Europe. Paul Woodage, who runs a company called Battlebus that tours the D-day beaches and battlefields of Normandy, accompanied fellow E/506th veteran Paul Rogers to Salty's grave in 2007 and notes that both Rogers and Guth shed a few tears over their lost friend. For me, to see the emotional effect of visiting a friend killed six decades earlier is moving beyond words. These men truly were a Band of Brothers.

23

GEORGE LAVENSON

Interview with Joel Lavenson, nephew

I am the oldest living relative of George Lavenson. I never met my uncle, and my parents and grandparents rarely spoke of him when I was growing up. But I knew of his existence when I was a boy, and in the years that have followed, our lives have connected in some highly unusual ways. It chokes me up today: it's such a passion for me now to talk about his life. My uncle never had any children of his own, and I feel like I'm the only one to carry on for him. He was being forgotten, and I had to go find out about him because I didn't want him to be forgotten anymore.

A Tree Struck by Lightning

Growing up, I had what I'd call several "brushes" with my uncle's life. There were occasional traces of conversation, little tokens of remembrance in our houses, that pointed to who he was.

I was the oldest boy in our family, and every once in a while my grandmother slipped and called me George by mistake. I didn't really get it.

I was a kid in the 1950s, and once as a Thanksgiving present my grandmother gave me some brown combat boots. I really liked them and was fascinated by them, but there was never a story attached to them that she told me about, or an explanation of why she got them for me. I felt like a soldier whenever I wore them.

In a hall closet, my grandmother kept her son's soft cap with the blue and white patch from the Airborne, and from time to time as a young boy I snuck in and wore it. I didn't know why I was fascinated with it, but I always was.

My grandfather had taken up painting after the Second World War, and he had painted my uncle twice: once in portraiture, and once symbolically in a picture that showed a lightning bolt hitting a grove of trees and striking one down, leaving the rest of the grove of trees standing. There was never any specific talk about the painting, but each of the trees represented a member of their family, I knew that much. There were two big trees that remained, the parents, then two little trees left, his two brothers, then one tree was being struck by lightning. I was always curious about that painting, and what the story was behind the tree struck by lightning.

My dad spoke occasionally about his brother. Even then, very few details emerged. He described him as a blue-eyed, handsome fellow, very well liked, very physically strong. My father was a wrestler, a lieutenant, and could certainly hold his own in a fight against most men. But when his brother got back from training with Easy Company, George quipped, "I don't think you want to wrestle me now."

"What do you mean?" my father asked.

My uncle snatched my father's lieutenant's bars off his shoulder and squashed them with his fingers. "That's how I'm going to treat you if you wrestle me," my uncle said.

My father told that story with great pride. His brother was a paratrooper, the best of the best.

Those were about my only brushes with my uncle until I was a grownup. Until recent years I never understood why they never spoke more about him. Now I know it was just too hard, too devastating. In 1985

I bought this summer camp in Maine. Camp Kennebec, it's called. Little did I know that owning this camp would change everything I knew about my uncle.

A Name on a List

For many years my father had worked for his father's business, which had been his grandfather's business, the Lavenson Bureau of Advertising. After that my father became the president of the Plaza Hotel in New York City. Then he owned one of the top fifty resorts in the world in Montecito, California, called the San Ysidro Ranch. John and Jacqueline Kennedy honeymooned there, and Churchill wrote his memoirs there. As a result of my dad's influence, I worked in the hospitality industry for many years.

I had another career influence as well. For many years my grandmother owned a children's camp in Maine. In fact, Millie Strayer, the wife of Colonel Robert Strayer, (2nd Battalion commander) was a nurse who worked for my grandmother at the camp during the war. So I had grown up learning the insides of the camp business. I loved it and always wanted to go into it as a career. After I had worked in the hospitality industry, I knew it was time. I searched all over New England and stumbled on Camp Kennebec. It wasn't the camp my grandmother had run, just another camp in the area. The camp was going through a hard time, almost empty, and available for sale. So I bought it and switched careers.

Here I was trying to resurrect this thing, and during my very first summer running it, early in the summer's activities—July 4, 1985, in fact—I was charged with the responsibility of reading the names of all the young men who went to Kennebec as campers who had died in the wars. It was an annual tradition. On Independence Day all the campers gathered in a place on the grounds called the Belltower Circle, and the director read the names in tribute. No one ever went into this ceremonial area except this one time each year.

So this very first summer I'm listening to myself speak the names of all these young men, and all of a sudden I come to a familiar name: George Lavenson. It was unmistakable. The realization hit me like a load of bricks. My uncle had gone to this very same camp when he was a kid—the camp I had just bought—and I didn't even know it. All these boys for years had been hearing his name read to them in honor. My family couldn't even speak his name out loud because of their grief. I saw my uncle's name on the page and couldn't continue. Right there, I started to cry. It was more than I could take. The ceremony ended early. Immediately I went to my office and phoned my father.

"Dad!" I said. "Did you know that Uncle George went to Camp Kennebec?"

"Yes," he said. "I went there with him when we were boys."

"How come you never told me this, particularly when I just bought the place?"

There was a silence on the phone. Some habits are hard to break.

"My brother was my best friend, you know . . . ," he said at last. Dad still couldn't talk about his brother in any detail, even so many years later.

Little by little, the story came out. Kennebec had been started in 1907. My grandfather had helped out at the camp in the 1920s, then my dad and uncles went there as campers in the 1930s. I searched around and found pictures of my uncle in the camp's yearbooks. His favorite activity was canoeing. He had been voted "best athlete" and "best looking." The camp was a traditional, old-time, rough-and-tumble, teach-people-how-to-be-resourceful-in-the-outdoors type of camp. The kids learned a lot of outdoor and survival skills. My father and uncle loved the place and it made many special memories for them growing up.

Here's the other twist to the story. As I talked with my father, he said that he and his two brothers had decided to run the place one day as a canoe camp. Not only was this a camp they had gone to as kids, this was the very same camp they had dreamed of owning one day.

I had bought the very camp that they wanted! I was living my uncle's dream!

To Whom Do I Owe Thanks?

From that moment on, I started doing everything I could to find out more about my uncle. I wanted to know as much as I could.

My uncle, George Lavenson, was born in Pennsylvania, graduated high school, and went to Haverford College in Philadelphia where he studied journalism. Before he enlisted he worked as a newspaper reporter in Philadelphia. All the family lived near each other not far from my father's farm. They were very close.

As young men, my uncle and my father both considered themselves pacifists. When war broke out, they initially talked about going off and holing up somewhere in the backwoods of Maine until the war was over. They figured they could come back then and start their camp—what they really wanted to do. But the tone in the country then was one of strong patriotism, and my father and uncle realized they needed to protect their country. It had been attacked, after all, and if they didn't step up, who was going to? They enlisted.

They both went to Officers Candidate School (OCS). My uncle heard about a new elite outfit, the paratroopers, and volunteered. He proved a capable, qualified soldier. He was one of the original Toccoa men. Winters notes, "Senior commanders only assign the most talented officers to headquarters staffs. Colonel Sink and Major Strayer were no exception," and within the first eight months of the company's existence, my uncle, along with Lieutenants Matheson, Nixon, and Hester, were all assigned to 2d Battalion staff.[1] There, my uncle became the battalion adjutant, a staff officer who assists the commanding officer in issuing orders. It meant he was often near the battle front.

Information trickled in over the years. Then, in the early 1990s, the book *Band of Brothers* came out. My father got a copy and gave it to me. I read it from cover to cover. It contained accounts of my uncle's life and death and added more fuel to my fire. My hobby turned into an obsession,

---

1. Winters with Kingseed, *Beyond Band of Brothers*, 27.

and I called all the people who knew about my uncle, including Stephen Ambrose. I couldn't even find a number for Ambrose, only a fax number, so I sent him a fax about my uncle, and he was kind enough to call me back right away. I had collected some stories about my uncle by then, and we both shared information. The story I told Stephen Ambrose made him gasp.

When my uncle first went to volunteer for the paratroopers, the waiting room was filled with soldiers all hoping to get in. The recruiter went through his list, then told the men, "It's all filled up this month, come back next month." Next month when my uncle came back, the captain again looked through his list and said to my uncle, "Sorry, you can't join. You're a Jew."

"What of it?" my uncle said.

"You can't be in this outfit," the recruiter, a captain, said. "Jews don't have enough guts."

My uncle was furious, grabbed the recruiter from behind his desk, punched him, and knocked him down. He was immediately called into the general's office. The general really ripped him up and down and said, "Don't you realize that you can be put in Leavenworth for the duration of the war, and even worse, for striking a superior officer during wartime? If you had been on the battlefield, you'd be shot!"

My uncle didn't say anything. The general calmed down and added, "Privately, I admire what you did, so I'm approving your papers, and I'm sending the captain off to be reassigned someplace else."

Ambrose was actually crying after I told him this. "My God," he said. "Fighting his way to get in—this is the kind of people we had back then!"

The original story was told by newsman Walter Winchell on his Sunday night radio broadcast. A Philadelphia area women's group picked up the story and decided to honor my grandmother for her son, who had the courage to fight his way into the outfit.

It was good to talk with Ambrose. I asked him why I was so obsessed with finding out information about my uncle. Was it just me, or did others feel the same way?

"We're all this way to one degree or another," Ambrose said. "It's a staggering thing to find out the last words, the last thoughts, the last breath, of someone who's disappeared so far away in combat. Of course you're going to wonder about your uncle. All men ultimately want to know two things—'To whom do I owe thanks that I should live in such opportunity?' And, 'Will I have the courage when the time comes?' Knowing about your uncle helps you answer those two questions."

On the Plane Home

The heart-wrenching story about my uncle is that he actually survived being shot in combat. After he was wounded, he was all set to return to the States and pick up with his wife where they left off.

He had met his wife, Joanne, when the men marched from Toccoa to Fort Benning, Georgia. She was stationed in Atlanta as part of the Red Cross. Her job was to welcome the troops when they arrived in the city. He met her there at the end of the hike, and they fell in love.

Herbert Sobel was my uncle's best man. I don't know what type of relationship he had with Sobel, but evidently it was good enough. Sobel gave them a forty-eight-hour leave. My uncle and his new wife were together for two weeks. Then he was shipped overseas.

I've spoken with my uncle's widow. She resented my grandmother for not allowing her the possibility of having any children with George. My grandmother convinced her to use birth control. They were only married for two weeks before he left, but at least it would have been possible for them to have conceived. She later remarried.

My uncle was shot just outside Carentan in the early morning of June 12, 1944, immediately prior to Easy Company attacking the town. The men were taking a break, and my uncle went to relieve himself. Colonel Strayer noted that George was out of position. A colonel observes the attack, and my uncle should have been next to the colonel, far away, observing the battle. But George apparently wanted to be as close to his buddies in Easy Company as he could. He was taking a crap in a field between E Company and F Company when a German sniper shot him in the butt. Ambrose notes the hour, that my uncle was hit just before six a.m., and the whereabouts, a field near the last one hundred or so meters of the road by the T junction leading into Carentan.[2]

My uncle was taken to England to recuperate. He was going to live, but evidently it was a serious enough wound that his fighting days were over. Then, flying back to Bangor, Maine, the Red Cross hospital plane he and twenty-one others were on was shot down, somewhere off the coast of Nova Scotia. You can imagine the emotions my family went through—hearing that he's been shot, which was a shock enough, but also a relief that he's still alive, then not being able to visit him when he's in the hospital in Europe, then the joy at hearing he's coming home, then the horror that his plane is lost over the Atlantic on the way home. It's like he was lost twice.

Newspaper articles describe the exhaustive search for the plane that followed. The wreckage was never found. It was the only Red Cross plane lost during the war. Authorities believe the plane was shot down by a German U-boat. Eventually it was discovered that a U-boat in that area had a habit of sending SOS signals. Planes would fly down low to see if they could help, then the U-boat would shoot them out of the sky. The date of my uncle's death is listed as July 26, 1944. There was a memorial service held for him back in America.

Living on Through Freedom

In 1994, the 50th anniversary of D-day was being held in Normandy, and a big spread was featured in the *Boston Globe* that showed where all the allied troops had landed. I saw the spread, and it was like a light bulb went off for me.

Right away I went to my father and said, "Let's go find the place!" But my father was still reticent to sift through the past. I decided to go anyway. I went over to France to the village of Carentan, found the town's mayor, and talked with him. With me, I had Ambrose's book that shows the picture of the town the morning Carentan was taken. The caption underneath reads, "Winters led the men down the road coming in from the left

---

2. Ibid., 94.

in a frontal assault against a German machine-gun position in the building to the right."[3] It was key for me to find that same scene in the present day. If I found that road, I could walk back from the town and find the field where my uncle was shot.

We were all standing in the lobby of the Hotel du Ville in Carentan when I showed the mayor the picture. Others were looking at the picture as well. They were mostly young people, and they said, "Oh, this is not Carentan, this picture. You see the name on this wall? This is St. Sauveur du Ville." (The conversation was all in French.)

I was heartbroken. I really wanted to find as close to the exact location he was shot as possible. But then someone got an idea and said, "Let's call in a man who was here the day the Allies came." So they called a man in who must have been in his mid-eighties. He came over to the hotel dressed up in a suit and tie. Someone said he dressed up just to come to talk with me. He looked at the picture and said, "No, no, this is here. We wrote 'St. Saveur du Ville' on the buildings to fool the Germans. We didn't want them to know what town they were in." He pointed to buildings. "You see those three smokestacks? Those are the same three smokestacks on the road that leads into Carentan."

I thanked him, jumped into my rental car, and headed down to the road he pointed out. Sure enough, the three smokestacks were still there, just like in the picture. I walked the length of the road and touched very near the same place where my uncle had fallen. It chokes me up even today when I think about it.

Several years after I visited Carentan, I was invited to Normandy with the Band of Brothers. I was on Utah Beach with many of the survivors, and met many of my uncle's friends, including Moose Heyliger, Richard Winters, Colonel Strayer, and John Martin—they all remembered my uncle and remembered his voice. They told me that he was generous, good, strong, and kind.

He wasn't buried because they never found his body, but his name is listed on a plaque in Westminster Abbey as missing in action. There's

---

3. Ambrose, *Band of Brothers*, 189.

another plaque that the Boy Scouts have made for him that says, "George Lavenson, March 26, 1917–July 26, 1944. Freedom Lives, and through it, he lives in a way that humbles the undertakings of most men."

That phrase means much to me, to think that he lives on in freedom. I guess I simply don't want my uncle to be forgotten, like I don't want any of the veterans killed in the war to be forgotten. I placed a small sign in his honor on the front of Camp Kennebec that reads, "The George, Jim, and Jay Lavenson Canoeing Camp," after my father and his two brothers. It's not an official name change; it's just one small way I'm keeping the memory alive.

One more thing: To this day I carry around his clicker, that one that the men used to identify themselves in Normandy. I've got it right here in my pocket. I click it often, and I'm still waiting to hear the return.

24

WARREN "SKIP" MUCK

Interview with Eileen LaFleur O'Hara, niece
With additional information from Ruth Muck LaFleur, sister,[1] and Richard Speight, actor

It's hard to talk about Warren "Skip" Muck, even today, more than sixty years after his death. He was my uncle, the brother of my mother, Ruth Muck LaFleur. So many people loved him, and he had so much potential—he must have been really incredible. I miss the man I never met.

For a long time our family didn't know much about the circumstances surrounding his death, so, naturally, when we began to meet the other veterans from Easy Company, we wanted to know as much as possible. But, it's funny, whenever my sister and I talked to the veterans about Skip, they would tear up. Even just being introduced to us seemed upsetting to them. I know Don Malarkey has a difficult time talking about Skip. He's always overcome by emotions. So even after we've discovered so much, we still don't know all we'd like to know.

It's not only his fellow veterans either. Tonawanda, where Skip grew

---

1. Ruth Muck O'Hara passed away before this book was researched. Her grandson, John O'Hara, had interviewed her on October 10, 2003, Ruth's eighty-first birthday. The information from her was gleaned from that recording.

up, is a fairly small town where a lot of people know each other. Years after his death, as I also was growing up in Tonawanda, if anyone found out I was Skip's niece, the first thing anyone said was how much they loved him. People couldn't speak beyond that one phrase. It was that way with anyone I met. *Everybody* simply loved Skip Muck.

Swimming the Niagara

As a little kid, Warren Muck never walked anywhere. He was a cheerful boy who found joy in the simplest of activities—like moving from point A to point B. Whenever he moved, he skipped. That's how he got the nickname. It stuck into his adult years.

Despite his sunny disposition, it wasn't like his family didn't have any problems. Skip's dad was a traveling musician and virtually abandoned his family for the sake of his career. Skip was the middle child of three children. He had an older brother, Elmer, and a younger sister, Ruth, and, as a natural leader, Skip assumed the role of man of the family from an early age.

He was especially close to his little sister, Ruth, who grew up to become my mother. She was eighteen months younger than Skip, and he was always good-hearted toward her. He worked two part-time jobs to bring in extra money for the family: delivering papers throughout the week and selling hot dogs at a stand downtown on weekends. If ever his little sister needed a few extra dollars, Skip always shared. He bought toys and roller skates for her when she was young.

Skip's older brother was different. Skip fought all his older brother's battles. One day Elmer came home from school all bloody.

"Where've you been?" Skip asked.

"I was in a fight," Elmer said. "Some bully beat me up."

"Well, where is he?" Skip asked.

Elmer told him. Skip went out, found the older bully, and beat him up on his brother's behalf. That was the last time the bully ever messed with Elmer.

Skip attended St. Francis of Assisi grade school, and then Tonawanda High School. He was very smart and skipped seventh grade. He loved sports, particularly football. In high school he played wide receiver and was also on the swim team. He was on the smaller side, maybe five-ten and 135 pounds as a senior in high school, but always athletic, and when he played football he was at his happiest—even when it hurt. Once, he got a concussion and came home with his head bandaged.

"You are never playing football again," said his mother.

"Ah, this is nothing," Skip said. He kept playing football.

It's mentioned in the series that Skip was Irish, but that's a mistake. The family was German, actually, and both Skip's grandparents spoke German at home. His grandparents immigrated to America and ran a dairy farm where Skip and his brother and sister spent summers while growing up. The kids were fluent in German, but no one's ever mentioned that about Skip, so he might have kept that quiet when he was in the service. It's one of those unanswered questions. I'm sure a complex set of emotions emerged for the family. My mom used to say that everyone stopped speaking German as soon as the war broke out. Whenever she visited her grandparents during the war years, they only spoke English.

During Skip's teen years, his sister used to cover for him whenever he broke curfew. The house's front and back doors had bells attached that would wake his mother, so his sister would wait up for him, then help haul him in through a bedroom window. They had a lot of friends in common and often double-dated. He always made sure she had a new dress for each dance. She made a point of ironing all his clothes "just right," as he was fussy about his appearance.

Once, his sister brought a new formal dress that was quite low cut in front. Skip was going to the same dance. When Ruth came down the stairs, their mother announced that there was no way she was going to the dance dressed like that—the dress was too low cut. Skip whispered to his sister, "Put on a damn jacket." She did, then when they got out on the porch Skip said, "Now, when you get to the dance, take the damn thing off."

Skip dated a cheerleader named Faye Tanner from a nearby high school. He wrote to her during the war that he hoped to marry her when he returned.

In the series it mentions briefly that Skip once swam the Niagara

River. That's true. It was part of an initiation to get into a fraternity, which they have even in some of the high schools around here. The river, as you can imagine, is very wide, and the current is extremely strong, even ten miles up from the falls, where Skip swam it. There's a certain place in the Niagara called the "point of no return," where, if you or your boat get to that point, there's no saving you. The current is too strong and you'll go over the falls. Skip crossed the river at night, and the river carried him almost two miles downstream before he made it across.

When Skip's mom found out, she really hit the roof, and his sister was also alarmed. Skip tried to calm them by saying that his friends had put a rowboat in the river in case he got into trouble—like that would have done much good. Skip's sister's comment was "I don't care if the entire $%#@ Coast Guard flotilla was in the river. Don't ever do that again!"

Skip went to Mass regularly and was a man of sincere faith. Growing up, he was an altar boy, and even in the service went to Mass whenever he could. The series shows actor Richard Speight (who portrays Skip) carrying a rosary in the pocket of his uniform. That was authentic, and veterans confirmed it with Richard. Today at the museum in Bastogne, they show a newsreel where one small scene shows several of the men kneeling in the snow to receive communion. The altar boy serving the communion is Skip. It flashes by so fast it's hard to see, but other veterans have confirmed it was Skip.

War Years

If you saw the movie *Saving Private Ryan*, you may have heard that the movie was based on a true account of the Niland brothers, four American soldiers from Tonawanda, New York, who served in World War II.

Of the four, two actually survived the war, (Robert and Pete Niland were both killed on D-day), but for some time it was believed that only one, Frederick "Fritz" Niland, had survived. Fritz was located in Europe and sent back home to the States to complete his service, which is featured as the main plot of the movie. Only later (in real life) did the family (and the military) learn that one other brother, Edward, was actually being held captive in a Japanese POW camp in Burma and still alive.

Well, Fritz Niland, the real "Private Ryan," was Skip's best friend in high school. They grew up five doors away from each other and did everything together, including joining the Airborne. Skip was seventeen when he graduated from high school. He wasn't old enough to join the paratroopers at first, and his mother didn't want to sign for him. They haggled back and forth for a few weeks. Then Fritz joined, and Skip said, "I'm going, too." She signed.

In Ambrose's book, he tells the story of Fritz, Skip, Don Malarkey, Chuck Grant, and Joe Toye getting passes to London on combat leave, where they met up with Fritz's brother, Bob Niland of the 501st PIR.[2] Ambrose later tells of Fritz finding Skip and Malarkey on the line near Carentan to explain why he was going home.[3]

Skip wrote to his sister with a story about Fritz. When they were practice jumping over England in 1943, Fritz got blown off course, and landed on the thatched roof of an English cottage. He landed hard, went right through the roof, and ended up sitting on the dining table of an English couple. Not missing a beat, they stood up, introduced themselves, and invited Fritz to join them for tea. He introduced himself, too, politely responding that he needed to return to his outfit, got out of his chute, and walked out the door unharmed.

A Foxhole in the Snow

Over the years I've attended several Easy Company reunions, and, despite their reticence to talk, the men have told me little things about Skip. These little things mean a great deal to our family. Don Malarkey said, "He was my best friend from day one at Toccoa." Johnny Martin described him as "totally real—he protected and took care of all the men in his

---

2. Ambrose, *Band of Brothers*, 59.
3. Ibid., 102.

squad." Les Hashey said simply, "We all loved him." Pete Toye, the son of Joe Toye, told me that his father admired very few people, but my uncle was one of them. Burr Smith has passed away, but his daughter, Susan Smith Finn, showed me where her father had written in his journal, "[Skip] had a magnetic personality that just drew people to him."

My mom has always found it very difficult to talk about Skip's military career. She mentioned that when Skip got his wings, he was so thrilled. Parachuting was really his thing. She said that it was very quiet in the house after he left. Their mom spent a lot of time baking cookies and sending them to the troops.

I know Skip was much more honest about what was going on with his sister than with his mother. From what I've seen of his letters to his mother, they're all like, "I'm fine. We're fine. Everything's fine. We're getting lots to eat. I'm going to church." But when he talked to his sister, he said things like, "I'm tired. We've lost a lot of men," that sort of thing. Letters were all censored, of course, so he couldn't say a lot about specifics, but the tone definitely changed when he wrote to his sister. In one letter, sent to his sister right after the fighting in Holland, Skip writes that he was so tired he "just wanted to lie down and stay down."

Unfortunately, there was a fire at their mother's house in 1948 and so much of their personal effects were destroyed, including most of Skip's letters. But there's one we've kept, written from Skip to his sister. It was postmarked on November 30, 1944, and sent from Mourmelon, France. The men were taking a brief respite there after fighting in Normandy and Holland. The men didn't know it yet, but they were just about to be sent to Bastogne, Skip's last battle. The letter reads, in part:

Dear Ruth:

. . . You mentioned Ann Brody in your letters. It seems funny she would ask about me. I thought she would be married like the rest of the girls I knew in school. I guess there can't be very many that aren't married that I used to run around with.

. . . I'm glad to hear Mom is feeling ok. I worry about her all the

*time. I wish this dam' war would end so I could get to see you and Mom
again. After leading the life I have for the last two years it even seems
hard for me to picture what our home looks like. It sure will take a lot to
settle me down for a while after this war ends. I've been used to a pretty
wild life in the army.*

*. . . I'm sorry to hear that Elmer will be coming overseas soon. I was
hoping that he wouldn't have to get in this awful mess. Let's hope that
it will end before he has a chance to see action. I have had my full of this
fighting too.*

*I've been busy all day working with the other sgts. on our new quar-
ters. There are five of us in one room. We have it fixed up pretty nice. We
have a swell radio that we bought.*

*I'm sending you some of this dam' foreign money I've been carrying
around. It's about the only souvenir I can pick up and hold on to.*

*Well Ruth I better close this now because I have to write Mom a
letter too.*

Love always
Skip

Tony Garcia was a new replacement in Skip's mortar squad, and under
Skip's command. Tony told me that he went off base one weekend while
in England to have a little fun, and Skip found out about it. Skip could
have turned him in and gotten him tossed out of Easy Company, but instead, he just chewed him out and ended it there. Tony always thanked
Skip for his flexibility, and never put Skip on the spot again.

Don Malarkey told me an incident that is in neither the book nor the
movie. After the 120-mile march that Easy Company made from Toccoa
to Atlanta, Malarkey's legs were so bad he had to crawl, and began to head
to the mess tent on all fours. When Skip saw Don he grabbed both mess
kits and said, "No friend of mine crawls anywhere." Skip went and filled
both with food and came back to the tent to eat with him.

We have a clipping from the *Buffalo Evening News* that names Skip
as part of a small force of 101st Airborne paratroopers who turned the ta-

bles on a larger group of German paratroopers. North of Nijmegena, four American paratroopers returned from patrol along the banks of the Neder Rhine and reported a large group of Germans at an important crossroads a short distance away. Dick Winters led a reconnaissance squad to within 250 yards of the German position, wiped out seven Germans trying to set up a gun emplacement, captured another worming his way through a drainage pipe, then charged the rest with their bayonets. Skip was awarded a Bronze Star for this battle.

That was the most detail we knew of Skip's action in combat.

Skip's death is shown in both the book and the movie. It's so sad. This is the part that we didn't know about until years later. Skip and Alex Penkala were in their foxhole during heavy shelling outside Foy on January 9, 1944. A shell hit their foxhole directly, killing them instantly. George Luz Sr. was out in the open when the shelling started, and Skip and Alex had yelled for him to jump into theirs. Fortunately, George had jumped in another hole. When the shelling finished, George ran to check on Skip and Alex. He found only some pieces of their bodies and part of a sleeping bag.[4]

We have a copy of the Western Union telegram that arrived from Washington, DC, on January 26, 1945. It reads simply:

> *The secretary of war desires me to express his deep regret that your son Sergeant Warren H. Muck was killed in action on ten January in Belgium. Confirming letter follows.*
>   *J.A. Ulio, the adjutant general*

A letter dated January 12, 1945, which my mother wrote to Skip, was returned to sender, marked simply, "Deceased, Co E 506, Lt. Ronald Speirs." We still have that letter. Unknowingly, Mom had written cheerily to her brother, "Hi, how are you? I haven't heard from you in a couple weeks. I hope everything is okay with you . . . I hope you will be able to come home soon."

Colonel Robert Sink wrote to Skip's mother March 23, 1945. The

---

4. Ibid., 204-205.

letter was kindly worded, and mentioned Skip had been buried in a United States military cemetery in Belgium, but didn't offer any details surrounding his death. I think Colonel Sink's letter explains why our family was confused about the details of Skip's death for so many years. Probably, Skip's friends thought we had been informed. But for fifty-five years all we had was the telegram and Colonel Sink's letter.

Years Later

When Skip died, his sister refused to celebrate holidays for some time. The only thing she ever mentioned about the experience was that when she saw the men in uniform walking up to the house with a telegram, there was no doubt in her mind her brother was gone. Skip's obituaries ran in the papers. After that, virtually nothing more was said. People simply found it too hard to talk about Skip.

All that changed in 1999 when our city's Chamber of Commerce phoned and said a man was trying to locate the relatives of Warren Muck. It turned out it was Richard Speight Jr., who was scheduled to portray Skip in the miniseries. We had never heard of the book *Band of Brothers*, and didn't know HBO was turning it into a movie. Richard had gone to great lengths to locate us. My mom had married in 1945 and had a different last name. Skip's folks had both passed away. So finding our family was not an easy task.

Richard was in boot camp in England for the series, and he and I started what became a long, amazing e-mail correspondence. Richard directed us to the book at first, which filled in details about Skip's death. Richard called my mom, letters flew back and forth across the Atlantic, and we developed an incredibly close relationship with him. Richard was able to get the story about Skip swimming the Niagara put into the script. My sister and I finally met him in Paris at the premiere. My folks met Richard at the Philly premiere. We've remained close to this day.

While *Band of Brothers* was in production, I wrote to our congressman John LaFalce to inquire about getting Skip's Purple Heart replaced. My grandmother had put it away for safekeeping and, when she passed away, it was never found. Congressman LaFalce responded with not only re-placing Skip's Purple Heart, but also providing seven other medals Skip had received including Bronze Stars, Distinguished Unit Citations, and more. The congressman came to my mother's house, along with media representatives, and presented the medals to her. It was really a thrill.

Faye Tanner, Skip's sweetheart during the war, married about five years after the war ended. When the story about my mom receiving Skip's medals aired on the local TV stations, she saw it. She was just up one morning and had the news on with the sound turned down, just puttering around the house, when she looked up and saw Skip's face on the televi-sion screen, after all those years. She was so stunned. She came over to see Mom later that week and brought over some of Skip's things that he had sent her from the war, his jump wings, and some photos. My Mom and this lovely lady got together again later that week to talk about the man they both loved very much. We stayed in contact with her from then on. She and Don Malarkey had corresponded after Bastogne, both devastated by Skip's death. But, as they lived on opposite coasts, they had never met. She bravely decided to join me on a trip to Fort Campbell. Skip's best friend and Skip's fiancée met for the first time. Introducing them to each other was a moment I'll never forget.

Something So Honest

About two years ago I received an e-mail from a soldier who was serving with his family in Germany. They have a Boy Scout troop on base, and every year they visit different American military cemeteries to do cleaning work on the crosses. He wrote me to say that his son specifically asked to go find my uncle's cross to clean it. He sent me a photo of his son cleaning Skip's cross. I mailed the Boy Scout troop a flag signed by Bill Guarnere as a thank you gift. Those types of things just keep happening year after year.

Skip was a remarkable man and I'm so proud to call him my uncle. I asked Richard Speight how people can best remember Skip Muck. Here is his eloquent reply:

I know you e-mailed me about this a while ago. I've been thinking about it a lot. It is quite a stumper—how to put it into words, I mean. Then it struck me . . . you know what is amazing? That people are still talking about your uncle and his impact on the world more than 60 years after his death. He never married, never had kids, was never elected to public office, never became a captain of industry. Yet here we are, discussing the impact he's had on us and the world we live in. And that right there sums up his legacy to me.

In a time that seems more selfish than any before it, the act of doing something selfless stands out like a lighthouse on a foggy sea. He knowingly entered a situation that put his life at risk, and he did it because he knew it was the right thing to do. He represents so many men and women who came before and after him, the men and women of the armed forces who do what needs to be done in spite of the danger. But I don't think his legacy is a military one. I believe it's more universal and grander in scope.

There seems to be something so simple about Skip, something so honest, so down to earth, so ubiquitously American about him that he serves as a constant reminder—an enduring example—that those who think not of themselves but rather of the people and the world around them are the ones who truly make a difference. It would be easy to attribute Skip's heroism to some special power, some unique gift he and others like him possess that we regular folk don't. But the truth is, he was just a man—maybe even just a boy—who dug down deep inside and found the courage and the strength and the drive to do what needed to be done. He has left me and countless others like me wondering if we would have made the same choice. Would we have found that courage in ourselves?

For me, Skip has taken heroism out of mythology. Do I have the strength of character to do what needs to be done? Skip did, and he inspires others like me to try and do the same. One thing is for sure. If every person in America could channel his "inner Muck," this country would be an amazing place. I think that is a pretty impressive mark to leave behind.

25

ALEX PENKALA JR.

Interview with Rudolph Tatay, nephew

I'm not old enough to actually remember my uncle. The last time he was home, I was just three years old, and I don't have any memories of the visit. But I grew up always knowing I had an uncle in WWII, and that his name was Alex Penkala, Jr. For a number of years, I thought he had been killed on D-day. I'm not quite sure why, because other family members knew he had been killed in Bastogne, although they didn't know the specific circumstances surrounding the death. It wasn't something people talked about much.

Then one day in the early 1990s, I got a phone call from my mother. My cousin Jimmy Lichatowich was in a bookstore and had picked up a copy of *Band of Brothers*. He called my mom and said, "Guess what, your brother's in this book!" I went down to the bookstore and picked up four copies, one for me, one for my mom, and two for other relatives. Everyone in our family read the book cover to cover. This was the first time our family found out the specific circumstances surrounding his death. From then on we began to research his life in more earnest. We talked to every-one we could who knew him. When the miniseries aired a few years later, it turned into a big family project. Everybody came over and we all watched each episode together, listing out the different scenes where my uncle was featured. As we were watching, my mom said, "I'm so glad they got somebody who was Polish to play him."

"Well, Mom," I said, "Tim Matthews"—the actor who played Alex—"could very well be Polish, but actually he's British."

"Well, he sure looks Polish to me," Mom said.

We went to the Easy Company reunion in Phoenix right after the miniseries. It was very well attended, and we talked to a lot of the vets there. We went to the next three reunions in a row.

When the Emmys came out, Merav Brooks from HBO invited fam-ily members to come to the celebration. HBO paid for our hotel rooms and meals. One of my cousins, Tim Penkala, and his wife live in San Diego, and he went to the Emmys to represent the family. They had a ball, and said everybody was so happy to meet them. His dad was Alex's brother, who served in the Pacific as a tailgunner on a B-24. He got a Purple Heart and came back. In 2005 we went to Europe to dedicate a monument at Bastogne with our uncle's name on it. Tim went along on that trip, too.

This is what we've found out about my uncle's life.

Tenth of Thirteen Children

To start at the beginning, my uncle's parents, Mary and Alex Penkala Sr., emigrated to the US from Poland in 1907. They knew each other back in Poland, then came to the States—I don't know if this was separately or together—and were married in 1908 in South Bend, Indiana. I found my grandfather's name in the Ellis Island information, but have never found my grandmother's. The problem is, no one is quite sure how she spelled her last name. It is either Mary Kinski or Mary Kencki, or perhaps spelled some other way, so that makes it more difficult. Basically they were just looking for a better life. In Eastern Europe they had been starving. They came to South Bend because there were people there whom they already knew.

Mary and Alex Sr. moved to Taylor Spring, Illinois, in 1910 where he worked as a coal miner. A few years later, around 1918, they moved back around South Bend, where he worked for Studebaker. He wasn't well educated and had only a third grade education. Obviously, their original language was Polish. I remember my grandfather: his English wasn't that great, even late in life.

Mary began having children soon after they were married and gave birth to thirteen children over the next twenty years, nine girls and four boys. My uncle, Alex M. Penkala Jr., was born August 30, 1924, the tenth of the thirteen children. Even to this day the family refers to him as Junior. My mother, Evelyn (her married name is Tatay), was born in 1921 and was one of Alex's older sisters. Today, my mom and the youngest girl are the only ones still alive from the thirteen kids in the family. My mother is eighty-eight. My Aunt Rose is eighty-two.

In 1928, Mary died in childbirth with her thirteenth child. The child, a boy, survived and was given to relatives to be cared for and raised under another name. After Mary died, the dad and the older daughters raised the family.

The family was devoutly Catholic. Sometime in the early 1920s, the family lived in a house near Notre Dame University, where Alex Sr. worked. As the girls got older, they went to work at Notre Dame in various jobs. Alex Jr. worked at Notre Dame also, when he came of age. During the Depression, the family wasn't rich by any means, but they were better off than a lot of people because of the steady work. All the kids spoke Polish first, then picked up English outside the home and at school. All of Alex's brothers and sisters were bilingual.

I have talked to people who knew Alex Jr. when he was young. He was a muscular, active kid, but not really talkative. He loved sports and played football and baseball, and was built on the shorter side, like the rest of the males in the family, about five-foot-seven.

Notre Dame owned a farm close to the campus. Alex and his friends would sneak to the farm and climb up the hayloft. A friend of Alex's told me they would build tunnels and forts out of hay bales. "We used candles and matches," the man said, "it's a wonder we didn't burn ourselves up."

When I was growing up, there were a couple of aunts who lived within walking distance of Notre Dame, and I used to play in the same barn that Alex Jr. played in when he was a kid.

From Cook to Paratrooper

Alex Jr. attended South Bend Catholic High School. My mother says he was a junior in high school when he enlisted, but his papers said he had only one year of high school. It wasn't unusual in those days for guys to go to high school for a semester or a year, then, if money was needed or if they got bored, they dropped out or worked for a year, then went back. So Alex could have easily been an eighteen-year-old sophomore in high school when he enlisted. I don't think high schools were very particular of a kid's age in those days.

His papers, which I got a copy of, read that he enlisted on February 27, 1943. For his civilian occupation, it lists "motorcycle mechanic or packer high explosives, munitions worker, or tool room keeper, or stock control clerk, or stock clerk." I'm not sure that's all the things he did, or if they put in a number that fit all these occupations. I know he did some work for Notre Dame, but other than that, I'm not sure exactly what.

Alex Jr. went through basic training, although I don't know where, then was assigned to cook school. All the daughters cooked in the family, not the sons, so I doubt it was due to his cooking ability. I think that was just where the military stuck him.

We have a number of letters that Alex wrote to my mother during that time. Alex wrote that he didn't think much of cook school, and wrote of his devotion to his girlfriend, Sylvia:

Dear Sis,

I received your letter and was I glad to hear from you. As you probably know by now I'm going to cook's school for eight weeks, so I'm going to make the best of it.

No, I don't need anything and I don't want anything for Easter. Thanks anyway. I'm not coming home for Easter because no one gets to go home during this time in school.

You should see the WACs [Women's Army Corps] here at camp! There are about 150 of them. You should know that Sylvia really doesn't know how much I love or should I say like her. I don't even go no place because I keep thinking of her so much.

Well, I am out of time so I'll have to say goodbye until I write again.

Your brother,
Alex
P.S. Send box candy if you want to.

In cook school he made some friends who told him about an elite unit called the paratroopers. He and two friends tried out. The two friends washed out, but Alex made it.

He wasn't a Toccoa man. I think he took his paratrooper training at Fort Bragg, but I haven't confirmed this.

The first picture of Easy Company I've seen with Alex is at Fort Bragg. He was one of the first replacements into the company. I have another picture of him and Skip Muck at Camp McCall. That's the only picture I have of those two guys together. Everyone I talk to said they were very good friends.

Alex wrote often—short, cheery, breezy letters, saying he was doing well, asking about family members, wondering if she had sent box candy because he didn't receive it, telling he had received her letters, promising to write again soon. One letter home, written in scrawled longhand, is dated March 30, 1943, and was probably written when Alex was at Camp McCall.

Dear Sis,

Well, I'm ok. Boy and do I like the army. . . . I might get shipped to some other camp. How do you like my writing? I'm in a hurry, so you'll have to excuse it. Write more often. I'll keep thinking of you.

So long,
Your brother
Junior

Regarding Skip Muck—the guys I talked to said he was the heart and soul of Easy Company. Everyone just loved him. I've asked Eileen O'Hara, his niece, why she thinks Alex and Skip might have become such good friends. They were both Catholic from large families, and had a lot in common that way. Skip was the mortar man and Alex was his assistant. Skip carried the gun sight and tube; Alex carried the base plate and bipod. I'm sure that base plate weighed thirty or forty pounds, so it wasn't much fun to carry that around. But everyone I've talked to said that Alex was muscular enough and carried it no problem.

Airborne vets have told me that whenever they jumped and went out on a mission, many of the guys carried four mortar rounds in their packs. The first thing they did after jumping was give all their rounds to the mortar squad and then deploy. It was a 60 mm mortar they used, smaller, but basically the mortars were their only weapons other than machine guns that could really reach from a distance. From all indications, both Alex and Skip were very good mortar men.

We know that Alex sailed for England September 15, 1943, aboard the troop ship *Samaria*. Sometime before that, Alex came home for the last time on leave. My mom still talks about the big party they had for him at their house. Alex seemed sad, mainly because he was leaving his family, and the men knew they were going overseas. He seemed to really like the paratroopers and talked about how much he loved jumping out of air-planes. I don't know if he ever actually landed in an airplane—I think he jumped out of every airplane he went up in. He never smoked before he went into the Army, but he was smoking at the party, my mom said, so he had developed that bad habit and they were all worried for him. Not about the smoking—they knew he was going in harm's way.

He wrote home just after arriving in Aldbourne:

Dear Sis,

Thanks for the candy you sent me. It sure is good. It's the third package I got since I'm in England. Boy, you can send me another one, don't hesitate.

Excuse my writing, I'm in a hurry tonight. Did you get my longest letter yet? Send me some air mail stamps if you get them. I hope to hear from you soon.

Your brother
Al

Like the other paratroopers, Alex Jr. simply did what he had to do. The men trained in England from September 1943 to June 1944. I talked to Frank Perconte, who stood next to my uncle in roll call because their names were close together. Frank said that one day they got a three-day pass. The big thing was to go up to Aberdeen, Scotland, and he and Alex went. Alex was helping a woman with her luggage, and Frank was trying to talk Alex into chatting her up. But Alex said, "Oh no, I can't do that, she's married."

Alex wrote more short notes over the fall, winter, and spring saying it had been constantly raining and how much he hated the weather in England, asking his sister to send him some candy bars and T-shirts, size thirty-six, and a pair of work gloves, size nine, and saying how much he missed not seeing his family over Christmas. He often talked about food. On December 5, 1943, he wrote:

Dear Sis,

Just a few lines to tell you I'm feeling alright. I got the package. Them cookies sure were good. If you have any time at all, send me some fudge. You know fudge. Oh, don't forget to send me some peanuts too.

    Is Clem married yet? Boy, I can't wait till this darn thing is over with.

Your brother,
Al

Sometime when Alex was in England, his girlfriend back home in South Bend sent him a Dear John letter. The breakup didn't seem to devastate him too badly, because he had another girlfriend in England pretty quickly afterward. It might have even been simultaneously, but knowing Junior, it was probably afterward. He was a pretty straight-arrow kind of guy. After the breakup, still in England, Alex wrote on April 10, 1944:

Dear Sis,

Just to let you know that I'm feeling alright, etc.
    . . . Did I tell you that I went out with a married girl? Boy was she ever nice, but it didn't last long after she told me she was married, because, well, you know me.
    I met this girl in Scotland. What a nice place Scotland is. They have everything there—nice girls, also nice dance halls, and did I ever dance a lot when I was up there. More than I ever did in my life. No fooling.
    Well, I'll have to close for now.

Your brother,
Alex
P.S. Don't forget to send me something to eat—anything!

Easy Company vet Joe Lesniewski joined E Company in England. It wasn't easy to come in as a replacement, and Joe said the first guy who ever talked to him was Alex. They got to be pretty good friends because they could both speak Polish. They hung around together with some other Polish-speaking guys, and Joe taught them all how to sing country and western songs.

Now, a lot of the details of what happened to Alex, from about D-day onward, we really don't know. The only information we have is what Ambrose put in *Band of Brothers.*

We know that Alex jumped on D-day and landed in Normandy on the roof of a barn. He climbed down. That's basically all we know of D-day. How he got back to his outfit, we don't know. That story is lost.

One of the vets, Les Hashey, talked in the miniseries about how he joined the squad with Corporal Penkala. We never knew my uncle was a corporal, so the first thing I did when I met Les was ask about that. Les remembered him as a corporal, but he said it might have been an acting corporal. In the squad Alex and Skip were in, they were the only two from that squad who weren't killed on D-day. So after D-day, they basically had to make up a new squad.

After D-day, June 6, 1944, the men fought in Normandy for about a month, then returned to England for a while. Alex wrote home after the fighting on July 22, 1944.

Dear Sis,

I guess I should say I'm sorry, but you know how it is when you're busy, don't you? I got one letter from you since D-Day and that was the other day. I didn't get much of a chance to write while I was in France.

Hey, I'm still waiting for that big package of apples and some good fudge.

Boy, that girl in Kentucky sure is a sweet kid. She writes to me almost every other day.

Well I guess I'll have to close now. Write soon.
Your brother,
Al

And once more, still in England, on August 20, 1944. The poignant line from that letter is:

> *Boy, when all of us guys get home we're really going to give one hell of a big party. I'm just waiting for that day.*

A few years back, Joe Lesniewski showed me a pilot chute—the one that comes out first and pulls out the main chute—that Alex had signed after D-day. I was really happy to see that. Sometime later, Joe asked if I wanted to have the chute. I said, sure, I'd love to. So I've got that.

The men jumped into Holland for Operation Market-Garden in September 1944. Alex made that jump as well. I contacted a woman in Eindhoven through the Internet who said a soldier named Alex Penkala signed a ration book she had when she was a child. We have one letter after that, made just after the Holland jump, where Alex mentioned everything was okay. That's the last letter home we have. As far as we know, Alex and Muck were the mortar squad all through Holland. Then came the Battle of the Bulge.

Bonded Forever

The way my uncle was killed in the miniseries was supposedly exactly how he died for real. It was January 10, 1945. The men were just outside of Foy, Belgium, in the Bois Jacques woods. They were being shelled heavily, and a shell landed directly in the foxhole where Skip Muck and Alex Penkala were, killing them both instantly. We're not really sure what they were hit with. It was probably a 105, but it may have been an 88. I think most artillery barrages were 105s. So that's probably what it was.

Alex was originally buried in France. He was exhumed and reburied in the American cemetery in Luxembourg, the same cemetery General Patton was buried in. There are five Easy Company KIA members buried there, including Skip Muck. We have two burial flags—it's possible one flag came from each cemetery. Alex was one of the many first generation Americans who ended up being buried in Europe, families who emigrated to America from Europe, then their sons went back to Europe to fight.

I told Eileen O'Hara, Skip Muck's niece, that our families were bonded together forever that one dark night in 1945. Recently we invited Eileen and her husband, Tom, to a Penkala family reunion. The Muck and Penkala families are close even today, more than sixty years later.

What's the one thing I'd want people to know about my uncle? All the vets I've talked to say these things: He was a good soldier. He always did his job. You could always count on him. Alex Penkala Jr. saw what he had to do and did it. He made the supreme sacrifice. That's how I'd want people to remember him.

26

ROBERT VAN KLINKEN

Interview with Gariann Wrenchy, great-niece
With information from Cora Bingman, niece

As a little girl, Gariann Wrenchey had always wondered about the picture on her Grandma Susie's bedside table. She knew she would never meet the dashing young man shown in the picture. He was gone. But Gariann always felt like she had a connection with her great-uncle, Robert Van Klinken. His sacrifice to his country was something the family had never forgotten.

When she was grown, Gariann began to ask questions. At first, no one wanted to talk. But her grandmother brought out from the closet a box with the young man's personal effects. The box hadn't been touched in fifty years, just a pile of photographs, news clippings, certificates, and documents with some other effects at the top. Gariann went to work.

Inside the box was an old wallet with a dollar bill inside that had been signed by a few buddies, a ring with the initial "R" on it, a few foreign coins with holes drilled through them, and an address for a veteran named Bill Wingett.

There was a patch torn from green military clothing. The patch showed a swastika surrounded with a red border with oak leaves above it. Gariann found it a bit creepy. It looked like the patch had been hacked with a bayonet from somebody's clothes. The bayonet was also still in the box.

An original set of paratrooper jump wings was there, along with a note to Gariann's grandmother. "Susie don't lose these, you have to realize what I went through to earn them."

Inside the wallet was a photograph of two young women eating an ice cream sundae and grinning. On the back of the picture was written, "Hello Cake Face."

Then there were letters. Most were still in their envelopes with postmarks from Toccoa, South Carolina, and England. They were written in clean, strong handwriting, often in pencil, and many on military stationery, now yellowed and fading. Gariann read them all.

Robert Van Klinken wrote to two sets of people. The first bunch of letters was to his parents. The information was shorter, tidier, and less revealing. The second set was addressed to Susie (Robert's sister and Gariann's grandmother), Johnny (Susie's husband and Robert's best buddy), and their young son, Walt. In this second bunch of letters, Robert spoke more freely.

What follows is the story of Robert Van Klinken, as revealed by family members and Robert's own letters.

Letters Home

Robert Van Klinken was born October 31, 1919, in Loomis, Washington, a city close to the Canadian border known for its mining. In the early 1920s, Robert and his family moved to Twisp, another small town in Washington State, where he grew up.

He was a country boy who loved to hunt and fish. Pictures show him dressed in overalls and standing next to chickens and old barns.

His parents had emigrated from the Netherlands and become tenant apple orchardists in the United States. They were very poor and never owned their own farm, but even during the Great Depression, they always had food. Robert's sister Susie was known to be spoiled, even though the family was so poor. Her father taught her horse how to jump fences because he didn't think his little girl should have to get off her horse and open gates. The kids didn't fight and got along well. Susie looked up to Robert like he was her hero.

Robert graduated from high school in 1939. There's a picture of him with his graduating class up on the wall in the old Twisp High School. Susie graduated the next year, 1940, and immediately married Johnny Klinkert, Bob's good friend. There was another brother in the family, Gene, but he was much younger, and Robert never addressed any letters to him.

Robert became a diesel mechanic who sometimes worked in logging. He was a good natured young man who dated a lot and dreamed of getting married someday.

When war broke out, he was in his mid-twenties and initially thought he was too old to go to war. That he went into the Army in the first place only makes his story more poignant. Right before he joined, he had a job offer with a defense industry company in Alaska. It would have meant a fortune for him, and it would have also kept him out of the war. Robert wrote:

Uncle Sam sure played a dirty trick on me when he put me in the army. I signed a contract with Deims Drake Company for 1 year to work as a mechanic in Kodiak Alaska at $450 a month. I bought a ticket for $87 on the steamship Yukon and $40 of clothes and was all ready to sail. Just about 15 hours before I was to leave, the Army called. If I'd got to Kodiak they would have given me a deferment as it was an air base for the Navy.

After being drafted, one of his first letters home was to Susie's new husband, Johnny, with whom Robert often fished and hunted. The letter was postmarked August 19, 1942, and sent from the reception center at Fort Lewis, Washington.

John,

I'm in. Better stick to the navy yard. I'm getting a better break than I expected. Signed up for the parachute troops. Don't write till you hear from me. Leaving here soon.
Bob

Robert made a prime candidate for the paratroopers. He was in good shape, certainly not afraid of shooting a rifle, and impressed with the fifty dollars a month extra pay.

A month later, September 28, 1942, Robert wrote again, this time from Camp Toccoa. Always the ladies' man, Robert talked about eating a meal at his girlfriend's house down in Georgia. He must have met her right away, because the men hadn't been at the camp for very long.

Dear Susie, Johnny, and Walt,

What happened to the Plymouth? Did it start using oil? Sounds good to hear that Johnny got a scope on his rifle. You shouldn't have any trouble getting a buck, you have two good guns. You should see the artillery we have here. Machine guns 30 cal. M1 Springfield Garand and carbines. I am training with an M1 now. It sure is a sweet pill squirter. I understand when we jump we will have the barrel strapped to one leg and the stalk to the other. Two fellows got killed jumping at Benning yesterday. They rolled up in their chutes when they hit the ground they were rolled up in the silk like a silkworm, so you see, jumping isn't easy.

Toccoa has a reputation for making Supermen, and it's not wrong. Everything is done on the double time around here. We take a run up a mountain about as steep as Twisp Pass two or three times a week along with the rest of our training. Every time I go up it gets easier. Boy I sure feel swell. Nothing to worry about, and got a swell bunch of fellows in our barracks. The last time I ran up the mountain I stood guard duty all night. I was up about 36 hours and kept up with the lieutenant, so you see I am getting in shape again.

If I wash out of this outfit, I'll go to the infantry and maybe later to the mechanics or truck driving. You should see my jumpsuits. They have 17 pockets and are full with knives and ammunition, grenades and such stuff. Also carry a pistol. A guy can't get any good drinking liquor, just Mt. Dew. All the girls want to do is sit at home or go to church. I had a home cooked meal last Sunday at my girlfriend's place. Boy it sure was good.

Be sure to get that buck for me. Nothing less than 4 points.

Bob

In another letter, Robert described being in E Company to his folks: "This is the best and toughest outfit in the army. It beats the regular army and the navy. It's like the Marines parachute troops. The definition of a paratrooper is a soldier who lands in hell in a parachute and runs the devil out with his own fork."

He talked about being on maneuvers in the "frying pan" in Alabama. He joked with his parents about not liking his uniform (evidently they had sent him a letter saying this in the meantime). "Well, the army's only got two sizes of clothes: too big and too small."

His letters were written on different camp stationeries to addresses with no streets or zip codes, often as simple as to "Mrs. W. Van Klinken, Pateros, Washington." He often wrote folksy, newsy notes home to his sister and brother-in-law. In one, postmarked October 12, 1942, from Toccoa, he wrote:

Dear Johnny, Susie, Walt, and Sleepy [Sleepy was Robert's dog]

Haven't anything to do tonight, so I'll write you a letter. I got stymied out of a pass tonight so I feel pretty ornery. After doing 7 miles marching last night and 13 miles of double time today I got a little blister on my foot. The C.O. sent me to the dispensary. The medical officer dumped a bucket of paint on it and gave me hell for bothering him. So I didn't get my pass.

I can't get used to this darned weather. It's hotter than hell in the day and frosty at night.

The nuts and persimmons are getting ripe and dropping. I and Dick—[probably PFC Dick Garrod, who was good friends with Van

*Klinken along with PFC Bill Wingett] he got hooked on his pass, too—
and are going out and getting a sack full tomorrow.*

*What do you think of the snapshot of my lady friend? She is going
to be madder than hell at me because I didn't go to see her and go to
church. I sho cain't figure out these Southern folks. All they want to do
is go to church. If a soldier goes to church he gets more invites out to dinner than he can keep in a month.*

So long,
Bob

More folksy letters followed with more news of training.

Dear Johnny, Susie, Walt

*Hi, you kids look like you got the breaks deer hunting. Sure wish I could
have been with you. I sure miss the steaks. Say, could you guys make up
a couple of pounds of jerky and send it down.*

*You're not the only ones getting the breaks. First I get a PFC rating,
then I am in the group of the 10 best men of Co E to run the qualifying
course against the battalion. Then I get picked out as 1 of the 5 men in
our company for demolition training. Boy, I am working like a cat on a
tin roof and really enjoying it.*

Robert's parents were known to be reserved and strict, people who didn't
show affection around each other. They spoke Dutch to each other when
they wanted to have private conversations. Robert's father was twenty
years older than his mother. His mother was a very religious and stoic
person who dug her own basement, canned her own food, and worked
hard around the farm.

Two letters described the march from Toccoa to Atlanta, both before
and after, one to his parents, one to Johnny and Susie:

Dear Folks,

Just received your letter. I got 2 days before we start marching to Atlanta on our way to Fort Benning. I just got off a 3 day march which covered about 50 or 60 miles. The day before yesterday I walked 31 miles with 20 pounds of T.N.T. on my back. Guess I haven't told you I am on the demolition squad.

I finished up my training here today and am leaving for Benning Monday. That's going to be a march of a hundred miles. I am dog tired now, so I'll be dead on my feet when I get there.

You asked if you could send me something. You could send me a box of oatmeal cookies, but wait till I write you from Benning.

Bob

Dear Johnny and Susie,

Just received your letter, was glad to hear from you. Just got the kinks shook loose in my hind legs after that march. You probably heard about it over the radio or through the newspapers. They sure gave us a write up about it. If you was in this outfit, you'd do more squawking than you do in the Navy Yard. We really catch hell down here. The first night was sure tough. It was raining when we went to bed and it cleared up so we had to climb into frozen clothes and shoes with 2 inches of mud in them. When we got into Atlanta, the "ole man" let us go in town and get cleaned up. You should have seen me and Dick drinking hot brandy while sitting in a hot bath of water.

Believe it or not but I have only been drunk once since I left home. I haven't anything to worry about and am getting fat on GI chow.

About Christmas the general will pin a set of silver wings on me.

We are having a hell of a lot of trouble with the other outfits. They are jealous as hell that the city of Atlanta gave us a big pennant.

Every time someone yells "currahee" there's hell a popping and the MPs make themselves scarce. Wish you were down here to join the excitement. I won't be home for Christmas. Don't expect me until you see me.

So long,
Bob

Right before Christmas 1942, Robert wrote his folks a short letter, which was inserted into a Christmas card, then wrote Johnny and Susie a longer letter describing his jumping and some information about a girlfriend he was becoming serious about.

Dear folks,

Well I am in Benning now. The biggest camp in the U.S. it's about the size of Wenatchee. I am jumping every day now. I'll make my last jump Christmas Day. The general will pin a pair of silver wings on me and give me my diploma. Then a bunch of movie stars will give us a big party and a dance.

I'll start my furlough December 31. I only get 10 days so I won't be home, but am going to New Orleans. After I get back we will be shipping out and leaving the U.S. I can't say when but it won't be long. That will give me a raise in pay to 138 bucks a month. The same as a lieutenant gets in the infantry.

Well, I have to sign off now as I have to go up and jump this morning. It takes me about 56 seconds to come down from 1,500 feet.

Don't worry about jumping me into combat as I'll only be in the air 5 or 6 seconds from about 350 to 400 feet. It will also be dark when we jump.

So long,
Bob

Dear Johnny and Susie,

Received your letter and was glad to hear from you guys. I am going to New Orleans as I can't get any traveling time, so I won't be home.

Well, I've made 6 jumps from a 300 foot tower and haven't hurt myself. A guy doesn't hit hard if he makes his downward pull at the right time. I landed pretty hard last night when we jumped in the dark. I couldn't judge the ground, so I got my feet in position and relaxed. A quite a few of the boys got hurt. Two guys got busted legs and about a dozen sprained ankles. It sure makes you feel funny standing up on the tower and watching them carry one of your buddies off the field on a stretcher. It makes you wonder if you're the next one.

The shock harness is a son of a gun. They take you up 150 feet. You lay on your belly to put the harness on and take you up in that position. When the sergeant counts 3 you pull the rip cord and freefall for 25 feet. When you hit, the risers hit you. It snaps you up straight and bounces you about 10 feet in the air. It almost shakes your teeth loose.

Well, tomorrow I go up for my first jump out of a plane. I got my chute all packed. We hook up to a 15 foot static line which snaps on the anchor cable in the plane, and stand in the door. When the jump-master says to, you let go of the static and jump out as far as you can, also make a left body turn. The static line rips off the pack cover and pulls out the chute. Then the break cord at the top of the chute breaks and lets the chute free. You fall about 100 to 125 feet before the chute opens.

It sure is a funny feeling. When you jump you are scared as hell. When the chute opens and jerks hell out of you and you start slowing up, it's the grandest feeling you ever felt. It's so peaceful and quiet, just like floating on thistle down. You wonder why you got so damned scared when you jumped. It's one extreme to the other.

I make my last jump Christmas day if my chutes open and don't break a few legs. The general is going to pin the silver wings on us then we'll have a big feed of turkey.

I am going to my girlfriend's house in New Orleans. I might get married, but I won't say for sure.

So long,
Bob
P.S. I had to fall out to police up, so I get a little more time to write.

We haven't made up our minds yet, we might wait till after I get out of the Army. I figure it's better that way as I'll be seeing action within a month and a half after I get back from my furlough. There is also a darned good chance of me not coming back.

We go swimming most every day in the Chattahoochee River, so you see the weather is warm. I'm sorry I can't come home, but I'll have a good time at my "ole lady's" house, so don't expect me.

Bob

He received his jump wings at last, and described some of the dangers in jumping:

December 29, 1942
Fort Benning, Georgia
Dear Johnny and Susie

Well, I got my jumps all made and got my wings and diploma which says I'm allowed to jump from a plane in flight. I am sure a happy guy. I've waited for those wings a long time.

They say the 2nd Bn. has the highest percentage of qualifications of any outfit that went through Benning. Our average was 87% for 650 men, that's pretty good. I've made 9 jumps so far from 3,000 to 800 feet. For some unexplainable reason you sweat every jump out. It's something like buck fever only there is a lot of fear to it. The first 2 or 3 times your mind goes blank from the time you hook up and start to the door till the chute opens. Then you have a good time guiding your chute and talking to your buddies around you. When you land it feels like you're going through the ground.

When I get back after the war, I'll be gray-headed and my legs will be all stove up. I've got 2 torn muscles now.

About 80% of this jumping is guts. Lots of the guys get up to the door and pass out. The prop blast grabs him and he goes out head first. I've seen more guys get hurt in the last week than I ever saw before. Anything from broken legs and necks to cracked minds. I saw one guy tear 2 fingers off and take all the flesh off the other three when he grabbed his static line as he went out. He came down alongside of me holding his hand. 12 men go out of the plane in 10 seconds—some speed, huh? Wish you could go out once, that's the only way of knowing how it feels. A guy just can't find the words to explain it.

I have to sign off now, so wish me good luck,
Bob

After the New Year he wrote to say he had quit demolitions, considering it too dangerous, and that he was in love with his girlfriend, Joyce. He also described an unorthodox way of commuting back to camp after furlough:

January 19, 1943
Dear Johnny and Susie,

I guess you think I am dead by this time, being I haven't written you since I left on my furlough. I had to go up to Tulsa Oklahoma to see Joyce. She's a riveter in the Douglas Aircraft in Tulsa.

Johnny, I am the happiest man in the U.S. The little lady is going to wait for me to get out of the Army. She is a girl any man could be proud of. If I don't get killed or shot up too bad, you'll see her and me coming back home. She is 23, the same age as I am. She has been married once. Her husband got killed about 2 years ago and she has been pretty lonesome. Johnny, maybe you think I am a damn fool for go-

ing with a girl that has been married. I don't care what you or any of my relatives think about it. Al that matters is that we love each other.

I darned near went AWOL. I sure hated to leave her. We both cried when I got in the plane in Oklahoma City. It cost me a buck for a chute. When I got over the camp I stood in the door and picked me a spot. I jumped out and said, "Joyce, this one's for you," and pulled the rip cord. The opening shock knocked hell out of me, but I am so darned happy that nothing can hurt me. I am sorry I didn't get home, but I think you understand how things are.

Say Johnny, I am doing all right. I hear a rumor I am getting a corporal rating in about a month.

Say Susan, will you make Johnny write me a letter. I want to know what he thinks about the situation. Just ride herd on him and make him write. Well so long.

Jump Happy,
Bob

Always Optimistic

In early 1943, Robert's father died. Robert received an unexpected furlough back home to Washington, then in February he wrote another letter. It showed some of the family man in him, about his endearment to his younger nephew, Walt, and how he wished to have children of his own someday.

Dear Johnny, Susan, Walt and Sleepy

Well I am back in camp again and found the rest of the outfit. Boy were my buddies tickled to see me. They thought I was AWOL. They didn't know about the extension.

I hope Susie doesn't feel too bad about my leaving there so soon. I hated to leave, too, but it's just one of those things that has to happen. I sure had a good time coming back.

How did Sleepy act when I left? Hope he didn't feel too lonesome. The poor little rascal.

Walt is sure a sweet little guy. I sure wish I was back home and had a cute little fellow like him to take care of.

Well, I have to sign off now. I have to write on to my "old lady" to-night. She only wrote 11 letters to me while I was on furlough.

So long kids,
Bob

There was a lapse of several months, then he wrote a letter dated simply "Spring 1943":

Dear Johnny and Susie

Boy, you should have seen the first platoon last night. We had to sleep out back of the hutment as a punishment. They let us go to town Saturday night and all day Sunday. Well when we came back we each had a pint or a quart of whiskey. Then we bought 5 cases of beer for chasers. Boy it really was a wild party. We sure got skunk drunk.

Say Johnny, I bought another guitar the other day. Gave 30 bucks for it. It sure is a honey.

So long,
Bob "Rip" Van Klinken

On April 17, 1943, Robert wrote to say he was dumped by his girl-friend, Joyce, who had met another guy. Bob remained upbeat and opti-mistic, or at least wrote through the lens of a paratrooper's bravado. He had also spent some time in the camp hospital, along with fellow para-trooper Wayne "Skinny" Sisk.

Dear Johnny and Susie,

Have only had about 8 hours of sleep in the last 2 nights and sleeping out on the ground. It's cold too. I am on guard tonight so I won't get any sleep. I am very unhappy as I got a date for tonight to go boat riding and can't get out of the camp. Who wouldn't be? You should see the Carolina moon.

We got 25 miles for next Monday with full pack. That's going to be tough.

You heard of that bobcat we swiped? Well we got another jump coming up around the 20th so we are going to jump him too. Sure wish you could see us hit the silk. It really is quite a sight. About 100 chutes in the air at once.

Well it looks like I got "outranked" by a 1st lieutenant from Fort Sill, Oklahoma. She figures the duration is too long to wait. Anyway, it's all over and it makes no difference. As Johnnie Rogers says, "I can get more women than a passenger train can haul."

I think I'll stay in the Army the next 30 years or so and get a pension. After all, it's a pretty soft life in peace time. That is if I am lucky enough to come back in one piece.

You should have seen me and Skinny when we were resting up in the barracks after we got out of the hospital. We really went on a good one. We were drunk for 3 days. The last night we had 3 quarts. We were so drunk we couldn't stand up, so we wound up shooting craps laying across a bed. We couldn't get up.

So long,
"Rip"

Life in the army continued. Robert moved around on maneuvers from Benning to Fort Mitchell in Alabama, then to Camp Hoffman in North Carolina, then to Camp Mackall. He wrote about getting into a bar fight:

Dear Johnny and Susie

Sure sorry to hear that Walt has the flu. Sure hope he is better.

There isn't much to write about except getting myself in a jam up in Raleigh a few weeks ago. I got fined 20 bucks and 3 weeks restriction. A civilian pulled a knife on one of the boys, so 3 of us 506th and 2 from the 505th cleaned out the joint. We did a pretty fair job too. I ruined my blouse in the deal so I have to buy a new one. It cost about 9 dollars. I've just pulled 17 hours K.P. in the officer's mess hall so I am pretty tired. Tomorrow we pull out for another week in the field. Go ahead and send the cookies to the address on the envelope.

So long,
"Rip"

The grueling training continued.

Dear folks,

I am back in camp again after being out in the field for 3 days. This is the first full night's sleep I've had in 7 days. I am so fried there's no feeling left in my legs and shoulders. Have been only getting about 2 hours sleep out of the 24 for 6 days.

I hear some of us are going to be shipped out this week. If I am in that bunch, it looks like I'll be long gone. I'll write and let you know where I am when I get across. Maybe I won't ever be called.

So long,
Bob

Wounded in Training

In late spring 1943, Bob was injured in a jump and initially told he would be washed out of the paratroopers. He wrote from Post Hospital ward B-108 in Camp Breckenridge, Kentucky, and let his disappointment show:

I bailed out about 350 feet and the next thing hit a tree. The thing that hurts most is that they have disqualified me, which means I won't jump anymore. I think they will keep me on jump pay till the outfit ships out and then send me to a replacement center.

Anyway, it has been nice knowing the 506th.

The last 4 jumps were hell anyway, everyone in trees, and we had about 80 pounds of equipment on.

Damn it all. I am stuck in a hospital and the rest of the outfit is down in Tenn or Ala. I'll have a hell of a time finding them.

So long and don't worry about me,
Bob

In summer 1943 he wrote from a different hospital in Fort Bragg, North Carolina:

Dear Johnny,

My papers came through and they read physically unfit as a soldier so that doesn't sound too good. I don't know where they are going to ship me or when. Most likely I'll spend a couple months in the hospital getting in shape again.

Johnny, I want you to do me a favor. Here's the setup. I got paid the other day and got 190 bucks. The first chance I get to town I'll send you $100. I want you to put it in the bank in your name or hold it for me.

When I get out of this outfit I may not be paid for 2 or 3 months if I go to a convalescence hospital.

So long,
Bob

Robert was eventually allowed back into the unit, but does not go into detail why. Altogether, he was hospitalized for 31 days. There were continued problems with his health, and he was not sure what his permanent status would be. He figured he would likely get transferred to limited service or receive a medical discharge, as reflected in the following three letters.

July 18, 1943
Fort Bragg, North Carolina
Dear Johnny and Susie,

The maneuvers are all over now. I got in on the last 2 weeks of them. Boy, it's pretty rough keeping up with the outfit after being in the hospital 31 days.

The last problem was pretty tough. We made a beach head on the Cumberland River and took Hartsville at daylight the next morning. We had to pack those damn boats ½ mile to get to the river. There wasn't a stitch of dry clothing on me when we got them in the water.

It's really hot down here and I've got a swell tan.

Well Johnny I got to drive one of those trucks last night. I drove one of those 6 wheelers up here from the other side of Nashville. They sure handle nice and lots of guts. I had 26 men and full equipment on it.

So long,
Bob
P.S. I am hiding out of skipping details so if they catch me I'll get Sunday K.P. That don't worry me because I am broke and I'll get my belly full of good chow once again.

Those maneuvers were pretty rough and the chiggers were terrible. My whole body is covered with bites. I got 27 bites on one ankle. The chiggers are worse than mosquitoes because they burrow under the skin and die. They become infected and really itch.

The rumor is I won't get a furlough until I get a transfer to limited service. You can't get anything definite. As I say, it's just a rumor.

August 8, 1943
Columbia, South Carolina
Dear Johnny and Susie,

I am on a 10-day furlough now. Out of a blue sky the C.O. called me into his office and asked me if I wanted a furlough. I took it. Something smells in this deal. You see, I am up for a medical discharge and they canceled a furlough for me 2 weeks ago. I can't tell you very much about it as it involves too much military.

I am having a swell time down here in Columbia. I am just taking it easy, out hitchhiking from one town to another. Say Johnny, I won't send that money home as I am using it on my furlough.

I am sending you a bag with some clothes I have to get rid of. That gabardine jacket is a present for you. It's a little large for me so should fit you.

So long,
Bob

August 22, 1943
Fort Bragg
Dear Johnny and Susie,

I am still going down to the dispensary and hospital every day. I can't seem to get any action on the situation.

It's so darn hot we can't hardly stand it. A lot of the men have heat rash all over their bodies. So far I've been lucky.

So long you all,

Bob

Sent Overseas to Fight

All Robert's health problems eventually get squared away and he was permanently reinstated in the company. Two letters were sent home, one from Robert, the other a form letter sent to Johnny from Captain Herbert Sobel. The men were at Camp Shanks in New York, set to board the troop ship *Samaria* and be sent overseas.

August 31, 1943
New York City
Dear Johnny and Susie,

I've changed my address again. Isn't this one beautiful? The weather is grand. It's cool just like home.

I can't say very much so this will have to be a short letter. There are a lot of things I'd like to tell you, but it's too involved with the U.S. here.

This may be the last letter I'll get to write to you in a long time.

Bob

The letter from Sobel to Johnny Klinkert has been circulated on the Internet. It's printed below, shown in its greater context. The letter was written in cursive on Company E letterhead.

27 August 1943
Dear Sir:

Soon your brother-in-law, Pfc. Robert Van Klinken will drop from the sky to engage and defeat the enemy. He will have the best of weapons and equipment and have had months of hard strenuous training to prepare him for success on the battlefield.

Your frequent letters of love and encouragement will arm him with a fighting heart. With that he cannot fail but will win glory for himself, make you proud of him, and his country ever grateful for his service during its hour of need.

Herbert M. Sobel, Capt.,
Commanding

There were no letters sent home during the months of training in Aldbourne.

Robert made the D-day jump on June 6, 1944, with Easy Company and survived but was wounded and sent to the hospital. He wrote a V-Mail home from England on June 14, 1944. (Note that he signed this letter "love Bob," when he signed all other letters "So long.")

Dear Susan and Johnny,

I don't know if I answered your last 2 letters or not. I received your package. Me and the boys ate the cake and cookies just before we got in the plane to make that jump in France.

I found plenty of fireworks over there but the Jerrys aren't as tough as I figured they were. They sure can't stop the paratroops.

Well Johnny I got a piece of shrapnel in my arm so they sent me back to England. My arm is okay as it's just a flesh wound.

You know Johnny, it's worse back here in the hospital than it is at the front. You get to thinking about your buddies you lost over there and you can't do anything about it. Hope they can send me back soon so I can get another crack at them. Tell the folks how I am getting along.

Love, Bob

Robert wrote next on September 7, 1944. He had been sent back to his unit from the hospital. He mentioned writing a girl named Phyllis who lived near his hometown.

Dear Johnny and Susie,

Received your Vmail a few days ago, was sure tickled to hear from you kids. I am getting along pretty well over here even if I do a little sweating once in a while.

How do you like living up at Holden? It sure is beautiful up there this time of year. Johnny should have a good time fishing. There is plenty of good lakes close there.

I haven't heard from Phyllis for a month and a half. It doesn't matter as there is too much to worry about over here, and there will be lots of girls left in the states when I get back.

I am sending you a money order for you to take care of. Also, get something for your birthday.

So Long,
Bob

Ten days after this letter was written, the men would jump during Operation Market-Garden. Bob would jump with his company and fight to liberate Holland.

That was the last letter home Robert ever wrote.

When the News Arrived

The next correspondence was dated October 9, 1944, sent to Johnny. It was a Western Union telegraph and read simply:

> *The secretary of war desires me to express his deep regret that your brother-in-law Pvt. Robert Van Klinken was killed in action of the 20th of September in Holland. Letter following.*
> *Ulio-adj. General*

The news followed on War Department letterhead. It was dated October 11, 1944, also sent to Johnny.

> *Dear Mr. Klinkert,*
>
> *It is with regret that I am writing to confirm the recent telegram informing you of the death of your brother-in-law, Private Robert Van Klinken, who was killed in action on 20 September 1944 in Holland.*
>
> *I fully understand your desire to learn as much as possible regarding the circumstances leading to his death, and I wish that there were more information available to you. Unfortunately, reports of this nature contain only the briefest details as they are prepared under battle conditions and the means of transmission are limited.*
>
> *I know the sorrow this message has brought you, and it is my hope that in time the knowledge of his heroic service to his country, even unto death, may be of sustaining comfort to you.*
>
> *I extend to you my deepest sympathy.*
>
> *Sincerely yours,*
> *J.A. Ulio*
> *Major General,*
> *The adjutant General,*

A Western Union telegram was dated the same day, sent by Johnny to inform Robert's mom. (Herman was Robert's uncle, who lived on the same ranch as his mom.)

> *Herman Van Klinken*
> > *Attendance Mrs. Alexander*
> > *Winthrop, Washington*
> > *Please advise Mrs. Walter Van Klinken personally that I received the following message last night. The sec of war desires to express his deepest regret that your brother-in-law Pvt Robert Van Klinken was killed in action the 20th of Sept in Holland. Letter following.*
> > *John F. Klinkert*

On December 27, 1944, Robert's father received a letter from the secretary of war, Washington, DC:

> *My dear Mr. Van Klinken:*
>
> *At the request of the president, I write to inform you that the Purple Heart has been awarded posthumously to your son, Private Van Klinken, Infantry, who sacrificed his life in defense of his country.*
>
> *Little that we can do or say will console you for the death of your loved one. We profoundly appreciate the greatness of your loss, for in a very real sense the loss suffered by any of us in this battle for our country, is a loss shared by all of us.*
>
> *When the medal, which you will shortly receive, reaches you, I want you to know that with it goes my sincerest sympathy, and the hope that time and the victory of our cause will finally lighten the burden of your grief.*
>
> *Sincerely yours,*
> *Henry L. Stimson*

Major General Maxwell Taylor wrote to Johnny on January 20, 1945, from the headquarters of the 101st Airborne Division:

Dear Mr. Klinkert,

I am sorry that I have not been able to write you before to express my deep personal sympathy to you in the loss of your brother-in-law, Private Robert Van Klinken.

He was killed in action on 20 September 1944 while fighting gallantly with our forces in Holland. His courageous example has had a profound influence on all who knew him and his memory will always remain with those who fought with him.

If it has not already done so, your brother-in-law's unit will furnish you with such details of his death and burial as are permitted under existing censorship regulations. I regret that the information is necessarily meager for the present.

The officers and men of this Division join me in extending to you our sincere sympathy in the loss of your brother-in-law and our Comrade-in-Arms.

Sincerely yours,
Gen. Maxwell Taylor

On April 13, 1945, Captain John R. Himes, chaplain with the 506th PIR, wrote to Robert's mother:

Dear Mrs. Van Klinken:

I believe I can answer some of the questions in your letter concerning the death of your son, Robert Van Klinken, who was killed in Holland, September 20, 1944. Robert was killed while voluntarily acting as a scout locating enemy positions during an attack. He was given a Christian burial in a military cemetery in Holland.

You asked for the names of some of his friends. I can give you these, Sgt. Denver Randleman, Pvt. William Wingett.

The Company Commander and I both extend our sympathy to you in Robert's passing. He was a fine soldier, and an expert rifle shot, and was aggressive and brave in action. He served his country very well. We pray that you may find a great measure of consolation in the cause of Liberty and Justice for which Robert gave himself.

Yours very truly,
John R. Himes
Chaplain

Four years later, on March 31, 1949, a final letter was sent from the War Department to Robert's mother, notifying her that Robert's remains were interred at the U.S. Military Cemetery in Margraten, Holland.

Robert's Legacy

The years passed, and Gariann notes that nobody in the family today specifically remembers having a service for Robert back in the States, but she assumes they did. There's a grave marker for him up at the Beaver Creek Cemetery in Twisp, although it lists the wrong year of Robert's death—1943 instead of 1944.

Susie's daughter, Cora Bingman, notes that her mother took the news hard for many years. Susie was a strong Christian woman and agonized with her feelings, mostly with the resentment she felt. Then, in the late 1980s, some forty-five years after her brother died, Cora went into her mother's house one day to find her sobbing.

"Mom what's wrong?" Cora said.

"Today is the day I finally have forgiveness in my heart," Grandma Susie said. The burden of hatred was finally gone from her life.

Grandma Susie always wanted to go to Holland to see her brother's grave, but was never able to. Then in 1995, Gariann and a girlfriend decided to backpack around Europe. Gariann asked her grandma if there was anything she wanted her to do while over there. Gariann still gets choked up when she thinks about it. Her grandmother said, "Tell him we love him and haven't forgotten." Then her grandma broke down and cried.

Gariann went to visit the family's Dutch relatives, then went to visit her great uncle's grave and whispered her grandma's words.

A neighbor of the Van Klinken family named Chuck Borg was just a young boy when news of Robert's death came to the town. Chuck's family lived across the road from the Van Klinken's cabin. The news of Robert's death left an impression on Chuck for years and he eventually went into the Army himself, rising to the rank of lieutenant colonel.

Years later, he was walking through a cemetery in Holland and saw the name Robert Van Klinken. It profoundly affected him. Chuck wrote home immediately and told his folks about it. When reading *Band of Brothers* several years later, he came across the name of his mom's old neighbor and friend once again. Chuck contacted the Twisp Chamber of Commerce and got in touch with my aunt and myself. Since then he has been an adopted part of our family. When he returned to the States to live, he established the Robert Van Klinken Memorial Scholarship at Liberty Bell High School in Twisp, where Robert went to school. The scholarship awards college money to hardworking, adventuresome country boys, similar to Robert's personality and drive.

This past year on Veteran's Day, Robert's great-grand-nephew, J. R. Matkins, took a picture of Robert Van Klinken to his third grade class along with the book *Band of Brothers*. The eight-year-old told his classmates about his relative who gave his life in the war so that generations could live in freedom. His classmates were impressed. J. R. also went to last year's Easy Company reunion along with his family.

For years, very few of the specific details of Robert Van Klinken's death were known to his family. Then, during the writing of this book, the family of Burton "Pat" Christenson and the Van Klinkens were connected, and details were shared for the first time. [To read the details, please see the essay about Pat Christenson.]

What's the one thing Gariann and her family would like people to remember about Robert Van Klinken?

"That he was a good man," Gariann said. "And that our family will always love him. He'll always be very much alive in our hearts."

EPILOGUE

Ambrose's Two Questions

This past September[1] I was in my home office one afternoon writing the essay about Lieutenant George Lavenson, when two ordinary events happened almost simultaneously that raised for me anew the two questions that Stephen Ambrose posed. One, I received an e-mail from my friend, Susie Krabacher, who had just written a letter to the United Nations special envoy to Haiti. And two, my wife came home with new school shoes for our six-year-old daughter.

You'll recall that Lavenson's nephew, Joel, had asked Ambrose if he had any theories about why he (Joel) was so passionate about researching his deceased uncle's life. Ambrose answered: "All men ultimately want to know two things—'*To whom do I owe thanks that I should live in such opportunity?*' And, '*Will I have the courage when the time comes?*'"

Answering Ambrose's questions can be difficult. Few of us today actu-

---

1. The epilogue was written prior to the events of January 12, 2010, when a 7.0 earthquake devastated Port-au-Prince and outlying areas of Haiti. Immediately following this tragedy, Haiti moved to the center of the world's thoughts and the world's compassion. My prayer is that we would all continue to help this devastated country.

ally jump out of airplanes into combat, or undertake any of the large-scale events that traditionally produce heroes. Sometimes the questions only tick quietly in the back of our minds. We need to strain to hear their subtleties.

Yet answering Ambrose's two questions reaches the heart of why we keep wanting to know more about the Band of Brothers. We read because of interest and to gather information, yes, but we also continually look to World War II for clues to the potential for our own heroics. We want to know if we've got the right stuff. We hope to live authentic lives that amount to something purposeful, and we're searching for examples that show us the way.

That's where Ambrose's questions connect with Krabacher's e-mail and my daughter's new shoes.

Of Gratefulness

Susie Krabacher is the CEO of the Mercy & Sharing Foundation, a philanthropic organization that runs orphanages, schools, and feeding centers in Haiti, the poorest country in the Western hemisphere. The situation in Haiti is continually desperate, and Krabacher's letter urged the Haitian government to take better, quicker action for their country's abandoned children.

In Haiti, where most people live on less than two dollars a day, these children are often left along roads and sewers or on hospital grounds, dumped like trash. Krabacher attached a picture that showed row after row of cribs in a Haitian hospital, three children in each crib. The children were dirty and disheveled and had likely spent most of their lives in those cribs. Some stared at the camera. Other children slept. Some looked off into space with large, vacant eyes.

In a contrasting culture, the shoes my daughter received that afternoon were everything a six-year-old could want. They were striped pink and brown, sparkly, with shiny hearts jangling from stretchy laces. I hugged my daughter as I admired her new shoes, and I couldn't help wonder why we live in a country so comparatively wealthy, when not more than five hundred miles off the coast of Florida there are abandoned babies sleeping three to a crib.

I couldn't help but hear Ambrose's first question, "*To whom do I owe thanks that I should live in such opportunity?*"

Of Bravery

Ambrose's second question, "*Will I have the courage when the time comes?*" is asked by people of all generations faced with the fight for ideals. The question deals with issues of justice, self-sacrifice, and compassion in action. It's about whether we have the stuff of heroics. And hero can be a tricky word, even when applied to the men of Easy Company.

When you read through the essays in this book, did you respond with mixed feelings? I know I did. All the men profiled fought heroically in the war, but reading about their lives after the war, we learn that not all the stories had happy endings. Some men survived and lived exemplary lives, caring well for their families and communities. They were heroes through the war and models of how to live afterward. Others floundered, drifted into addictions or despair, and never seemed sure of the right road. Were they heroes, too? Perhaps the definition of hero needs to be broadened. Some of the men were so broken that they did not do well after the war, but that does not negate what they did in those vital years of conflict. They did not live perfect lives, and yet they still did mighty things.

Hero is a concept that beckons us. Most of us today, if we are not military personnel or third world humanitarians, will never fight in conditions anywhere close to the terror of Bastogne. Still, we face battles that we hope matter. We take actions that we hope have significance. We don't aspire necessarily to be international heroes; we just want to do more than sit on the couch watching reruns of *Matlock*.

Ambrose's questions mean most for us today when we remember that the soldiers who fought in the battlefields of Normandy, Holland, and Bastogne indeed gave much. And they gave it for a reason—so that we could live for what matters. The liberty that the Band of Brothers fought for was not a freedom to do whatever we want whenever we want, but rather a freedom from tyranny, a freedom of self-determination, a freedom to make something of our lives.

Answering the Two Questions

The men of Easy Company were everyday guys, kids like those we grew up with, yet they reached way beyond themselves and way beyond their home turf. Because they were ordinary men who chose to live extraordinarily, their examples inspire us to make deliberate decisions for right action. They invite us to be courageous in our commitments, to provide security for our families, to be noble in our careers and communities, and to be engaged on a global front. They fought and bled and some of them died on foreign soil, and part of their legacy to us is an unselfish global perspective.

Here is one way to make a fitting and tangible tribute to their heroics and to begin ours: write a check to our charity of choice in honor of the Band of Brothers. We might consider organizations that help the families of our fallen military people. Or we might follow the global vision and reach out to another battle that matters, such as the abandoned children in Haiti. Here is a land where innocents are still waiting for people who will be their heroes and offer them the tools for opportunity. I can vouch that the goal of Krabacher's organization is to help alleviate human suffering for this generation and the generations to come, a principle the men of Easy Company continually stood for.

Scenes and lines from the essays we've just read will stay with us for some time. For me, there's a scene from the story of Pat Christenson: a telephone call, the announcement, "Pat's home," his ten-year-old nephew, Gary, sprints out of the house without his jacket, running down the street to meet his hero home from the war. Maybe in some small way we can be some child's hero, too.

A check is not the same as spilling blood. But this much we can do as evidence of the potential for heroics in us all. I suggest as a good place to start, writing in the amount of a new pair of shoes.

For more information see www.haitichildren.com.

ACKNOWLEDGMENTS

This book originated at the 2008 Easy Company reunion in Salem, Oregon. I had written another book called *We Who Are Alive and Remain*, and, at the back of that book, had invited four adult children of Easy Company members to talk about their deceased fathers. The section acted as an appendix and was meant to convey the idea that many more stories could be told. Advance copies of the book were circulating at the reunion, and the appendix garnered a good amount of attention from the E Company men and their wives, many of whom said things like, "There are so many guys from the company whose stories need to be told, you should do a whole book about this."

Ed Tipper and Amos "Buck" Taylor, although neither was able to attend that year's reunion, both phoned later and strongly encouraged another book. Thanks go to both men.

I am always grateful for Natalee Rosenstein, Michelle Vega, Caitlin Mulrooney-Lyski, and the excellent staff at Penguin, who care deeply about the men of Easy Company's legacy and championed this project from the start.

Thanks go to my agent and friend, Greg Johnson, Rachelle Gardner, and the team at the WordServe Literary Group for making projects happen.

Tracy Compton introduced me to Chris Langlois, the grandson of Doc Roe. Chris invited me to join a closed Internet forum for children and relatives of Easy Company men. I joined the forum, explained the project, and right away several Easy Company relatives expressed eagerness in participating, which got the ball rolling. We corresponded about how we wanted to do this book for three reasons: 1) as a tribute to their fathers or loved ones, 2) as a remembrance book for future generations, 3) for current readers' enjoyment, inspiration, and leadership. This book could not have been made without all the contributors. Thank you so much.

George Luz Jr., C. Susan Finn (daughter of Burr Smith), Bill Guarnere—who organized and kept records of Easy Company reunions for years—and Herb Suerth Jr., current president of the Men of Easy Company Association, helped put me in touch with other contributors.

Thanks go to many others who helped along the way, including Rich Riley, a WWII 101st Airborne historian and friend of Easy Company, historian Jake Powers, Joe "Mooch" Muccia from www.MajorDickWinters .com, Peter van de Wal in Holland, Marci Carson, Joe Toye, Vance Day, Carol Pulver—who regularly writes letters of encouragement to the troops—Colonel Susan Luz, Merav Brooks, Robyn Post, Michael Pohlman, PhD, Paul Woodage from www.Battlebus.fr, and Bryan and the gang from Valor Studios.

Gratefulness is continually expressed to Stephen Ambrose, Tom Hanks, Steven Spielberg, and HBO.

Lieutenant Buck Compton remains a strong source of personal inspiration. Thank you, Buck. None of this would have happened without your book starting it all.

Newspaper journalists Dorothy Brotherton and H. C. Jones went through each essay line by line and offered valuable suggestions along the way.

Karen Clark and Bob Craddock, two great lifelong friends, encouraged me in many ways throughout the writing of the book.

I'm thankful for friendship, love, and support from Mike and Judy, Jon and Alison, Japheth and Elly, David and Carrie, Addy and Zach, Peter Sheldrup, Roger Chamberlin, David Kopp, and our friends at the Tuesday night dinner club.

I am ever grateful to my wife, Mary Margaret Brotherton, for her strong support in this project and her love always.

Thanks go to my father, D. Graham Brotherton, who has acted heroically throughout his life and career.

Final thanks go to the international community of fans who continue to preserve the legacy of the Band of Brothers and hold closely what it means to live in freedom.

All honor goes to him who holds our lives in his hands. Daniel 5:23b.

UNDERSTANDING
EASY COMPANY'S PLACEMENT
Easy Company 506th Regiment, 101st Airborne,
World War II

101ST AIRBORNE DIVISION/THE "SCREAMING EAGLES"
12,000–15,000 MEN

General Maxwell Taylor commanded the four regiments that made up the 101st Airborne Division. The United States began World War II with 6 divisions (5 infantry and 1 cavalry). By the end of the war, there were nearly 100 divisions.

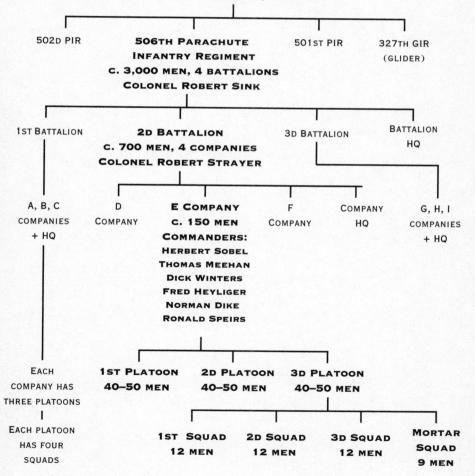

502D PIR

506TH PARACHUTE INFANTRY REGIMENT
c. 3,000 MEN, 4 BATTALIONS
COLONEL ROBERT SINK

501ST PIR

327TH GIR (GLIDER)

1ST BATTALION

2D BATTALION
c. 700 MEN, 4 COMPANIES
COLONEL ROBERT STRAYER

3D BATTALION

BATTALION HQ

A, B, C COMPANIES + HQ

D COMPANY

E COMPANY
c. 150 MEN
COMMANDERS:
HERBERT SOBEL
THOMAS MEEHAN
DICK WINTERS
FRED HEYLIGER
NORMAN DIKE
RONALD SPEIRS

F COMPANY

COMPANY HQ

G, H, I COMPANIES + HQ

EACH COMPANY HAS THREE PLATOONS

EACH PLATOON HAS FOUR SQUADS

1ST PLATOON 40–50 MEN

2D PLATOON 40–50 MEN

3D PLATOON 40–50 MEN

1ST SQUAD 12 MEN

2D SQUAD 12 MEN

3D SQUAD 12 MEN

MORTAR SQUAD 9 MEN

KNOWN MEMBERS OF EASY COMPANY
506 PIR, 101ST AIRBORNE

Aldrich, PFC
Alley, James H. Jr., Sgt.
Andrews, Owen L., Pvt.
Ansell, Keith

Bain, Roderick G., T/5
Baker, Pvt.
Baldwin, Kenneth T., Cpl.
Ballew, Raymond, L., PFC
Barnwell, Archibold Smith, 2nd Lt.
Bealke, Frederick G., Pvt.
Becker, Paul. L., Sgt.
Bellino, Salvator F., PFC
Benton, James V., Cpl.
Berg, Richard F., Pvt.
Bernat, Edward J., PFC
Blake, Homer T., Pvt.
Blithe, Albert, PFC
Bloser, Robert J., Pvt.
Bond, Donald S., Pvt.
Bay, Conrad M., PFC
Boyle, Leo D., S/Sgt.
Bray, Richard L., Pvt.
Brewer, Robert B., Col.
Broska, Charles F., Pvt.
Bruce, Earl V., Pvt.
Burden, PFC
Burgess, Thomas H., PFC

Campbell, James
Campbell, James D., Cpl.

Capoferra, John J.
Carlino, Matthew J., PFC
Carillo, Leopollo P, Alex., T/5
Carson, Gordon F., Sgt.
Childers, Ora M., Pvt.
Chow, Pvt.
Christenson, Burton "Pat," T/Sgt.
Cipriano, Robert, Pvt.
Clark, Maxwell M., PFC
Cobb, Roy W., PFC
Coleman, James F., Pvt.
Collette, Vincent S., PFC
Collins, Herman F., T/5
Comba, James
Compton, Lynn D. "Buck," 1st. Lt.
Connell, John G., Pvt.
Conway, Pvt.
Coombs, James Tex., Sgt.
Coviello, Phillip., Pvt.
Cowing, Robert, H., 1st Lt.
Cowthu, Samuel, M., Pvt.
Crosby, Seth, O., PFC
Cunningham, Bernard S., Sgt.
Cushman, Pvt.

Damon, Pvt.
Dassault, Barry J.
Davenport, Richard P., PFC

Davis, James K. 1st Lt.
De Tuncq, Edward R.
Dickerson, Jay S., Pvt.
Diel, James L., 2nd Lt.
Dike, Norman S. Jr., Capt.
Dittrich, Rudolph R., Pvt.
Doe, John, Pvt.
Dominguez, Joseph P., PFC
Donahue, Edward J., PFC
Dukeman, William H. Jr., Sgt.

Eckstrom, Carl F., PFC
Eggert, Walter F.
Elliott, George L., Pvt.
Ellis, Taskel, Sgt.
Eschenbach, Chester, Pvt.
Eubanks, John L., Pvt.
Evans, William S., 1st Sgt.

Fenstermaker, Carl L., PFC
Fernandez, PFC
Fieguth, John F., Cpl.
Flurie, Gerald L., PFC
Foley, Jack E., Capt.
Ford, Norman A. [Cadre 2nd Pl.], S/Sgt.
Freeman, Bradford C., PFC

Garcia, Antonio, PFC
Garrod, Richard R., PFC
Gates, Roy, 2nd. Lt.

Gathings, Johnnie E., PFC

Geraghty, John L., Pvt.

Gier, William D.

Giles, Terry G., Pvt.

Gilmore, Eugene S. "Bob," Pvt.

Ginn, Jack O., PFC

Glass, Milton B., Pvt.

Gordon, Walter S. Jr "Smokey," Cpl.

Grant, Charles E. "Chuck," Sgt.

Grant, Frank B., Pvt.

Gray, Everett J., PFC

Griffith, Genoa H., Pvt.

Grodski, Stephen E., Pvt.

Guarnere, William J., S/Sgt.

Guth, Forrest L., Sgt.

Guy, Lloyd D., Sgt.

Hagerman, Stanley L., Pvt.

Hale, Earl L., S/Sgt.

Hale, Franklin W., Pvt.

Haley, Robert, Lt.

Hanes, Sgt.

Hansen, Walter E., PFC

Hanson, Herman E., S/Sgt

Hargroves, Elwood, Pvt.

Harrell, Thomas A., Pvt.

Harrellson, Siles E., PFC

Harris, Terrence C. "Salty," S/Sgt.

Hartley, Dale L., PFC

Hartsuff, George B., Pvt.

Hashey, Lester "Hash," 1st. Sgt.

Hawkins, Verlin V., Pvt.

Hayden, Sgt.

Hayes, Harold G., Pvt.

Haynes, Sgt.

Heckler, Cyril B., Pvt.

Heffron, Edward J. "Babe," PFC

Henderson, J. D., Sgt.

Hendrix, Walter "Black Jack," T/Sgt.

Hensley, Robert C., Pvt.

Herron, A. P., PFC

Hertzog, Elwood, PFC

Hester, Clarence, Lt. Col.

Hewitt, George W.

Heyliger, Frederick T. "Moose," Capt.

Hickman, PFC

Higgins, George, Cpl.

Hite, Paul A., Pvt.

Hogan, Joseph E., PFC

Holbrook, Owen V., Pvt.

Holland, John R. [Medic], Pvt.

Holton, David L., Pvt.

Hoobler, Donald B., Cpl.

Howard, Walter G., PFC

Howell, Clarence S., PFC

Howell, William A., T/5

Hudgens, Bruce A., Pvt.

Hudson, PFC

Hudson, Charles A., 2nd Lt.

Hughes, Richard H. II, 1st Lt.

Hughes, Richard J., Pvt.

Huntley, Warren C., PFC

Hussion, Charles F., Pvt.

Irish, Sherman M., Sgt.

Ivie, Eugene E., PFC

Jackson, Eugene E., Pvt.

Janovec, John A., PFC

Jarrett, Robert, Pvt.

Johnson, Coburn M., PFC

Joint, Edward J., Cpl.

Jones, George E., PFC

Jones, Hank, 1st Lt.

Jordan, Joseph M., PFC

Jordan, Vernon, Pvt.

Julian, John T., PFC

Kiehn, William F., Sgt.

King, Donald L., Cpl.

Kohler, PFC

Korb, John R., Pvt.

Kratzer, William N., Pvt.

Kudla, Steven A., [Cadre 3rd Pl.] S.Sgt.

Lager, Harry, PFC

Lamoureux, Paul E., PFC

Lampos, Lewis "Bob," Pvt.

Lavenson, George, 1st Lt.

Leonard, Robert T., PFC

Lesniewski, Joseph A., PFC

Liebgott, Joseph D., T/5

Lindler, Quinton E., PFC

Lipton, C. Carwood, 1st Lt.

Longo, Philip E., Pvt.

Lowery, Dewitt, PFC

Lusty, John, Pvt.

Luz, George, T/5

Lyall, Clarence O., Sgt.

Lynch, John C., 1st Sgt.

Mahmood, A., Pvt.

Maitland, Thomas, Cpl.

Malarkey, Donald G., T/Sgt.

Mampre, Albert L., S/Sgt.

Mann, Robert A., 1st Sgt.

Marsh, Robert K., Sgt.

Martin, John W., Sgt.

Martin, Walter E., Pvt.

Massaconi, Michael V., Pvt.

Mather

Matheson, S. L., Maj. Gen.

Mathews, Robert L., 2nd Lt.

Matthews, Jack F., Pvt.

Matz, Leo J., Lt. Col.

Mauser, Edward A., PFC

Mauzerall, Arthur J., PFC

Maxwell, Robert, Pvt.

Mayer, John G., T/5

Maynard, William C., T/5

McBreen, John, PFD

McCauley, Carl F., Pvt.

McClung, Earl J. "One Lung," Cpl.

McCreary, Thomas A., Sgt.

McGrath, John, T/5

McKay, Walter L., PFC

McMahon, James A., PFC

McGonigal, William T. Jr., PFC

Medved, William E., PFC

Meehan, Thomas, 1st Lt.

Mellett, Francis J., Cpl.

Melo, Joachim, Pvt.

Mendoza, Ynez M., Pvt.

Menze, Vernon J., PFC

Mercier, Kenneth D., Sgt.

Meth, Elmer T., Pvt.

Meth, Max M., Pvt.

Metzler, William S., PFC

Miller, James W., PFC

Miller, John N., PFC

Miller, William T., PFC

Milo, Franklin, Pvt.

Minne, Elmer T., Pvt.

Montes, Alfred B., Pvt.

Moone, Donald J., Pvt.

Moore, Walter L., 1st Lt.

More, Alton M., PFC

Morehead, Harvey H., [Cadre] 1st Sgt.

Morris, David E., PFC

Morris, William E., Pvt.

Motowski, Stanley F., Cpl.

Motz

Moya, Sergio G., PFC

Muck, Warren H. "Skip," Sgt.

Murray, Elmer L. Jr., Sgt.

Neitzke, Norman W., PFC

Nelson, Henry E., PFC

Neumann, Pvt.

Nevenfeldt, Gordon, Pvt.

Nixon, Lewis "Blackbeard," Capt.

O'Brien, Francis L., 1st Lt.

O'Keefe, Patrick S., Pvt.

Oats, Ernest, L. [Medic], PFC

Oien, Gordon H., Pvt.

Orth, Ralph J. [Medic], PFC

Owen, Richard E., Sgt.

Pace, Cecil M., Pvt.

Pace, Ledlie R., T/5

Peacock, Thomas A., 1st Lt.

Penkala, Alex M. Jr., PFC

Pepping, Edwin E., PFC

Perconte, Frank J., PFC

Perkins, Ben M., 1st Lt.

Peruginni, Philip P., PFC

Petty, Cleveland O., PFC

Pickel, Roy E., Pvt.

Pierce, David R., Pvt.

Pisanchin, John E., 1st Lt.

Plesha, John Jr., Cpl.

Pomely, Pvt.

Potter, George L. Jr., Pvt.

Powers, Darrell C. "Shifty," Sgt.

Pyle, Charles W., Pvt.

Raczkowski, Alex R., Pvt.

Rader, Robert J., S/Sgt.

Rajner, George J., Pvt.

Ramierez, Joseph, PFC

Randleman, Denver "Bull," Sgt.

Ranney, Myron "Mike," S/Sgt.

Reese, Lavon P., Cpl.

Rexrode, Charles E., 2nd Lt.

Rhinehart, Charles E., T/4

Rice, Farris O., PFC

Richey, Ralph D. Jr., Major

Riggs, Carl N. Sgt.

Robbins, Woodrow W., PFC

Roberts, Murray B., S/Sgt.

Robinson, Harvey G., Cpl.

Roe, Eugene G. [Medic], T/5

Rogers, Clifford E., Cpl.

Rogers, Paul C., Sgt.

Rossman, John W., PFC

Rotella, Gregory C., Pvt.

Roush, Warren R., 1st Lt.

Rowles, Richard C., T/4

Sabo, Edward F., PFC

Sarago, James

Sawosko, Carl C., PFC

Schmitz, Raymond G., 1st Lt.

Schuyler, Elmer N., PFC

Serilla, William D., Pvt.

Sewell, John P., Pvt.

Shames, Edward D., Col.

Sheehy, John L., PFC

Sheeley, John P., PFC

Shindell, John E., Pvt.

Shirley, Urbon M., Pvt.

Sholty, James B., Sgt.

Sisk, Wayne A, "Skinny," Sgt.

Smith, Campbell T., T/5

Smith, Garland R., PFC

Smith, George H. Jr., Pvt.

Smith, John D., Pvt.

Smith, Robert "Burr," Lt. Col.

Smith, Robert T., [Supply Sgt.] S/Sgt.

Snider, Gerald R., PFC

Sobel, Herbert M., Major

Sobeleski, Frank

Sowell, James L.

Speirs, Ronald C. "Killer," Major

Spina, Ralph F., [Medic] PFC

Stafford, Ralph I., T/5

Stedman, Joe E., [Cadre 1st Pl.] S/Sgt.

Steele, Robert L.

Stein, Edward H., Cpl.

Stickley, Joseph, Pvt.

Stokes, J. B., Sgt.

Stoney, Benjamin J., T/4

Strohl, Roderick G., PFC

Suerth, Herbert J., Sgt.

Sullivan, Paul J., PFC

Supko, Paul

Sweeney, Patrick J., 1st Lt.

Talbert, Floyd M., 1st Sgt.

Taylor, Amos J., "Buck," T/ Sgt.

Telstad, Elmer L., PFC

Thomason, George W., Pvt.

Thompson, Raymond H., Pvt.

Tipper, Edward J., PFC

Tokarzewski, Felix J., PFC

Toner, John, Pvt.

Toye, Joseph D., Sgt.

Trapuzzano, Ralph J., PFC

Tremble, Eugene R.

Tremonti, Norman, Pvt.

Tridle, Clarence M., Sgt.

Uuban, Andrew, PFC

Van Klinken, Robert, PFC

Vest, Allen E., Jaws, PFC

Vittorre, Alexander, PFC

Wagner, Paul, PFC

Wagner, William H., T/5

Warren, Thomas W., PFC

Webb, Harold B., PFC

Webb, Kenneth J., PFC

Webster, David Kenyon, PFC

Welling, James W., PFC

Welsh, Harry F., LTC

Wentzel, Jerry A., T/5

Wentzel, Walter H., Pvt.

West, Daniel B., PFC

Wheeler, James W., Pvt.

Whitecavage, Joseph P., S/ Sgt.

Whitwer, Roland, M., P.F.C.

Whytsell, Elijah, Pvt.

Wimer, Ralph H., T/5

Wingett, William T., PFC

Winn, Melvin W., PFC

Winters, Richard D., Maj.

Wiseman, Donald S., Pvt.

Woodcock, William H., PFC

Wright, Richard M., Sgt.

Wynn, Robert E., "Popeye," PFC

Yochum, George F., PFC

York, Ronald V.,

Youman, Arthur C., Sgt.

Young, Jerry G., Pvt.

Zastavniak, Frank J., PFC

Zimmerman, Henry C., PFC

[*source: Men of Easy Company Association*]

KILLED IN ACTION, EASY COMPANY 506TH, PARACHUTE INFANTRY REGIMENT, 101ST AIRBORNE DIVISION

Robert J. Bloser
June 7, 1944

James D. Campbell
October 8, 1944

Herman F. Collins
June 6, 1944

James L. Diel
September 19, 1944

William H. Dukeman
October 5, 1944

George L. Elliot
June 6, 1944

William S. Evans
June 6, 1944

Everett J. Gray
June 8, 1944

Terrence C. Harris
June 18, 1944

Harold G. Hayes
December 1944

A. P. Herron
January 13, 1945

Donald B. Hoobler
January 3, 1945

Richard J. Hughes
January 9, 1945

Eugene E. Jackson
February 15, 1945

John A. Janovec
May 1945

Joseph M. Jordan
June 6, 1944

John T. Julian
January 1, 1945

William F. Kiehn
February 10, 1945

Robert L. Matthews
June 6, 1944

William T. McGonigal
June 6, 1944

Thomas Meehan
June 6, 1944

Francis J. Mellett
January 13, 1945

Vernon J. Menze
September 20, 1944

William S. Metzler
June 1944

James W. Miller
September 20, 1944

John N. Miller
June 6, 1944

William T. Miller
September 20, 1944

Sergio G. Moya
June 6, 1944

Warren H. Muck
January 10, 1945

Elmer L. Murray
June 6, 1944

Patrick H. Neill
January 13, 1945

Ernest L. Oats
June 6, 1944

Francis L. O'Brien
December 1944

Richard E. Owen
June 6, 1944

Alex M. Penkala
January 10, 1945

Murray B. Roberts
June 6, 1944

Carl N. Riggs
June 6, 1944

Carl C. Sawosko
December 1944

Raymond G. Schmitz
September 23, 1944

John E. Shindell
January 13, 1945

Gerald R. Snider
June 6, 1944

Benjamin J. Stoney
June 6, 1944

Elmer L. Telstad
June 6, 1944
Robert Van Klinken
September 20, 1944
Thomas W. Warren
June 6, 1944

Harold D. Webb
January 13, 1945
Kenneth J. Webb
January 13, 1945

Jerry A. Wentzel
June 6, 1944
Ralph H. Wimer
June 6, 1944

[source: Men of Easy Company Association]

INDEX

Marcus Brotherton is a journalist and professional writer known internationally for his literary collaborations with high-profile public figures, humanitarians, inspirational leaders, and military personnel.

Other military nonfiction books authored or coauthored by Marcus Brotherton are *Call of Duty* (with Lieutenant Buck Compton), *The Nightingale of Mosul* (with Colonel Susan Luz), *We Who Are Alive and Remain* (with twenty of the still-living Band of Brothers), and *Shifty's War*. For more information, please see www.bandofbrothersbooks.com.